Surveillance and Democra ,

This collection represents the first sustained attempt to grapple with the complex and often paradoxical relationships between surveillance and democracy. Is surveillance a barrier to democratic processes, or might it be a necessary component of democracy? How has the legacy of post-9/11 surveillance developments shaped democratic processes? As surveillance measures are increasingly justified in terms of national security, is there the prospect that a shadow "security state" will emerge? How might new surveillance measures alter the conceptions of citizens and citizenship which are at the heart of democracy? How might new communication and surveillance systems extend (or limit) the prospects for meaningful public activism?

Surveillance has become central to human organizational and epistemological endeavours and is a cornerstone of governmental practices in assorted institutional realms. This social transformation towards expanded, intensified and integrated surveillance has produced many consequences. It has also given rise to an increased anxiety about the implications of surveillance for democratic processes; thus raising a series of questions – about what surveillance means, and might mean, for civil liberties, political processes, public discourse, state coercion and public consent – that the leading surveillance scholars gathered here address.

Kevin D. Haggerty is editor of the *Canadian Journal of Sociology* and book review editor of the international journal *Surveillance & Society*. He is Professor of Sociology and Criminology at the University of Alberta, Canada.

Minas Samatas is Associate Professor of Political Sociology in the Sociology Department at the University of Crete, Greece, and author of *Surveillance in Greece: from Anticommunist to the Consumer Surveillance*, Pella, NY, 2004.

Surveillance and Democracy

Edited by
Kevin D. Haggerty and Minas Samatas

Routledge·Cavendish
Taylor & Francis Group

First published 2010 by Cavendish Publishing

Transferred to digital printing 2010
by Routledge-Cavendish
2 Park Square, Milton Park, Abingdon, Oxon, OX14 4RN

Simultaneously published in the USA and Canada
by Routledge-Cavendish
270 Madison Avenue, New York, NY 10016

Routledge-Cavendish is an imprint of the Taylor & Francis Group, an informa business

© 2010 editorial matter and selection Kevin D. Haggerty and Minas Samatas, individual chapters the contributors

Typeset in Sabon by Integra Software Services Pvt. Ltd, Pondicherry, India

British Library Cataloguing in Publication Data
A catalogue record for this book is available from the British Library

Library of Congress Cataloguing in Publication Data
A Catalog record for this book has been requested

ISBN 10: 0-415-47239-3 (hbk)
ISBN 10: 0-415-47240-7 (pbk)
ISBN 10: 0-203-85215-X (ebk)

ISBN 13: 978-0-415-47239-5 (hbk)
ISBN 13: 978-0-415-47240-1 (pbk)
ISBN 13: 978-0-203-85215-6 (ebk)

Dedicated to the memory of Richard V. Ericson

Contents

Acknowledgements

Most of the chapters of this book were originally presented at the international research workshop "Surveillance and Democracy" at the University of Crete, Rethymno, Crete, Greece, on June 2–4, 2008. The workshop was organized in the context of the postgraduate program in "Sociology" at the University of Crete, by Associate Professor Minas Samatas.

We acknowledge the economic support provided by the programme (EPEAEK II, MIS 91297), which was co-funded with European Union and National Funds.

The editors would like to thank the Department of Sociology at the University of Crete and EPEAEK for funding and hosting this international academic event and the participants and other contributors for their papers.

The editors would also like to thank Laura Botsford and Carla Ickert for their excellent editorial assistance. Thanks also to Ariane Ellerbrok and Greg Eklics for their help with the index.

Contributors

Kirstie Ball is Senior Lecturer in Organization Studies at the Open University Business School. Her research interests comprise surveillance in and around organizations and society, data protection and privacy in call centers, and the electronic monitoring of employees. She is the author of a number of scholarly articles and book chapters around these issues. She is co-founder of the journal *Surveillance and Society*, and co-founding director of Surveillance Studies Network, a charitable company which owns the journal.

Andrea Mubi Brighenti is a Postdoctoral Research Fellow at the Department of Sociology, University of Trento, Italy. He researches both empirically and theoretically issues of space, power and society, with specific concern for the processes of control and resistance. Besides contributions to edited volumes, he has published articles in several Italian and international peer-reviewed journals, including *Critical Sociology, Ethnography and Qualitative Research / Etnografia e Ricerca Qualitativa, Quaderni di Sociologia, Current Sociology, Polis, Rassegna Italiana di Sociologia, Sociologia del diritto, Sortuz, Canadian Journal of Law and Society / Revue Canadienne de Droit et Société, Thesis Eleven*, and *Law and Critique*. Currently, he is working on a monograph on the notion of visibility. He is a member of the International Sociological Association and editor of the independent online web review *lo Squaderno* (www.losquaderno.net)

Elizabeth Daniel is Professor of Information Management and Associate Dean, Research and Enterprise at the Open University Business School (OUBS), UK where she researches in the field of information systems in business. Prior to joining OUBS in 2005, Elizabeth worked in the IS Research Centre at Cranfield School of Management. She has published numerous papers in leading academic journals and a number of management reports. Prior to joining academia, she spent over ten years in industry and continues to advise both private and public sector organizations about IS investments.

Sally Dibb is Professor of Marketing and joint Head of the Marketing and Strategy Research Unit at the Open University Business School, Milton Keynes, UK. She was awarded her PhD (Marketing) from the University of Warwick, where she was previously a member of faculty for 19 years. Sally's research interests are in marketing strategy, target marketing, segmentation and customer relationship management (CRM). She has published extensively in these areas, including articles in the *Journal of the Academy of Marketing Science, European Journal of Marketing, Industrial Marketing Management, International Journal of Advertising, Journal of Marketing Management, Journal of Service Industry Management, Journal of Strategic Marketing, Long Range Planning,* and *OMEGA,* among others. Sally founded and currently chairs the Academy of Marketing's Special Interest Group in Market Segmentation. She has also co-authored seven books, including *Marketing Planning, Market Segmentation Success: Making It Happen!* and *Marketing Essentials,* all of which were published in 2008.

Kevin D. Haggerty is editor of the *Canadian Journal of Sociology* and book review editor of the international journal *Surveillance & Society*. He is Professor of Sociology and Criminology at the University of Alberta and a member of the executive team for the *New Transparency* Major Collaborative Research Initiative. He has authored, co-authored or co-edited *Policing the Risk Society* (Oxford University Press), *Making Crime Count* (University of Toronto Press), and *The New Politics of Surveillance and Visibility* (University of Toronto Press).

Dr. Ben Hayes is associate director of the London-based civil liberties group *Statewatch,* where he has worked since 1996. He also works for the *Transnational Institute* in Amsterdam on their "Militarism and Globalisation" program and as a consultant for a number of international human rights organizations. He obtained his PhD from the Department of Social Policy of the University of Ulster in 2007 and is currently working on a book on human rights and democracy in the European Union.

Deborah G. Johnson is the Anne Shirley Carter Olsson Professor of Applied Ethics and Chair of the Department of Science, Technology, and Society in the School of Engineering and Applied Sciences of the University of Virginia. Trained in philosophy, Johnson's scholarship focuses broadly on the connections between ethics and technology, especially the ethical issues arising around computers and information technology. Two of her books were published in 2009: the fourth edition of *Computer Ethics* (Prentice Hall), and *Technology and Society: Engineering our Sociotechnical Future,* co-edited with J. Wetmore (MIT Press). As an interdisciplinary scholar, Johnson has published over fifty papers on a wide range of topics and in a variety of journals and edited volumes. Currently Johnson serves as co-editor of the journal *Ethics and Information Technology*, published by Springer, and on the Executive Board of the Association for Practical and Professional Ethics. Johnson received the John Barwise prize from the American Philosophical Association in 2004; the Sterling Olmsted Award from the Liberal Education Division of the American Society for Engineering Education in 2001; and the ACM SIGCAS Making a Difference Award in 2000.

Michalis Lianos is Professor at the University of Rouen-Haute Normandie and Director of the Groupe de Recherche Innovations et Sociétés (GRIS). He was previously Lecturer at the University of London (Goldsmiths College) and Director of the Centre for Empirically Informed Social Theory (CEIST) at the University of Portsmouth. Michalis' publications include Le nouveau contrôle social (Paris, L'Harmattan, 2001) and "Social Control after Foucault," *Surveillance and Society*, 1:3, 2003.

Dr. Maria Los is Professor Emerita at the University of Ottawa, where she was Professor of Criminology. She is a Research Adjunct Professor at the Institute of European and Russian Studies and the Department of Legal Studies, Carleton University. Her books include *Crime and Markets in Post-Communist Democracies* (Special Issue of *Law, Crime and Social Change*, 2003), *Privatizing the Police-State: the Case of Poland* (Palgrave/ Macmillan Press, with A. Zybertowicz, 2000), *The Second Economy in Marxist States* (Macmillan / St. Martin's Press 1990), *Communist Ideology, Law and Crime* (Macmillan / St. Martin's Press 1988), *Multi-Dimensional Sociology* (Routledge and Kegan Paul, with A. Podgorecki, 1979). She has published numerous scholarly articles and chapters in books in several languages as well as poems, including a volume of collected poems, in her native Polish. Her interests have included sociology and philosophy of law; crime, law and order in communist and post-communist countries; women and the law; mechanisms of total domination, and theorizing surveillance in late modernity. Professor Los has been a Visiting Fellow at Fitzwilliam College and the Institute of Criminology, University of Cambridge, England (1989); Research Scholar at the Woodrow Wilson Center for International Scholars, Smithsonian Institution, Washington, DC, USA. (1988); Research Fellow in Socio-Legal Studies, Social Science Research Council, England (1978–79); Ford Foundation Fellow, USA (1973–74).

David Lyon holds a Queen's Research Chair and is Professor of Sociology and Director of the Surveillance Studies Centre at Queen's University, Canada. His most recent books are *Surveillance Studies: an Overview* (Polity 2007) and *Identifying Citizens: ID Cards as Surveillance* (Polity 2009).

Maureen Meadows is Senior Lecturer in Management at the Open University Business School, and Centre Head for Strategy and Marketing. Previously she held a Lectureship in Operational Research at Warwick Business

School. Her commercial experience was with National Westminster Bank, initially in an internal consultancy role, and subsequently as a Strategic Marketing Manager for Personal Financial Services, with responsibility for market segmentation and distribution channels. She holds a BA in Mathematics from the University of Oxford and an MSc in Management Science and Operational Research from Warwick. Maureen's current research interests focus on the use of methods and models in strategy development, including scenario planning and visioning. She is exploring the use of strategy tools to support strategic conversations in groups, and the role of managers' cognitive styles in determining their experiences of strategy tools. Maureen has also published on the progress of a range of strategic projects in retail financial services and other sectors, including market segmentation, relationship marketing and customer relationship management.

Anthony Minnaar is a Senior Researcher and postgraduate student coordinator for the Department of Security Risk Management at the School of Criminal Justice in the College of Law at the University of South Africa (UNISA). In the early 1990s he published largely on issues of political violence and conflict, *inter alia* hostel violence, warlordism, massacres, and the proliferation of firearms and self-defense units. In the mid-nineties his research interests turned to other forms of violence such as land disputes, informal settlements, illegal squatting and evictions, taxi-industry conflicts, violence around witchcraft, xenophobia and undocumented migrants and vigilantism. In more recent times he has researched border controls, illegal motor vehicle importations, migrants' rights, vehicle hijackings, use of force by police, informers and witness protection programs and most recently the struggle to legislate for stricter gun controls, the declarations of persons unfit to possess a firearm; and security measures at ports of entry. His current research interests are in the broad field of criminal justice, dealing with the specific issues of corruption prevention, border controls and undocumented migrants, use of firearms in violent crime, civilian oversight of public and private policing, private-security industry issues (specifically crime prevention and private policing; and security at ports of entry) and CCTV open-street surveillance. His most current research project looks at the function and role of the Private Security Industry Regulatory Authority (PSIRA) in regulating and monitoring the private-security industry in South Africa.

Dr. Lilian Mitrou is Assistant Professor at the University of the Aegean, Greece (Department of Information and Communication Systems Engineering) and Visiting Professor at the Athens University of Economics (Postgraduate Studies Program). She teaches information law and data protection law. Dr. Mitrou holds a PhD in Data Protection (University of Frankfurt, Germany). Her thesis concerned the so-called institutional control of data processing and more specifically the Data Protection Models and Authorities in the Federal Republic of Germany and France. She has served as a Member of the Hellenic Data Protection Authority (1999–2003) and as Advisor to former Prime Minister Simitis in the sectors of Information Society and Public Administration (1996–2004). From 1998 to 2004 she was the national representative in the EC Committee on the Protection of Individuals with regard to the Processing of Personal Data. She served as member of many committees working on law proposals in the fields of privacy and data protection, communications law, e-government etc. Her professional experience includes senior consulting and researcher positions in a number of private and public institutions on national and international level. Her research interests include: Privacy and Data Protection; e-democracy and e-government services; internet law. Dr. Mitrou has published books and chapters in books (in Greek, German and English) and many journal and conference papers.

Torin Monahan is an Associate Professor of Human and Organizational Development and Associate Professor of Medicine at Vanderbilt University. He is the editor of *Surveillance and Security: Technological Politics and Power in Everyday Life* (Routledge, 2006) and the author of *Globalization, Technological Change, and Public Education* (Routledge, 2005). He is trained in science and technology studies (STS), which is an interdisciplinary, social-science field devoted to studying the societal implications of and design processes behind technological systems and scientific knowledge. Monahan's main theoretical interests are in social control and institutional transformations with new technologies. He is a member of the international Surveillance Studies Network and is on the editorial board for the primary academic journal on surveillance, *Surveillance & Society*.

Minas Samatas is Associate Professor of Political Sociology in the Sociology Department of the University of Crete, and has a PhD in sociology from the Sociology Department of the Graduate Faculty of the New School for Social Research, New York, USA. His doctoral dissertation, "Greek Bureaucratism: A system of socio-political control," received the Albert Salomon Memorial Award as the best PhD thesis of the New School for 1986. He has published in international and Greek journals on issues such as "Greek McCarthyism," "Greece in 'Schengenland'," "Security and Surveillance in Athens 2004 Olympics", "Surveillance Expansion and Resistance in Post-Olympics Greece," and so on. Based on his research and book *Surveillance in Greece: From Anticommunist to the Consumer Surveillance*, Pella, NY, 2004, he is a participant in various international surveillance study groups.

Kent A. Wayland is an anthropologist, and a Postdoctoral Research Associate in the Department of Science, Technology, and Society at the University of Virginia. In addition to a new project analyzing surveillance and transparency as accountability systems, his research areas include the cultural politics and technological practices of restoring Second World War planes and conceptions of cultural exchange in undergraduate service-learning projects.

Jennifer R. Whitson is a Sociology PhD student at Carleton University. She holds a Canada Graduate Scholarship and was co-editor of the 2005 special double volume of the journal *Surveillance & Society* on "Doing Surveillance Studies." Her current research interests include digital identity management, governance in online domains, identity theft, and software development processes. Her most recent work includes a chapter, co-authored with Aaron Doyle, on virtual world governance in Stéphane Leman-Langlois' edited collection, *Technocrime,* and an article on identity theft, co-authored with Kevin Haggerty, in the November 2008 issue of *Economy and Society.*

Introduction

Surveillance and democracy: an unsettled relationship

Kevin D. Haggerty and Minas Samatas

Surveillance, when positioned on a normative continuum, tends to sit at the polar opposite of democracy. Democracy rests with the angels, signifying all that is laudable and promising about government. At the other extreme lurks surveillance; a sinister force that threatens personal liberties. What could be more self-evident than the fact that surveillance curtails personal freedoms, inhibits democracy, and ultimately leads to totalitarianism (Haggerty, 2009; Rule, 2007)? That said, readers looking to rally around the mantra "surveillance is undermining democracy" will only scratch the surface of this volume. While contributors accentuate the challenges that surveillance poses to democratic forms of governance, this book is more generally an opportunity to hold these two ostensibly antithetical phenomena in creative tension; to deepen our thinking about the various relationships that exist between democracy and surveillance.

The first difficulty that arises when thinking about surveillance and democracy is that both concepts are complex. If we start with democracy, we quickly recognize the truth of George Orwell's (1946) observation that there are forces aligned against attempts to provide a meaningful definition: "… not only is there no agreed definition, but the attempt to make one is resisted from all sides. It is almost universally felt that when we call a country democratic we are praising it: consequently the defenders of every kind of regime claim that it is a democracy, and fear that they might have to stop using that word if it were tied down to any one meaning." Moreover, as we will see, democracy is a multi-faceted phenomenon, meaning that there can be considerable variability amongst countries with a legitimate claim to being democratic.

Notwithstanding such variability and contestation, democracy can succinctly, if not unproblematically, be characterized as power exercised by the people. Democracy involves a system of open procedures for making decisions in which all members have an equal right to speak and have their opinions count. Democracy is appealing, in part, because it promises to contribute to effective decision-making informed by the interests of a wide group of people while also protecting individuals from the corrupting effects of power. Consequently, democracy is commonly associated with practices designed to ensure the fair and equitable operation of participatory decision-making. Ideally, it recognizes the interests of the majority while also trying to protect the concerns of the minority.

Democracy, however, is much more than a system for making decisions; it is also an idea, a doctrine, a set of institutional arrangements, and a way to relate to others. Some of the wider constellation of democratic practices include open discussion between competing views; the equal right of members to have a say, to elect office holders and to influence their deliberations; and the freedom to associate with others.

A vital aspect of democratic governance with a direct bearing on surveillance issues is that democracies are accountable to their citizens, meaning that they have to produce accounts for various constituencies (the media, legislature, citizens), and also that governments face a meaningful prospect of sanction if they act illegally. Accountability therefore implies that citizens need access to a range of information about the actions of their representatives and a free press to assess the behavior of their government. Civil liberties and human-rights legislation aim to protect such arrangements and strike an appropriate balance between competing interests. Liberal democracies consequently emphasize individual rights, as the smooth operation of a democratic systems is presumably enhanced when we protect rights of communication and democratic participation. The rights pertaining to privacy and freedom of expression therefore have pride of place in discussions about surveillance.

As is apparent at several points in this volume, democracy can also be associated with a more substantive ends-orientation, meaning that democratic governments are evaluated on the degree to which they provide citizens with security of the person and of his or her possessions. Based on such an understanding, democratic governments are expected to improve citizens' quality of life, an ambition that is either implicit in the concept of democracy itself or a natural by-product of including "the people" in policy considerations and political rhetoric. This more tangible understanding of democracy also means that many forms of social critique are themselves founded on a comprehensive notion of democracy. So, for example, irrespective of whether a citizen lambastes her government because its institutions have not followed proper procedures, because some groups unfairly bear the burden of social policies or because the rights of identifiable minorities have been downgraded, all such critiques can be formulated as faulting the government for failing to live up to a democratic ideal. The upshot is that democracy, understood as a flexible and historically specific standard for evaluating what is just, fair and right, has increasingly become the rhetorical ground from which many, if not most, social criticisms are launched in liberal societies.

Turning our attention from democracy to surveillance, we also find a series of ambiguities at play. Definitionally, surveillance involves assorted forms of monitoring, typically for the ultimate purpose of intervening in the world. While this definition is very broad, it usefully moves us beyond the common fixation on cameras and espionage, which is what tends to immediately come to mind when thinking about surveillance. Difficulties start to emerge, however, when we move beyond precise definitions and try to contemplate the enormous range and variability of surveillance practices that now operate. The most familiar and longstanding of these are the routine forms of interpersonal scrutiny which are an inevitable component of human interaction (Goffman, 1959). Today, such informal face-to-face scrutiny has been augmented by a raft of initiatives designed to make people more transparent. Indeed, surveillance is now the dominant organizing practice of late modernity, and is used for a multitude of widely divergent governmental projects, by turns both laudable and disconcerting (Gandy, 1993; Haggerty and Ericson, 2006; Hier and Greenberg, 2007; Lyon, 2007).

Western nations are undergoing a world-historical transformation in the dynamics of social visibility. Institutions are capitalizing on technologically augmented scrutiny of different categories of people (citizens, motorists, workers, students, consumers, international travelers, military adversaries, welfare recipients, and assorted other groupings) to enhance such things as rational governance, corporate profit, social regulation, entertainment and military conquest. We can appreciate the centrality of surveillance to organizational and epistemological endeavourers if we simply step back and survey how various manifestations of watching have become a central institutional preoccupation. Just a quick listing of surveillance-related initiatives culled from the newspaper would include databases, espionage, military satellites, bureaucratic files, Internet monitoring, and assorted personal spying devices.

The picture becomes even murkier when we realize that these different practices and technologies can be used for highly variable projects of control, regulation, care, governance, scientific advancement, profit, entertainment, and the like. A global community of scholars has produced excellent case studies of the dynamics and normative implications of different surveillance practices, but run into more difficulty when it tries to make generalizations about surveillance *tout court* (Haggerty and Ericson, 2006), often because the surveillance dynamics and implications of, say, spy satellites, are wildly different from those of DNA testing.

As citizens start to become attuned to the pervasiveness of surveillance, we suspect that they will recognize that most Western nations would now qualify as surveillance societies given the centrality of surveillance to myriad institutional practices (Murakami Wood, 2009). This is itself related to what appears to be a fairly remarkable change in public sentiments. The existence of such things as CCTV cameras on the streets, transponders in cars, and detailed mobile-phone records, have made monitoring a routine and often prosaic attribute of social existence. While there is public debate on surveillance's excesses, the envelope has been pushed strongly in the direction of normalized and routinized surveillance.

As the world becomes increasingly transparent to public and private agencies alike, what does this mean for key attributes of democratic practice, such as civil liberties, political dialogue, citizenship and trust in political authority? Does a society configured for surveillance give rise to nightmare totalitarian scenarios, or, alternatively, offer unprecedented opportunities to care for our most needy and foster an inclusive public sphere?

The remainder of this chapter sets the stage for this collection by drawing attention to some of the central themes in the relationship between surveillance and democracy. While we could not begin to address the full scope of issues involved, we have highlighted some topics that repeatedly emerge in such discussions. We do so by dividing our comments into three parts. First, we analyze some of the ways that surveillance can inhibit democracy. We then discuss how surveillance in different forms can, perhaps paradoxically, be a key precondition or vital attribute of democratic processes. Our third section touches upon the question of whether the opportunities for democratic practices to shape surveillance dynamics are receding. The concluding section provides a brief synopsis of the book itself.

Surveillance as corrosive barrier

By far the most common way that commentators understand the relationship between surveillance and democracy is as surveillance hindering democracy, alternately inhibiting the growth of representative institutions, corroding established democratic traditions and undermining patterns of sociability and trust that are essential preconditions for fostering democratic practice.

The fascist governments of the twentieth century and the new millennia's totalitarian states provide the most telling examples of how massive state-conducted surveillance can become a tool of state repression. Ostensibly democratic nations have also been guilty of such behavior, and there are too many examples to begin to list them all here. Some of the more infamous examples include the American Cold-War scrutiny of labor organizations, Civil Rights activists and the more recent attention that many Western nations are directing at Muslim groups.

Such monitoring is typically framed and criticized from within a liberal framework which distinguishes between a public realm of political action and a private sphere of personal fulfillment and family intimacy (see Brighenti in this volume). Intrusive state surveillance can destroy that distinction, undermining the private realm and in so doing limiting a person's ability to develop a unique sense of self and of his or her political interests. Such scrutiny can also have more straightforward implications for democracy. Citizens need a space comparatively free of governmental oversight if they are to engage in political action. Surveillance is therefore anti-democratic to the extent that it prevents individuals from coming together to identify common interests, forge alliances and develop political strategies. Such a result is sometimes the explicit aim of conducting surveillance, or alternatively, can be an unintended by-product of monitoring. In either scenario, such surveillance can corrode the interpersonal trust required for democratic governance (Tilly, 2005).

Intrusive surveillance is typically used by political elites to suppress different viewpoints and in so doing limit the possibility for alternative political constituencies to emerge or become effective. As such, surveillance can be one component in wider practices of state censorship. Keeping in mind how vital open public debate and a free press are for democratic governance, surveillance that operates to quench dissent can have disastrous consequences for the prospect of nurturing a democratic public sphere (Habermas, 1989). Consequently, surveillance can not only violate personal privacy, but can inhibit freedom of expression.

Today, there is much concern about how surveillance might chill democratic participation. As citizens become more attuned to the increased transparency of their actions and communications, recognizing that there is an (always unknowable) potential that in the future officials will act upon things they said or did, people will self-censor, withdraw from public life, and in so doing render democratic debate and participation anaemic (see Mitrou in this volume).

In thinking about these dangers, activists and academics are understandably fixated on the monitoring capabilities of contemporary information technologies. It is worth remembering, however, that some of the most manifestly repressive and anti-democratic forms of state surveillance—such as was conducted by East Germany's notorious secret police, the Stasi—did not rely on cutting-edge technologies, but instead drew upon extensive networks of informers; common citizens who were either enticed or coerced into informing on others (Schmeidel, 2008). We mention this as a reminder of the need to foreground ongoing efforts by the state's security establishment to initiate and coordinate forms of interpersonal monitoring. Perhaps the most well-known, recent initiative was the Bush administration's ill-fated proposal in the aftermath of the 9/11 attacks to create Operation TIPS (Terrorism Information and Prevention System). This legislation would have empowered a wide array of American citizens (postal employees, telephone repair workers, cable installers, and the like) to report "suspicious" behavior of citizens to the federal government. The scale of that program would have meant that the United States would "have a higher percentage of citizen informants than the former East Germany through the infamous Stasi secret police" (Goldstein, 2002).

Another reason to keep in mind the dynamics of state-coordinated interpersonal scrutiny is because they provide the most familiar and well chronicled example of how repressive state surveillance can create anti-democratic legacies. Citizens of nations trying to transition from a totalitarian past to a more democratic future often find themselves confronting revelations that they were spied on by family, friends, and lovers on behalf of the previous regime. Beyond the destructive effects that such discoveries can have on communities, they have also created a context in Eastern Europe where established interests have fortified their hold on power by blackmailing prior informants (Funder 2003; Garton Ash 1997; Los in this volume; Samatas 2004)

Enhancements in information technologies have prompted their own surveillance-related anxieties. Beyond the well-documented fears about how such systems allow for intensified monitoring of citizens, making them transparent to a previously unimaginable degree while also allowing for complex behavior modeling, there is also a concern about how new forms of surveillance, particularly dataveillance (Garfinkel 2000), tend to disaggregate populations. Initially developed in the private sector, such monitoring is used by corporations seeking to carve out precise market segments in order to maximize the effectives of their marketing and to orient their businesses model to identifiable consumer niches. In the process, the notion of a singular "consumer" has given way to a proliferation of detailed market segments that are the product of ongoing surveillance of consumer purchases, survey responses and service use patterns (Gandy 1993; Turow 1997; Turow 2007).

In recent years this form of surveillance has also moved into the public realm, being used to target service delivery or in the increasingly unrelenting practice of electioneering. As such disaggregating forms of surveillance move into the electoral sphere there is a danger that standards of equal citizenship are starting to evaporate. Individualizing surveillance fractures the aggregate "public"—leading to increasingly narrow political appeals. As Ball et al. (in this volume) point out, such surveillance subtly changes how people are conceived of within a democratic system, moving from a notion of "citizen" to one of "consumer." In the process the incentive to contemplate the aggregate needs of the citizenry recedes, in favor of appealing to the desires of disproportionately significant electoral niches.

The second difficulty that this disaggregating tendency of surveillance poses for democracy is that it also fosters a form of informational narrowcasting. As citizens come to be identified with specific market or political niches, the tendency both for the citizen and for informational systems is towards replication. That is, the surveillance system identifies their existing preferences and serves them more of the same: the same news, political appeals, and the like, cumulatively limiting the variety of information to which citizens are exposed (Sustein 2001). Such a development is particularly disconcerting given that it works against the desire to nurture an electorate with a broad vision and sensitivity to other points of view.

Surveillance as necessary, inevitable or desirable?

While much public commentary focuses on the challenges that new forms of surveillance pose for democracy, there is also a sense that surveillance, when understood broadly, is both an inevitable attribute of democracy and a key component of liberal forms of governance. Indeed, even among civil libertarians most concerned about, for example, police surveillance, few would argue that the police should completely eschew wire taps, informants, under-cover work and other comparable components of police work. Such surveillance is now required, given that it is near impossible to penetrate complex criminal organizations through more traditional police work. Moreover, it is often imperative for a functioning democracy to curtail the illegal behaviors that are investigated using such measures, as these activities can pose a threat to democratic institutions. For the police, the ongoing challenge is to balance their need for surveillance against the often-corrosive consequences of such measures.

Not every individual who physically resides in a state's territory is necessarily entitled to the same democratic rights. States discriminate amongst members of the population to determine who can and cannot vote, who is to be afforded additional rights and entitlements, and so on. The state's need to identify citizens and make discriminations among the population has contributed to the growth of systems that essentially create the informational structures of citizenship (see Lyon in this volume). Whether in a democratic nation or else-where, citizenship is marked by a host of identity documents, and to be a citizen is to be identified as such on the appropriate bureaucratic systems (Groebner, 2007; Torpey, 2000).

The extent to which such officially recognized citizens can provide politicians with meaningful or binding direction is today blunted by many factors. The sheer scale of contemporary societies makes it impossible for the entire polity to physically come together to debate issues and cast their vote. The rise of the party system was at least partly a response to this issue of scale, but it also kept citizens several steps removed from the levers of power. These and comparable developments have produced a sense that democratic participation, even in the most exemplary democratic societies, has become thin and formulaic. Public input is often reduced to an intermittent opportunity to choose parties or leaders, something that can amount to choice among barely distinguishable options. Low levels of voter turnout in many of the world's ostensibly leading democracies testify to the public apathy that such a situation can produce.

A series of countervailing developments have introduced opportunities for citizens' views to play a more direct role in shaping political decisions or, more cynically, becoming the target of conscious political manipulation. Governance, particularly in its liberal form, depends on knowledge and is contingent on producing official, typically quantified, facts (Haggerty, 2001; Rose, 1999). Before programming is initiated both problematic situations and problem people must ideally be known, and known in empirical detail. As Scott (1998) has accentuated, the state has a built-in tendency to embrace a form of optics conductive to ways of making problems legible to centralized authorities, culminating in efforts to document, standardize and register the social (and natural) world. Hence, we experience the routine deployment of a style of political discourse and practice that privileges appeals to certain forms of empirical facts perceived to be actionable by government officials. These facts are typically the product of a surveillance infrastructure.

Official attempts to learn about a problem involve establishing or drawing upon an attendant surveillance regime. Fears of a pandemic prompt new forms of disease surveillance. If the problem is adolescents using drugs, parents can compel their progeny to urinate in a bottle so that they can use home drug-testing kits to scrutinize their behavior (Moore and Haggerty, 2001), and so on. In each instance a specific problematization prompts a political demand for more and better governmentally relevant knowledge, which, in turn, depends upon a specific monitoring regime. In many cases the causal arrow points in the opposite direction, as proponents of new surveillance technologies work to foster an official interest in the type of knowledge that their devices can generate. The point is that surveillance is an inevitable facet in producing governmentally relevant knowledge.

One of the most important of these surveillance infrastructures for the operation of contemporary governmental practices is the public opinion polling industry that now feeds an insatiable political machine. While there were public opinion polls as early as the 1820s, the practice only proliferated in Western societies in the 1940s with the pioneering work of George Gallup (Herbst, 1993; Page, 2006). While few would suggest that these surveys represent an ideal way for political authorities to learn about citizens' views, the knowledge that they generate has nonetheless fundamentally altered political dynamics in Western nations, and they are now an inescapable attribute of policy development and campaigning. Indeed, beyond the intermittent exercise of the vote, opinion surveys are now the most significant and institutionalized form of political knowledge generated about citizens' attitudes and preferences.

The rise of the survey industry was itself contingent on exponential increases in computing power. As networked computers have become a common household item, they have also become a groundbreaking political technology. We are still in the midst of the transformations flowing from the embrace of these tools, so it is difficult to discern the precise contours of how computers have shaped and will continue to shape politics. Few, however, doubt that their impact will be anything less than monumental—which is not necessarily the same as being desirable.

For some, computers are harbingers of a new era of democratic participation, given their combined ability to provide near immediate feedback on policy options while allowing officials to scrutinize individual's online behavior to ascertain public preferences and priorities. As computers become more interactive, and as individual citizens (often inadvertently) come to signify more about their preferences, desires and inclinations through their daily electronically recorded activities, policy will inevitably be informed by the knowledge generated about such actions. For the optimists, these changes promise to usher in a world of greater democratic practice and political accountability.

Others are less sanguine about these developments, suggesting that the utopians are naïve about the real-world dynamics of power and are initiating yet another round of technocentric hyperbole in celebrating the emancipatory political potential of computers. Instead of seeing greater political participation altering the nature of established social hierarchies, critics suggest that the surveillance capacities inherent in computers allow private institutions and political interests to cynically manipulate the populous, offering in the guise of "interactivity" little more than a series of highly circumscribed choices crafted by elites and powerful special-interest groups (Andrejevic, 2007).

In democracies there is an expectation that citizens will be able to scrutinize governmental affairs. Under the rubric of "accountability," a proliferating number of bureaucratic monitoring systems have been established, contributing to the normatively ambiguous rise of an audit society (Power, 1997). Both public and private institutions are under increasing pressure to provide formal accounts of their actions, something that also relies on systems designed to scrutinize personal behavior and institutional routines (see Johnston and Wayland in this volume). This quest for political visibility has also come at a cost, as auditing, for example, can distort organizational mandates and privilidge phenomena simply because they are easily measured.

Perhaps the most extreme argument for the necessity or desirability of surveillance to contemporary democratic systems is provided by David Brin (1998) in his book *The Transparent Society*. Brin starts from the assumption that surveillance is becoming ubiquitous. In such a context appeals to privacy tend to reinforce a form of non-reciprocal visibility, with authorities and elites being able to secure some limited privacy protection while the lives of the masses are opened up to ever-greater scrutiny. Brin's provocative proposal is for a form of radical transparency, a situation whereby all parties would have equal access to all of the information generated by different surveillance and administrative systems. The key point is that the watchers would be as open to scrutiny as the common citizen. Rather than presenting this as a dystopia, Brin sees this as a measure that could reduce the positional advantage elites have in maintaining their privacy while also allowing for the development of reciprocal surveillance norms which would dictate when it is and is not appropriate to examine revealing information. While Brin might be guilty of trying to make a virtue out of a necessity, his focus on the non-reciprocal nature of visibility accentuates one of the most recurrent concerns about contemporary surveillance.

Limits to democratic oversight

Greater democratization often appears to be a panacea for individuals concerned about the continuing expansion of surveillance; democracy promises to introduce systems of accountability that will provide some bulwark against our nonchalant drift towards a despotic surveillance society. With that in mind, we conclude our brief introduction on a regrettably despondent note, accentuating some of the factors that limit the prospect for meaningful democratic accountability as it pertains to surveillance.

The first point to note is that today many surveillance developments are technological. Groundbreaking surveillance initiatives emerge out of laboratories with each new imputation of computer software or hardware. These augmented technological capacities are only rarely seen as necessitating explicit policy decisions, and as such disperse into society with little or no official political discussion. Or, alternatively, the comparatively slow timelines of electoral politics often ensure that any formal scrutiny of the dangers or desirability of surveillance technologies only occurs long after the expansion of the surveillance measure is effectively a *fait accompli*.

By default, then, many of the far-reaching questions about how surveillance systems will be configured occur in organizational back regions amongst designers and engineers, and therefore do not benefit from the input of a wider range of representative constituencies. Sclove (1995) has drawn attention to this technological democratic deficit, and calls for greater public input at the earliest stages of system design (see also Monahan in this volume). And while this is a laudable ambition, the prospect of bringing citizens into the design process confronts a host of pragmatic difficulties, not the least of which are established understandings of what constitutes relevant expertise in a technologized society.

Even when surveillance measures have been introduced by representative bodies this is no guarantee that these initiatives reflect the will of an informed and reasoned electorate. One of the more important dynamics in this regard concerns the long history whereby fundamental changes in surveillance practice and infrastructure have been initiated in times of national crisis. The most recent and telling example of this process occurred after 9/11 when many Western governments, the United States most prominently, passed omnibus legislation that introduced dramatic new surveillance measures justified as a means to enhance national security (Ball and Webster, 2003; Haggerty and Gazso, 2005; Lyon, 2003). This legislation received almost no political debate, and was presented to the public in such a way that it was impossible to appreciate the full implications of the proposed changes. This, however, was just the latest in the longstanding practice of politicians embracing surveillance at times of heightened fear. At such junctures one is more apt to encounter nationalist jingoism than measured debate about the merits and dangers of turning the state's surveillance infrastructure on suspect populations.

The example of 9/11 accentuates the issue of state secrets, which can also limit the democratic oversight of surveillance. While few would dispute the need for state secrets, particularly in matters of national security, their existence raises serious issues insofar as the public is precluded from accessing the information needed to judge the actions of its leaders. In terms of surveillance, this can include limiting access to information about the operational dynamics of established surveillance systems, or even simply denying the existence of specific surveillance schemes. Citizens are asked (or simply expected) to trust that their leaders will use this veil of secrecy to undertake actions that the public would approve of if they were privy to the specific details. Unfortunately, history has demonstrated time and again that this trust is often abused, and knowledge of past misconduct feeds a political climate infused with populist conspiracy theories (Fenster, 2008). Indeed, one need not be paranoid to contemplate the prospect that, as surveillance measures are increasingly justified in terms of national security, a shadow "security state" is emerging—one empowered by surveillance, driven by a profit motive, cloaked in secrecy and unaccountable to traditional forms of democratic oversight (see Hayes in this volume).

A central dilemma in trying to establish democratic oversight of surveillance measures concerns larger dynamics in the international system of states and corporations. Over the past quarter century a neoliberal project of globalization has resulted in the steady decline of national sovereignty. One upshot is that the bodies which effectively govern a host of matters, including concrete affairs of security and surveillance, are effectively unaccountable to the citizens who will be subject to these policies. One example of this is the internationalization of domestic policy-making in the European Union where "around seventy per cent of new legislation in the UK originates in Brussels, where it is subject to the approval of a ministerial council drawn from all member states" (Beetham, 2005:59). This is itself part of what Vibert (2007) characterizes as the "rise of the unelected," a process whereby assorted private institutions ranging from banks, international organizations and regulators operate a form of post-democratic governance.

The internationalization of surveillance can also occur more informally, as smaller states are pressured to bend to the sway of the surveillance-infused agendas of the remaining superpower and corporations aligned with its geopolitical aspirations. In the domain of realpolitik, small democratic nations can have little opportunity to resist the hegemony of major states and an increasingly international surveillance industrial complex (see Hayes and Samatas, both in this volume).

All of this points to one of the most intractable dilemmas pertaining to surveillance and democracy, which is the play of private corporations on the surveillance landscape. Democracy is not the operative principle of private companies, but these entities initiate an ever greater percentage of surveillance measures. Moreover, with the ongoing corporate appropriation of the internet, assorted informational spaces where people spend an increasing amount of time socializing are being revealed to be legally private spaces, and not subject to principles of democratic accountability (see Whitson in this volume). In an era of globalization, it is hard to bring such companies under the sway of national interests, with the upshot being that large swathes of our lives are lived in the confines of surveillance-infused institutions where claims to democratic representation have no purchase.

All of the above could be read in many different ways. For the most optimistic, these developments can be interpreted as a self-evident case for why we need ever more democratic accountability on matters of surveillance. For the pessimist, this reads like a litany of reasons why the prospect of a democratic check on surveillance is receding to a vanishing point on the horizon. Irrespective of how one interprets these trends, it is undeniable that the issues of surveillance and democracy are now more unsettled than at any time in the recent past, making the need to address such concerns all the more compelling.

Structure of this book

While the different contributions to this volume inform one another and present occasionally overlapping and reinforcing insights, we have divided the chapters into three sections to greater accentuate thematic continuity. The first section, "Theorizing Surveillance and Democracy," sets the stage by providing theoretical tools and analytical distinctions useful in contemplating the relationship between surveillance and democracy. Johnson and Wayland usefully interrogate two key themes that run throughout the entire collection. In particular, they make the novel move of differentiating between surveillance and transparency systems. Although both are understood as sociotechnical systems of accountability, the nature of how this accountability operates is quite different in each realm. For them, surveillance is positioned as a more intrusive act of watching individuals, typically conducted by state operatives. In contrast, transparency systems are often directed at private and governmental organizations, and designed to ensure that these institutions adhere to established administrative protocols.

David Lyon's contribution accentuates a central tension inherent in the relationship between citizenship and surveillance. That is, the paradoxical situation whereby administrative forms of surveillance are needed to establish rights and obligations, but that these same systems of identification can be used to more arbitrarily coerce or manipulate individuals. Following on from this insight, Lyon considers ID cards in the context of questions about democratic citizenship, detailing the history of modern identification and the emergence of new forms of social sorting that derive from such measures. He explores how these processes can affect the operation of governance and how individual citizens might alter the dynamics of identification.

Brighenti abstracts up from the unique manifestation of surveillance to frame these issue unders the larger concept of "regimes of visibility." He differentiates between how visibility is understood to operate in terms of democratic theory versus Foucauldian studies of governance. Rather than public visibility being anathema to democracy, Brighenti argues that regimes of visibility help constitute political regimes. Consequently, the established liberal notion that privacy is valuable because it protects a form of private life free from scrutiny is misleading. Indeed, a key attribute of democracy is that it involves others being visible in prescribed ways. We should therefore contemplate visibility regimes as involving an emergent internal organization of social relations by means of visibility arrangements that shape both public and private realms.

For Lianos, the fundamental question of how surveillance might relate to democracy emerges obliquely from his analysis of the dynamics of social control in Western societies. He demarcates a historical periodization whereby forms of value-based control characteristic of democratic and interpersonal forms of sociality are receding as more and more of social life is coordinated by and through a complex web of institutions. One implication of this development is that the longstanding opposition between control and democracy is defused, as control becomes built into the institutional structures that make sociality possible. Consequently, the scope for individuals to negotiate the dynamics of surveillance-based forms of control recede in favor of the ceaseless production of a web of competing utilitarian functions.

The second section of the book is entitled "Surveillance Politics and Practices of Democratic Governance." Here the contributions are slightly more applied explorations of both the operation and regulation of surveillance in light of democratic concerns. Torin Monahan's chapter focuses on the role of surveillance in routine forms of anti-democratic social control. Building upon work in science and technology studies he accentuates how technologies can be inherently political. In terms of how this applies to surveillance, Monahan notes that surveillance technologies typically operate through the dynamics of both differential and automated control, and how these can undermine democratic aspirations. To counter these anti-democratic tendencies, he advocates measures to incorporate citizens in the design and creation of surveillance technologies, and offers intriguing examples of how this can work in practice.

For their part, Ball and her colleagues also follow the insight that technologies can be inherently political to explore the anti-democratic tendencies of customer relationship management (CRM). These tools were initially developed in the private sector to use dataveillance to foster relationships between corporations and consumers. In recent years, such techniques have also become appealing to governments, something encouraged at least in part by the rise of a pervasive market sensibility in Western nations. That said, the authors note that providing government services does not neatly mimic market dynamics, raising questions about the desirability of applying CRM in the public sector. One of the more disconcerting attributes of such tools is that CRM is based on a drive to treat individuals differently, and when applied in the public sector this can work against the democratic ethos of equality.

Mitrou's chapter also explores the possible anti-democratic implications of measures that make the average citizen more transparent. She analyzes new

European measures designed to retain information about a citizen's electronic communications. While some see this development as innocuous given that they do not store actual communication content, Mitrou accentuates how much potentially sensitive information can be derived from the data that is collected. As the public becomes more aware of such measures there is a risk that this will produce an anti-democratic chilling effect, as individuals wary of how their information might be used in the future start to self-censor any communications that could be construed as having political implications. Mitrou interrogates how these measures can limit the democratic rights to privacy, expression and freedom of movement.

Whereas most analysts of surveillance typically concentrate on the implications of one unique practice or technology, Hayes presents a disturbing vision of the overall direction of how assorted surveillance measures are being aligned in the ostensible service of securing the European Union. Rather than surveillance expanding in an ad-hoc fashion, he details an explicit agenda being pushed by non-representative agencies with strong ties to large international military and security firms. Their aim is to establish a form of domestic "full spectrum dominance" that relies on new information technologies to create a form of largely unaccountable control over all risks that different groups are imagined to pose.

The contributions in the final section of the book are organized under the heading "Case Studies in the Dynamics of Surveillance and Democracy." Here the emphasis is on specific examples of the unsettled relationship between surveillance and democracy. Maria Los outlines some of the lingering deleterious effects of the totalitarian forms of surveillance that were a mainstay of Europe's Communist regimes. As these nations have sought to become more democratic they have also had to grapple with how to regulate the social and political risks inherent in opening up the secret archive to reveal who informed on friends, colleagues and loved ones. These developments have also raised questions about the contemporary effectiveness of the strategies for resisting surveillance that were practiced under Communism.

Anthony Minnaar's chapter concentrates on anti-crime surveillance in South Africa, a country that is also still struggling with the historical legacy of repressive surveillance practices. Minnaar focuses on the rise of both official and informal gated communities in South African neighborhoods, and situates this development in the context of an escalating crime problem and lingering anxieties about race-based forms of exclusion. As he notes, these new physical barriers, and their attendant surveillance systems, smack of a form of privatized racial segregation. What is particularly intriguing about such developments is how debates about their propriety have been framed according to assorted democratic rights, a comparatively novel development given the fairly recent genesis of South Africa's constitution.

In Greece — yet another country trying to come to grips with the legacy of a political regime that used coercive surveillance — more technologically sophisticated forms of surveillance have recently become front-page news. This involved a political scandal that erupted after authorities revealed that the cellular telephones of senior Greek officials had been tapped in the lead-up to the Summer Olympic Games in Athens. Samatas provides a compelling account of the political intrigue surrounding this development, and accentuates the dilemma faced by comparatively small democratic nations who seem incapable of resisting the surveillance intrusions of some of the world's institutional giants, which consist of both nations and corporations.

Appropriately, the final contribution offers us a glimpse of a setting where questions about surveillance and democracy are apt to become paramount in the future. Whitson's analysis of the dynamics of the online community Second Life reveals a world essentially created through and for surveillance, but one that is nonetheless populated by millions of individuals who socialize, shop and engage in political activities within its transparent informational confines. At the same time, Second Life and a range of comparable "digital enclosures" are essentially private legal entities, meaning that notions of democratic account-ability or oversight are alien or non-existent, notwithstanding the democratic aspirations that can occasionally emerge among many denizens of these communities. As online communities continue to proliferate we can expect that questions of democratic accountably on such sites will become evermore prominent.

Ultimately, the contributors to this volume directly engage with some of the myriad ways that democratic issues arise in any consideration of surveillance. At a minimum, they reveal that while the relationship between surveillance and democracy may be unsettled, it also raises some of the most pressing political questions of our day.

References

Andrejevic, Mark. 2007. *iSpy: Surveillance and Power in the Interactive Era*. Lawrence: University Press of Kansas.

Ball, Kirstie and Frank Webster. 2003. "The Intensification of Surveillance." London: Pluto.

Beetham, David. 2005. *Democracy*. Oxford: One World.

Brin, David. 1998. *The Transparent Society: Will Technology Force Us to Choose Between Privacy and Freedom?* Reading, Mass.: Perseus Books.

Fenster, Mark. 2008. *Conspiracy Theories: Secrecy and Power in American Culture*. Minnesota: Universiiyy of Minnesota Press.

Funder, Anna. 2003. *Stasiland: True Stories from Behind the Berln Wall*. London: Granta.

Gandy, Oscar Jr. 1993. *The Panoptic Sort: A Political Economy of Personal Information*. Boulder: Westview.

Garfinkel, Simson. 2000. *Database Nation: The Death of Privacy in the 21st Century*. Sebastopol: O'Reilly.

Garton Ash, Timothy. 1997. *The File: A Personal History*. New York: Vintage.

Goffman, Erving. 1959. *The Presentation of Self in Everyday Life*. Harmondsworth: Penguin.

Goldstein, Ritt. 2002. "US Planning to Recruit one in 24 Americans as Citizen Spies." *Sydney Morning Herald*.

Groebner, Valentin. 2007. *Who Are You: Identification, Deception and Surveillance in Early Modern England*. Translated by M. Kyburz and J. Peck. New York: Zone Books.

Habermas, Jurgen. 1989. *The Structural Transformation of the Public Sphere*. Cambridge, Mass.: MIT.

Haggerty, Kevin D. 2001. *Making Crime Count*. Toronto: University of Toronto Press.

———. 2009. "'Ten Thousand Times Larger ... ': Anticipating the Expansion of Surveillance." pp. 159–77 in *New Directions in Surveillance and Privacy*, edited by D. Neyland and B. Goold. London: Willan.

Haggerty, Kevin D. and Richard V. Ericson. 2006. "*The New Politics of Surveillance and Visibility*." Toronto: University of Toronto Press.

Haggerty, Kevin D. and Amber Gazso. 2005. "Seeing Beyond the Ruins: Surveillance as a Response to Terrorist Threats." *Canadian Journal of Sociology* 30:169–87.

Herbst, Susan. 1993. *Numbered Voices: How Opinion Polling Has Shaped American Politics*. Chicago: University of Chicago Press.

Hier, Sean and Josh Greenberg. 2007. *The Surveillance Studies Reader*. Maidenhead: Open University Press.

Lyon, David. 2003. *Surveillance After September 11*. London: Polity.

———. 2007. *Surveillance Studies: An Overview*. Cambridge: Polity.

Moore, Dawn and Kevin D. Haggerty. 2001. "Bring It On Home: Home Drug Testing and the Relocation of the War on Drugs." *Social and Legal Studies* 10:377–95.

Murakami Wood, David. 2009. "The 'Surveillance Society': Questions of History, Place and Culture." *European Journal of Criminology* 6:179–94.

Orwell, George. 1946. "Politics and the English Language." *Horizon* 13:252–65.

Page, Christopher. 2006. *The Roles of Public Opinion Research in Canadian Government*. Toronto: University of Toronto Press.

Power, Mike. 1997. *The Audit Society: Rituals of Verification*. Oxford: Oxford University Press.

Rose, Nikolas. 1999. *Powers of Freedom: Reframing Political Thought*. Cambridge: Cambridge University Press.

Rule, James B. 2007. *Privacy in Peril: How We are Sacrificing a Fundamental Right in Exchagne for Security and Convenience*. Oxford: Oxford University Press.

Samatas, Minas. 2004. Surveillance in Greece: From Anticommunist to Consumer Surveillance. New York: Pella.

Schmeidel, John C. 2008. *Stasi*. London: Routledge.

Sclove, Richard. 1995. *Democracy and Technology*. New York: Guilford.

Scott, James C. 1998. *Seeing Like a State*. New Haven: Yale University Press.

Sustein, Cass. 2001. *Republic.com*. Princeton: Princeton University Press.

Tilly, Charles. 2005. *Trust and Rule*. Cambridge: Cambridge University Press.

Torpey, John. 2000. *The Invention of the Passport: Surveillance, Citizenship and the State*. Cambridge: Cambridge University Press.

Turow, J. 1997. *Breaking Up America: Advertisers and the New Media Order*. Chicago: University of Chicago Press.

Turow, Joseph. 2007. *Niche Envy: Marketing Discrimination in the Digital Age*. Cambridge, Mass.: MIT.

Vibert, Frank. 2007. *The Rise of the Unelected: Democracy and the New Separation of Powers*. New York: Cambridge University Press.

Part I

Theorizing surveillance and democracy

Chapter 1

Surveillance and transparency as sociotechnical systems of accountability

Deborah G. Johnson and Kent A. Wayland

In this paper we argue that surveillance can be illuminated by framing surveillance regimes as sociotechnical systems of accountability, and then comparing surveillance to transparency regimes also framed as sociotechnical systems of accountability. We begin by grounding our understanding of accountability in the relationship between technology and democracy. We next explore surveillance and transparency regimes as traditionally and separately conceived and then show how they both function as mechanisms of accountability in democratic societies. The framing allows us, first, to compare the systems and ask a set of questions about how each kind of system constructs and positions individuals, what role information technology (IT) plays in constituting the system, and how relationships of power are arranged and maintained.

STS, IT, and the technology-democracy connection

Research and scholarship in the field of science and technology studies (STS) has, in the last several decades, converged on a thesis generally referred to as "co-construction" or "mutual constitution." The thesis holds that technology both constitutes and is constituted by society. It grew out of early work (Bijker et al., 1987; Bijker and Law, 1992), and has been used to explore a myriad of topics, such as gender (Wajcman, 2004), the role of users in constituting technology (Oudshoorn and Pinch, 2003), issues in medical and biomedical technologies (Oudshoorn, 2003), and the role of technical expertise in decision-making (Jasanoff, 2005). This literature gives a rich and nuanced view of the mutual creation of technology and culture.

One implication of STS theory and the co-construction thesis in particular is that the unit of analysis in technology studies should be sociotechnical systems (rather than artifacts). Technology and society are so intertwined that technology should be understood to be the combination of artifacts, social practices, social arrangements, and meanings. Society or particular social practices must, as well, be understood to be combinations of artifacts, cultural meanings, and social arrangements. In other words, the co-construction thesis goes hand-in-hand with understanding that systems are almost never merely technological or merely social.

Another implication of the co-construction thesis is that values — social, moral, and political — are part of this mutual constitution. Early in the development of the field of STS, Winner's seminal work, "Do artifacts have politics?" (1986) drew attention to the connection between values and technology, but the field subsequently went through a period of neglect (Winner, 1993; but see Bijker, 1993). In recent years, however, interest in the connection has returned (Hackett et al., 2008) and more attention is being given, broadly, to the normative implications of STS scholarship.

Scholars in the field of computer ethics and, more broadly, those who study the social implications of IT have readily taken up normative issues and brought attention to values being promoted, undermined, or simply transformed through information technology. However, while normative scholarship in these fields has been robust, only recently have these scholars begun to draw on work in STS. For recent work in computer ethics drawing on STS see, for example, Verbeek (2006), Keulartz et al. (2004), and Introna (2007).

The value that most concerns us here is democracy. Scholarship in STS, computer ethics, and the social implications of IT has, in varying ways, addressed the link between technology and democracy, though more often than not the link is presumed or hinted at rather than explicitly addressed. The most prominent technology–democracy themes found in the STS literature are those focused on the role of expertise and of public / citizen participation in democratic decision-making, or, more broadly, how to understand citizenship in technocratic societies. Thorpe (2008), for example, suggests that STS scholarship has tended to focus on democratizing expertise and on the implications of STS scholarship for democratic / public participation (see also Kleinman, 2000; Hamlett, 2003). Another related stream of analysis in STS is focused on social movements and activism (Hess et al., 2008). Significant progress has been made in these areas and the scholarship continues to reveal new possibilities for technological decision-making in democratic societies.

Scholarship in the fields of computer ethics and the social implications of computers has taken the technology–democracy connection up specifically with regard to IT. Bimber (2003) examines the effects of the internet on democratic politics while Johnson (2007) addresses technological literacy. Here there is also important work on values in design that has not explicitly addressed democracy but points in that direction by noting how technological decisions can be value decisions and value decisions can be technological decisions (Friedman and Nissenbaum, 1996; Brigham and Introna, 2007; Flanagan et al., 2007). Perhaps the most explicit discussion of the technology–democracy connection is that about the internet and whether it is a "democratic technology" (Johnson, 1997, 2000; Best and Wade, 2007).

The work that most directly examines technology and democracy as a matter of co-construction is Sclove's *Democracy and Technology* (1995).

Sclove's analysis begins with the idea that technology is social structure, provides an analysis of technology as multivalenced, and then goes on to focus on democratic procedures for decisions about technology. Our analysis expands upon this and the previous STS literatures by addressing how sociotechnical systems of accountability function to constitute and maintain democracy.

Accountability and democracy

"Democracy" is at once a simple and a complex idea. Perhaps the most straightforward expression of the idea is the principle that individuals should have a say in decisions that affect their lives. The simplicity disappears quickly when we realize that this principle can be manifested in many different forms—at different places, in different times, with differing institutions, in different cultures. Democracy has been, and continues to be, interpreted and reinterpreted, invented and reinvented as the world changes, in relationship with new technology, new ideas, new circumstances, and many other kinds of change.

Nevertheless, even given this complexity, systems of accountability are essential components of democratic societies, especially representative democracies. Here "having a say in decisions that affect one's life" entails that representative decision-makers be accountable to those for whom they make decisions, and that institutions set up to achieve social goals are accountable to the public they aim to serve. This means that citizens must be informed about the activities and decisions of their representatives and that they must have opportunities to provide input to these representatives. The ultimate consequence of accountability in political systems is, of course, that citizens vote for or against re-electing a representative, or call for the resignation of an untrustworthy bureaucrat. Institutional accountability is more complex but also involves information flow from institutions to citizens and processes by which public input can be received. All democracies devise systems of accountability involving information flows between citizens, representatives, and institutions. Thus, a first claim of our analysis is that democratic societies are constituted in part by systems of accountability, systems in which individuals and institutions are held to standards of behavior and expected to explain failures to conform to those standards.

Increasingly, these systems of accountability are mediated through information technologies (IT). Government agencies use websites to disclose their practices; law-enforcement officials hold citizens accountable by means of various IT tracking systems; corporations monitor their employees and provide information to auditors through IT systems. In other words, the accounts created and provided in these systems are either constituted in or translated into data which can be accessed, processed, and/or searched. Our second claim is, then, that systems of accountability are sociotechnical systems. Information technology is used to gather, use, and display information in these systems, and hence these accountability systems are constituted by (and in turn constitute) IT.

Our third claim is that surveillance and transparency practices are both systems of accountability. This allows us to frame surveillance and transparency as parallel systems. Such an approach has not, to our knowledge, been undertaken before. Indeed, although accountability is implicit in most discussions of transparency and some discussions of surveillance, rarely is accountability used as the dominant framework or lens through which to describe and evaluate such systems.

Typically "accountability" refers to practices in which individual actors (elected officials, government bureaucrats, professionals, judges) and institutions (government agencies, corporations, organizations of various kinds) are expected to behave in specific ways (i.e., according to certain formal or informal standards) and to "answer to" particular constituents. Government officials and institutions are expected to function in the public interest; corporations are supposed to abide by the law; professionals and professions are supposed to be worthy of the trust that clients must put in them. Citizens (as individuals or related groups) are expected to play a role in the process if in no other way than by responding (or not responding) to the accounts given by institutional actors. Generally "accounts" must be given when actors fail to meet given standards, but often they are also expected to "give accounts" to demonstrate that they have adhered to standards or fulfilled their responsibilities even when there is no failure.

Transparency readily fits the notion of accountability: in transparency regimes, institutions provide accounts of how they operate to demonstrate that they are fulfilling social or legal standards (expectations). The idea that surveillance regimes are systems of accountability might, however, seem somewhat odd, especially when it comes to marketing research and other forms of non-state surveillance. Yet, in these surveillance regimes an account of an individual is developed and then decisions are made on the basis of that account. The account (a digital profile) is put together by linking data from any number of sources to a specific person/identity. The decision may be as significant as making an arrest or as trivial as sending marketing information. In either case, the profile amounts to an account of the person, based on their behavior, and usually predicts future behavior. In this respect, and despite the fact that the person is not personally providing the account, surveillance practices fit the accountability framework.

We propose, then, to read the notion of "giving accounts" broadly here, to include any kind of data collection that seeks to characterize or categorize an actor and use that collection (a profile) as the basis for treatment. Thus, our framework of accountability includes the following key elements: the giving or creation of an account, which is based on one's behavior or characteristics, is compared with some set of norms or categories and the comparison is then used as the basis for some kind of treatment—the granting or denial of a loan, the imposition of a fine for violating an environmental standard, further scrutiny of auditing reports, the offering of special marketing deals.

With this framework in hand, we can now begin to examine surveillance and transparency as sociotechnical systems of accountability.

Surveillance

From the early days of computing to the present, concern has been expressed about the threat particular uses of information technology can pose to personal privacy. However, the first computers were large mainframes and public concern was based on the expectation that computers would be used primarily by large bureaucratic organizations, especially government agencies, to amass huge quantities of data on citizens. Worries about the threat to personal privacy waned somewhat with the development of personal computers, for small computers were thought to put information in the hands of many (and not just large and already powerful organizations). With the development of technology, however, a much broader and more powerful set of computer-based tools has been created for tracking and sorting individuals and regulating their behavior, including data-mining tools, biometrics, facial recognition, intelligent highways, cookies (to track web browsing), and RFID (radio-frequency identification). In the end, then, although the development of personal computers complicated the issues, public concern and scholarship on privacy has persisted with attention turning from one new technological development to another.

The theoretical literature on privacy has focused on conceptualizing privacy and understanding its value and its variations (Marx, 2001). Broadly, the literature might be described as moving through stages in which privacy was understood as an individual good to understanding it as a social or public good. Regan (1995) argued for this move in *Legislating Privacy*. More recently, scholarship seems to have shifted from privacy to surveillance as a better paradigm for understanding institutional practices configured around IT, personal data collection, and personal data manipulation (Lyon, 2001). This shift of focus to surveillance extends the switch in emphasis that Regan and others made from individual goods to social goods. Studies of surveillance draw attention to inequality and social justice in addition to violations of individual rights. Increasingly, the paradigm of surveillance as social sorting has become central (Gandy, 1993; Lyon, 2003a, 2003b; Gilliom, 2006; Haggerty and Ericson, 2006).

The literature on surveillance as social sorting is therefore the starting place for our analysis of surveillance as a sociotechnical system of accountability. We understand surveillance to be a set of practices that gather and collect data about individuals or entities, with or without their knowledge or consent, for purposes of an analysis which sorts those individuals or entities on the basis of their behavior or characteristics. Surveillance systems collect data, categorize individuals, and treat them in particular ways based on these categorizations.

The justification for this collection and sorting involves holding individuals accountable for their behavior but not, as already indicated, in the ways we ordinarily think about the operation of accountability. Here the individuals may not even know they are being watched, let alone be asked to give an account. Nevertheless, accounts of them are being created as they go about their daily lives. The various data are merged to form a profile that is used to sort the individual, putting him or her into categories relevant to the decisions the data collector wants to make: Should we give a loan to this person? Should we hire her? Can he board the airplane?

The key element in surveillance, then, is that a watcher develops an account of a watched person, an account that serves the watcher's purposes in making decisions about the watched. As already acknowledged, this is not typically understood as accountability but it has the features characteristic of accountability structures since an account is created and used to respond to behavior.

Transparency

At the same time that the literature on surveillance has expanded, a good many changes have taken place in transparency practices and scholarship. The term "transparency" is used in a variety of ways—to refer to personal openness and authenticity, to governments' revelations of their workings—that all play metaphorically on the literal meaning of "seeing through." Transparency has been explicit in discussions of governance at least since Bentham, but it echoes earlier ideas going back to the ancient Chinese and Greeks (Hood, 2006). Here it can carry two different meanings: first, operating according to established policies and procedures, and second, "openness" in the sense that all dealings either occur in public or are made public. In corporate contexts, on the other hand, transparency is often termed "disclosure," and refers to an increasing demand for information from corporations about their financial dealings and about the possible risks their operations pose, such as potentially hazardous releases from chemical plants. In international transparency regimes, such as arms control or trade, transparency entails a nation providing data to some defined community to establish that it is abiding by agreed-on policies. Non-governmental organizations working in economic development have also adopted the push for "good governance" involving transparency, and they have, in turn, been pushed to become more transparent themselves. For our purposes then, transparency encompasses the voluntary or required release of entity-specific information about actions, states, or intentions, where the information is used to evaluate that entity.

The literature on transparency does not seem to have coalesced into a central theme; indeed, transparency carries different meanings in different contexts. Like surveillance, an increasingly common feature of transparency regimes is their use of information technology. IT is shaping practices whereby information is collected, distributed, and displayed for constituents, investors, donors, and other users.

Although transparency can be seen as an individual virtue, the policies with which we are concerned are normally understood as serving social ends: the trust of the polity in its government, the trust of investors in a market, the prevention of self-dealing and corruption, and so on. In this sense, transparency practices are a form of accountability, but they are quite different from surveillance. Transparency requirements come about because institutions are expected both to operate within the confines of civil society and to demonstrate that they are doing so. The point is not to give an account of why you have failed to meet a standard but rather to give an account of what you are doing (be it fulfilling formal and informal requirements or surpassing them).

Surveillance and transparency compared

We concluded the section on surveillance by identifying the key elements as follows: in surveillance there are watchers and the watched; the watchers develop accounts of those who are watched, accounts that serve the watchers' interests in making decisions. Our brief discussion of transparency suggests an overlapping set of elements. In transparency there are also watchers and watched but here the watched develop accounts of themselves. These accounts are targeted at the interests of the watchers but here the accounts given (provided) respond to or aim to fulfill legal requirements or more loosely defined public concerns. In effect, the interests of the watchers are either formulated into legal requirements or loosely interpreted by the watched, for example when corporations reveal information about their environmental policies.

With this brief structural comparison as the backdrop, we can now dig more deeply into the similarities and differences between these different types of regimes. We begin by considering the rhetorical framing of each, go on to consider the power relations within each type of system, touch briefly on the role that IT plays in constituting the systems, explore the role of "information doubles" in both, and end by examining the degree of activity each system affords to its participants.

Although surveillance and transparency regimes both involve watchers and watched, the rhetorical frames of each type of system are generally distinct. Surveillance carries negative connotations, while transparency carries positive connotations. "Surveillance" suggests the operation of authority, while "transparency" suggests the operation of democracy, of the powerful being held accountable. As well, in discussions of the rationales for the different systems, surveillance is often said to be in the name of diminishing crime or collecting marketable information, and transparency is required to assure clients or the public that rules are being followed (promises adhered to). The rhetoric of security, risk, and safety pervades surveillance, while the language of public responsibility pervades transparency. One "protects" democracy, while the other "demonstrates" its proper functioning.

These rhetorical frames indicate radically different understandings of the watching that takes place in each kind of system; the rhetoric shapes (and reflects) how these systems are understood. If, for example, corporations were to launch a successful campaign that described the requirements of the "Sarbanes–Oxley Act of 2002" as a form of surveillance, rather than transparency, the understanding of that law's provisions might change dramatically.[1] Similarly, if marketing firms or credit agencies were to advocate the personal transparency of their customers, their activities might be understood quite differently.

Looking beyond these different discursive frameworks, however, the systems seem to involve different arrangements of power, arrangements that are consistent with, but not the same as, their rhetorical frames. Much of surveillance studies grows from Foucault's analysis of the panopticon as a system of control, a negative exercise of power. In this framework, the power of surveillance regimes operates directly, either by intervening to stop, to encourage, or to channel behavior (as with airport security checks and CCTV in public areas) or by limiting individual opportunities (as with credit reporting). Focusing on social sorting, these systems channel individuals' actions and, ultimately, their life chances, often without the individuals' awareness. Yet the power relations in surveillance can, as well, be understood to rest on a continuum of care to control, with watchers having varying degrees of, or motives for, an interest in the good of the watched (Lyon, 2003a). Surveillance of hospital patients and surveillance of airline passengers span the continuum here; care-based surveillance can be seen in the concern about the patient and the aim of providing better medical care (the monitoring of medical patients), but also in the claim of marketing companies to offer better customer service (by knowing as much as possible about that customer), and the concern in airport security for the security of citizens and of the nation (especially after 9/11). On this analysis, all surveillance systems contain some ambiguity with respect to their power relations, with a least some care-based exercise of power inherent in what might otherwise be thought of as simply control-based power.

Transparency regimes have not escaped criticism. Especially in the corporate sector, those who must meet the requirements of transparency have complained about the costs of doing so (Anonymous, 2006). Nevertheless, as a general approach (a form of public policy) used to protect against the excesses of both corporate and public authority, transparency requirements are embraced as positive, democratic exercises of power and are necessary in the post-Cold War, globalizing world (Florini, 1998). According to Florini, the various forms of "government in the sunshine" laws and corporate disclosure requirements have both fostered citizen and investor confidence and reduced health-and-safety risks. Transparency regimes are often seen as a limitation placed on the powerful: corporations, government officials, product manufacturers, and so on. Lyon's care–control continuum might be used here, but only indirectly. In other words, the watchers—often figured here as the public, rather than some specific authority—in this context might be seen as exercising only indirect power over the watched, whether in the form of elections, continued participation in agreements or some form of market power. The subtlety of this indirect power has been most thoroughly considered in discussion of transparency in transnational economic development regimes. In those arenas, the "new development" has made transparency a key component of programs to promote good governance and institutional integrity (instead of the former efforts merely to directly fund large development projects, like dams) (Mosse, 2003). Critics have analyzed these "capacity-building" programs as a form of governmentality, with the implication that they serve to remake the watched, not necessarily into the docile subjects of panoptic control, but into ready participants in the globalization of neoliberal capitalism (Anders, 2003; Gould, 2003). Of course, it may be that docility is less the issue than compatibility with outside powers when previous systems followed a more locally defined logic. The critique suggests that promoting this form of governmentality has negative effects overall, helping to incorporate cultural Others into a political–economic system which does not benefit them. Extrapolating from this case, we can ask if the indirect control (or care) that takes place through transparency is really that benign.

If we focus on the difference in power relations between these two types of systems, it seems that the powerful and the marginal can demand different types of accountability. The powerful are required to be transparent, while the less powerful—the poor and other marginalized groups—are required to endure surveillance, even if such surveillance is meant to be part of an ethics of care. The asymmetry goes deeper; despite the growing prevalence of transparency policies, it is often the powerful who can demand transparency, not the poor. Wealthy investors, for example, can demand corporate transparency, while welfare and social services for the poor are notoriously opaque (Gilliom, 2001). The same international NGOs that push good governance on foreign governments have not themselves (until recently) been transparent (Fox and Brown, 1998; Woods and Narlikar, 2001).

Both types of systems constitute the "watched" individuals (or entities) by creating "information doubles" of them (see also Haggerty and Ericson's discussion of "data doubles", 2000), while at the same time constituting a set of watchers who will analyze these information doubles according to some pre-established or emergent normative criteria. In the case of surveillance, the information double refers to the profile of collected information about a person that represents (constitutes an account of) a person. Your credit report is one of many information doubles you may have. In the case of transparency, the audit is a major component of the corporation's information double. In either case, the representation consists of selected data pertaining to particular aspects of the person or corporation. The information doubles aim to capture the characteristics of interest to the watchers. Often these characteristics are presumed to be durable, so that they predict future behavior. Both the relevance/salience of the information double and its predictive value are open to critique, though such critiques have focused much more on surveillance systems than transparency systems.

As already mentioned above, both surveillance and transparency systems have undergone major transformation because of information technology. One crucial change has been the creation of richer, faster, and more nuanced (fine-grained) information doubles. While information doubles existed before in various kinds of paper records, IT affords the chance to build profiles of much greater depth, from many more sources, with more speed, and with more immediate utility. Data mining of consumer habits, employer monitoring of employee email, the U.S National Security Agency's email wire-tapping, online corporate financial statements, and instant legislative updates have all developed in concert with these technological changes. In contrast to previous surveillance and transparency systems, IT enables a much finer grained analysis of subjects and a capacity to merge information from different streams. Data mining was not impossible prior to the digitization of the information, but IT makes possible a much greater scale of analysis. Credit reports, for example, can now instantly survey the breadth of an individual's finances. Further, IT enables a broader and faster distribution of the information, as, for example, with the searchable maps of campaign donations that one can find online. Despite this enhanced capability, however, we should not lose sight of the fact that all information reduces complex phenomena to particular data forms. Some aspects of life do not lend themselves to easy reduction and measurement. So it is with individual profiles; individuals are understood simply in terms of the categories by which institutions measure them.

In thinking about this measurement, perhaps the most striking difference between surveillance and transparency practices is that in surveillance practices the individuals being watched are in many ways passive and in transparency practices those being watched are active. In many surveillance schemas, the individuals being watched may not be aware that information about them is being gathered since the data collection is a seamless part of an activity such as shopping, swiping a card to gain access to a building, or working on a computer. Even when subjects have been told in advance that they are being watched (as in computer monitoring or monitored telephone conversations), there may be no obvious indicator or reminder that data are being collected. While surveillance may be negotiated and contested, the subjects of transparency practices often have a more active role in providing and displaying information for the watchers. Formal transparency policies require institutions and corporations to "produce" information according to specified requirements. Informal transparency practices involve institutions or corporations "presenting" information to demonstrate that their activities serve the public interest or do not threaten public safety.

Of course, we have glossed over the details here. Institutions are more complex than our comparison suggests. We need to dig more deeply into the social practices and individual behaviors that constitute the production of "accounts" in both transparency and surveillance. How, we need to know, do institutions produce their audit reports to fulfill the requirements, say, of Sarbanes–Oxley? How do marketing firms make decisions about what information to collect and what IT tools to use to create individual profiles?

Although the role of the watched is different in surveillance as compared with transparency, the watchers in both cases are implicitly active, receiving the information, checking it against standards, fitting it into categories or processing it in some way that allows the watched to be categorized. Although the nature and degree of activity varies with context, the watchers in both types of systems are expected to respond to information about the watched even if it is "no response," i.e., the watched is not of interest, the company is worthy of trust, etc.

Even though the watched in surveillance seem to be more passive as compared with the watched in transparency, it is important to note that the revelation of information is not entirely out of the hands of the people being surveilled. Those who are surveilled can negotiate conditions of invisibility, for example, through collective protest using whatever market value they have as consumers, or their electoral power as citizens. Arguably these responses to surveillance may be understood as navigating the conditions of visibility rather than negotiating invisibility, but negotiation is possible. Numerous "weapons of the weak" can disrupt surveillance (Monahan, 2006; Gilliom, 2006); for example, individuals can plot their movements based on the known locations of surveillance cameras. In another case, the Surveillance Camera Players have staged performances to problematize the presence and use of cameras in public places (Schienke and Brown, 2003). Some activists resist surveillance by engaging in countersurveillance, or "sousveillance"; for example, some community groups videotape the actions of police officers, while other activists wear cameras into stores to record surveillance equipment (Mann et al., 2003). We can look to the successful pushback against Facebook's "beacon" program as an instance of the subjects of surveillance negotiating the cancellation of a surveillance program. In that program, Facebook was able to register a member's purchases and automatically broadcast them to that person's network of friends. In the face of tremendous user outrage, Beacon was changed from an automatic to an "opt-in" program (Story and Stone, 2007).

Still, there is another way we might consider the active/passive role of the watched in these systems. How active are the subjects of surveillance and transparency in setting the norms and standards of the accountability system, that is, the categories or standards by which they will be evaluated? In systems of transparency, there is often a process to establish policies or public expectations. Here the watched may have a significant role in negotiating the conditions of their being watched (Fung et al., 2007). By contrast, the watched in many surveillance systems have little say. Indeed, many surveillance systems have not been negotiated with the public. In these cases, information technology made data collection possible and companies and institutions took advantage of it without any public discussion or formal public decision. Of course, even in surveillance, standards can be contested, as in the case of racial profiling, but only when such standards become public knowledge (i.e., are transparent).

Before offering concluding thoughts on this analysis, we must add that a number of accountability systems straddle the surveillance–transparency distinction (Heald, 2006). Indeed, a bright line dividing the systems does not exist. This blurriness reinforces the structural parallels between the two types of systems and the potential value of examining the two together. Indeed, it raises an interesting question about why some systems are perceived as surveillance and others as transparency. Perhaps the richest example here is social-networking sites. Framing such systems as transparency regimes seems the most congenial to users' interpretations of these systems, as means to keep in touch with friends—by revealing information about where they are going, what they are doing, who they are dating, and so on. On the other hand, a series of recent incidents suggests that these systems are being used as sites for surveillance. As discussed earlier, users of social networking sites were surprised to find that their attempts at personal transparency fed into the surveillance regimes of potential employers, campus police, and corporate marketers (Story and Stone, 2007; Hass, 2006; Finder, 2006). Although one might dismiss this as a case of "function creep," whereby the function of a system changes from one use to another, the fact that a transparency system can easily be switched to a surveillance system reinforces our claim that the two types of regime have important structural similarities.

Conclusions

In systems of accountability, individuals and institutions are expected to achieve specified goals or adhere to particular rules and standards; generally, consequences ensue from failure to achieve the goals or adhere to the standards. Such systems require that individuals give an account when they fail in either respect and/or to demonstrate that they are achieving the goal or adhering to the standards. We have framed surveillance and transparency regimes as systems of accountability in order to break out of established ways of thinking about these systems and in the hope that the alternative framing will lead to new insights and new questions. Admittedly, surveillance does not fit the standard description of accountability because while accounts of individuals are created and used, the surveilled individuals do not "give" the account. Nevertheless, the comparison between surveillance and transparency as sociotechnical systems of accountability has helped us to elicit some of the nuances of the relationships of power in these systems. In future work, we will have to attend more carefully to how these relationships operate, especially in the area of setting norms for the data used to create information doubles and how those information doubles are in turn employed. The comparison within the frame of accountability has the advantage of facilitating evaluative questions about how the systems constitute democracy. We can ask whether or how systems of surveillance do and do not constitute accountability that is appropriate for democratic societies. Indeed, since the accountability constituted by transparency systems meshes well with the ideals of the public good, as long as those systems are well tailored to that end, the comparison suggests the possibility of a new critique of surveillance addressing the democratic concerns at stake in many transparency systems.

Note

1 The Sarbanes–Oxley Act of 2002, also known as the Public Company Accounting Reform and Investor Protection Act of 2002, was a package of accounting reforms passed by the United States Congress to enhance corporate transparency following the Enron scandal.

References

Anders, Gernard. 2003. "Good governance as technology: Towards an ethnography of the Bretton Woods Institutions." In *The Aid Effect: Giving and Governing in International Development Anthropology, Culture and Society*, edited by D. Mosse and D.J. Lewis, 37–60. London: Pluto.

Anonymous. 2006. "The trial of Sarbanes-Oxley: Regulating business." *The Economist* April 22:59.

Best, Michael L. and Keegan W. Wade. 2007. "Democratic and anti-democratic regulators of the internet: A framework." *The Information Society* 23 (5):405–11.

Bijker, Wiebe E. 1993. "Do not despair—There is life after constructivism." *Science Technology & Human Values* 18 (1):113–38.

Bijker, Wiebe E., Thomas P. Hughes, and Trevor J. Pinch, eds. 1987. *The Social Construction of Technological Systems: New Directions in the Sociology and History of Technology*. Cambridge, MA: MIT Press.

Bijker, Wiebe E. and John Law, eds. 1992. *Shaping Technology/Building Society: Studies in Sociotechnical Change*. Cambridge, MA: MIT Press.

Bimber, Bruce A. 2003. *Information and American Democracy: Technology in the Evolution of Political Power*. Cambridge: Cambridge University Press.

Brigham, Martin and Lucas D. Introna. 2007. "Invoking politics and ethics in the design of information technology: Undesigning the design." *Ethics and Information Technology* 9 (1):1–10.

Finder, Alan. 2006. "When a risqué online persona undermines a résumé." *New York Times* June 11.

Flanagan, Mary, Daniel C. Howe, and Helen Nissenbaum. 2007. "Embodying values in technology: Theory and practice." In *Information Technology and Moral Philosophy*, edited by J. van den Hoven and J. Weckert, 322–53. Cambridge, UK: Cambridge University Press.

Florini, Ann. 1998. "The end of secrecy." *Foreign Policy* 111:50–63.

Fox, Jonathan A. and L. David Brown. 1998. *The Struggle for Accountability: The World Bank, NGOs, and Grassroots Movements*. Cambridge, MA: MIT Press.

Friedman, Batya and Helen Nissenbaum. 1996. "Bias in computer systems." *ACM Transactions on Information Systems* 14 (3):330–47.

Fung, Archon, Mary Graham, and David Weil. 2007. *Full Disclosure: The Perils and Promise of Transparency*. Cambridge: Cambridge University Press.

Gandy, Oscar H. 1993. *The Panoptic Sort: A Political Economy of Personal Information*. Boulder, CO: Westview.

Gilliom, John. 2001. *Overseers of the Poor: Surveillance, Resistance, and the Limits of Privacy*. Chicago: University of Chicago Press.

——. 2006. Struggling with surveillance: Resistance, consciousness and identity. In *The New Politics of Surveillance and Visibility*, edited by K. D. Haggerty and R. V. Ericson, 111–29. Toronto: University of Toronto Press.

Gould, Jeremy. 2003. "Timing, scale and style: Capacity as governmentality in Tanzania." In *The Aid Effect: Giving and Governing in International Development Anthropology, Culture and Society*, edited by D. Mosse and D. J. Lewis, 61–84. London: Pluto.

Hackett, Edward J., Olga Amsterdamska, Michael Lynch, and Judy Wajcman, eds. 2008. *The Handbook of Science and Technology Studies*. 3rd ed. Cambridge, MA: MIT Press.

Haggerty, Kevin D. and Richard V. Ericson. 2000. "The surveillant assemblage." *The British Journal of Sociology* 51(4):605–22.

——, eds. 2006. *The New Politics of Surveillance and Visibility*. Toronto: University of Toronto Press.

Hamlett, Patrick W. 2003. "Technology theory and deliberative democracy." *Science Technology & Human Values* 28 (1):112–40.

Hass, Nancy. 2006. "In your Facebook.Com." *New York Times* January 8, 2006.

Heald, David. 2006. "Varieties of transparency." In *Transparency: The Key to Better Governance?* ed. C. Hood and D. Heald, 25–43. Oxford: Oxford University Press.

Hess, David, Steve Breyman, Nancy Campbell, and Brian Martin. 2008. "Science, technology, and social movements." In *The Handbook of Science and Technology Studies*, edited by E.J. Hackett, O. Amsterdamska, M. Lynch and J. Wajcman, 473–98. Cambridge, MA: MIT Press.

Hood, Christopher. 2006. "Transparency in historical perspective." In *Transparency: The Key to Better Governance?* ed. C. Hood and D. Heald, 3–24. Oxford: Oxford University Press.

Introna, Lucas D. 2007. "Maintaining the reversibility of foldings: Making the ethics (politics) of information technology visible." *Ethics and Information Technology* 9(1):11–25.

Jasanoff, Sheila. 2005. *Designs on Nature: Science and Democracy in Europe and the United States*. Princeton, NJ: Princeton University Press.

Johnson, Deborah G. 1997. "Is the global information infrastructure a democratic technology?" *Computers and Society* 27 (3):20–26.

——. 2000. "Democratic values and the Internet." In *Internet Ethics*, edited by D. Langford, 181–96. London: Macmillan Press, Ltd.

——. 2007. "Democracy, technology, and information societies." In *The Information Society: Innovation, Legitimacy, Ethics and Democracy*, pp. 5–16. edited by

P. Duquenoy, P. Goujon, K. Kimppa, S. Lavelle, and V. Dumont. New York: Springer-Verlag.

Keulartz, Jozef, Maartje Schermer, Michiel Korthals, and Tsjalling Swierstra. 2004. "Ethics in technological culture: A programmatic proposal for a pragmatist approach." *Science Technology & Human Values* 29(1):3–29.

Kleinman, Daniel Lee, ed. 2000. *Science, Technology, and Democracy*. Albany, NY: State University of New York Press.

Lyon, David. 2001. "Facing the future: Seeking ethics for everyday surveillance." *Ethics and Information Technology* 3(3):171–80.

———. 2003a. *Surveillance after September 11*. Cambridge: Polity Press.

———, ed. 2003b. *Surveillance as Social Sorting: Privacy, Risk, and Digital Discrimination*. London: Routledge.

Mann, Steve, Jason Nolan, and Barry Wellman. 2003. "Sousveillance: Inventing and using wearable computing devices for data collection in surveillance environments." *Surveillance and Society* 1(3):331–55.

Marx, Gary T. 2001. "Murky conceptual waters: The public and the private." *Ethics and Information Technology* 3(3):157–69.

Monahan, Torin. 2006. "Questioning surveillance and security." In *Surveillance and Security: Technological Politics and Power in Everyday Life*, edited by T. Monahan, 1–26. New York: Routledge.

Mosse, David. 2003. "Global governance and the ethnography of international aid." In *The Aid Effect: Giving and Governing in International Development Anthropology, Culture and Society*, edited by D. Mosse and D. J. Lewis, 1–36. London: Pluto.

Oudshoorn, Nelly. 2003. *The Male Pill: A Biography of a Technology in the Making*. Durham, NC: Duke University Press.

Oudshoorn, Nelly and Trevor J. Pinch, eds. 2003. *How Users Matter: The Co-Construction of Users and Technologies*. Cambridge, MA: MIT Press.

Regan, Priscilla M. 1995. *Legislating Privacy: Technology, Social Values, and Public Policy*. Chapel Hill, NC: University of North Carolina Press.

Schienke, Erich W. and Bill Brown. 2003. "Streets into stages: An interview with surveillance camera players' Bill Brown." *Surveillance & Society* 1(3):356–74.

Sclove, Richard. 1995. *Democracy and Technology*. New York: Guilford Press.

Story, Louise and Brad Stone. 2007. "Facebook retreats on online tracking." *New York Times* November 30, 2007.

Thorpe, Charles. 2008. "Political theory in science and technology studies." In *The Handbook of Science and Technology Studies*, edited by E.J. Hackett, O. Amsterdamska, M. Lynch, and J. Wajcman, 63–82. Cambridge, MA: MIT Press.

Verbeek, Peter Paul. 2006. "Materializing morality—Design ethics and technological mediation." *Science Technology & Human Values* 31(3):361–80.

Wajcman, Judy. 2004. *Technofeminism*. Cambridge: Polity Press.

Winner, Langdon. 1986. "Do artifacts have politics?" In *The Whale and the Reactor: A Search for Limits in an Age of High Technology*, 19–39. Chicago: University of Chicago Press.

———. 1993. "Upon opening the black-box and finding it empty—Social constructivism and the philosophy of technology." *Science Technology & Human Values* 18(3):362–78.

Woods, Ngaire and Amrita Narlikar. 2001. "Governance and the limits of accountability: The WTO, the IMF, and the World Bank." *International Social Science Journal* 53(170):569–83.

Chapter 2

Identification, surveillance and democracy

David Lyon

Identification, surveillance and democracy stand in paradoxical tension with each other. Democratic participation, as it is understood within liberal democracies, requires that everyone be registered to vote. This ensures fairness: everyone eligible within a nation-state has the opportunity to vote, but only once, within an election. The list of voters, however, must include some means of identification to distinguish between one voter and another, as well as some basic details such as residential address and citizenship status. The election system must verify the identification to maintain the "one person, one vote" rule. But that means of identification and its placement on the list is a way that the government department concerned may keep tabs on the population, if only for election purposes. It is, in other words, a surveillance system as well, for better or for worse (Abercrombie, et al., 1986).

This paradoxical situation, exemplified by voter lists but visible in many other forms of identification and classification in the modern state, gets to the heart of the dilemma of democracy and surveillance. The very instruments that are intended to ensure equality of treatment for all, or fair and appropriate treatment for each group, as in cases such as health-care or education, may also provide opportunities for authoritarian or arbitrary treatment. These sometimes occur as unintended consequences of particular ways of organizing a given system, but they may also arise from, say, racially or nationalistically skewed policies, or from the re-use of government data for purposes different from those for which they were gathered. The use of census data for population control in Israel (Zureik, 2001) or for targeting specific population groups for negative treatment, such as the internment of Japanese Americans during World War Two (Ng, 2002) are cases in point.

In democratic societies, citizenship depends upon some sort of national identification system. By identifying who is and who is not a citizen—or who might have intermediate or temporary status, such as a permanent resident—governments may determine not only who may vote but also who has access to certain rights and who may be expected to fulfill certain responsibilities. The bureaucratic systems for regulating citizenship that emerged in the nineteenth century became increasingly subject to computerization in the later twentieth, processes which were also both cause and consequence of growing mobility. A combination of technological and commercial pressures, and a tilt towards "national security" priorities in the early twenty-first century converged in a number of proposals, plans, and procurements for national identification systems integrated by citizen registry databases, often referred to simply as "national ID cards" (Lyon and Bennett, 2008).

Given the importance of electronic records in national identification registries, a development that enhances surveillance capacities significantly, it is crucial to understand how national ID cards are being developed today. While it is important to be aware of their genuine benefits, it is also vital to consider their possible negative effects and uses. The same goes for all new ID systems, dependent as they are on networked computer databases and—especially since 9/11—harnessed to goals such as national security, understood as "anti-terrorism." Critics argue that numerous values, taken for granted in Western liberal democracies, are jeopardized both by reducing identification to abstract personal data and by various post-9/11 measures. In the latter case, the monitoring of movement, encouraging spying on neighbors, detention without trial, and even the use of torture are now countenanced, along with the massive processing of personal data in quest of "national identification." Even those systems that downplay the relationship between identification and national security still raise questions about democracy and citizenship because they touch directly on governance and the terms of membership in the nation-state.

Considering ID cards in relation to citizenship requires attention to four questions. First, how has citizenship been understood in modern times? This must be answered in order to see how contemporary modes of identification may affect citizenship, for better or for worse. Second, what aspects of identification and social sorting are enabled by new ID systems? New identification methods affect citizenship especially in relation to how Others are defined and treated. Third, how might citizenship be affected when the sorts of governance represented by new identification systems go well beyond the nation-state, across different nations but also across different institutional spheres? Fourth, under what conditions can ordinary citizens make a difference to how they are classified and administered through new ID systems? Before turning to these questions, however, a few comments are needed about how citizen identification might be evaluated.

Evaluating citizen identification

"Citizens" are always the products of specific times, cultures, and polities. Today's citizens may be thought of increasingly as the product of new information-technology-based modes by which governments register and interact with the populations of nation-states. On the one hand, this may offer new vistas for accuracy and efficiency, and for citizen access to government departments and information. On the other, such "citizenship," often associated with "e-government" policies, may also place an attractive gloss on how stereotypes and cumulative disadvantage are reinforced, as the feedback loops created serve purposes inimical to democratic recognition and participation (see, for example, the discussion in Hague and Loader, 1999).

New "national" ID systems and their surrogates—such as the "Enhanced Driver's Licenses" being developed in Canada and the "Real ID system" in the USA—relate directly to citizenship and indirectly to democracy. But how should these systems be evaluated with respect to citizenship and democracy? The polarized options offered above clearly will not do, not least because it is unlikely to be a zero-sum game between greater efficiency and greater disadvantage. Social advantage or disadvantage may be reproduced more or less efficiently. Access to government information may be strategically sanctioned or shut down, very effectively in either case. Nor can researchers point to established systems to indicate what sorts of experience other countries have had with large-scale national ID systems. Japan, for example, has an advanced registration system but few corresponding "cards" as yet and Malaysia, for all the technological sophistication of its multi-purpose card system, has had very limited roll-out to date. The most advanced systems are scarcely off the ground.

The only way to obtain some kind of evaluative stance is to place such emerging systems in context, both historical and comparative. If we view new ID systems in the context of administrative development and the technological upgrading of bureaucratic processes, then the best that can be said is that their likely outcomes are ambiguous with respect to citizenship and democracy. Seen more consequentially as a crucial moment in the shift towards a generalized surveillance that is rapidly becoming the dominant organizing principle of contemporary institutions, ID systems deserve closer scrutiny. Could they be part of a sea change in modes of governance?

Pressing this question, from historical and comparative angles, another picture starts to take shape. This one may be far less benign than the bureaucratic–technical one—already a cause for concern in some quarters— and whose origins and consequences may be disturbing to democratically minded citizens. After all, much that comprises new ID systems, such as biometric techniques, originates in colonial, crime-control, and wartime conditions, each of which suggest that something perceived to be deeply abnormal necessitates extraordinary measures. Moreover, identification is a basic component of surveillance systems that today are overwhelmingly characterized by a desire to place people in different categories so that each group may be treated differently. How much of this is understood by "ordinary citizens" going about their everyday lives? Also, classification is carried out in part by means of biometrics, which prefers body data to personal narrative, especially in those cases for which biometrics is often said to be superior—relating to vulnerable groups such as those on welfare, parole, or seeking refugee or asylum status.

The larger frame of all this is an interconnected global enterprise in which governments, corporations, and indeed the technologies themselves work together to create a new context for whatever is left of the concepts of citizenship and democracy. This context was clearly forming from the 1980s, and by the 1990s the very discourses of citizenship were shaped by consumer sensibility. As understood by Zygmunt Bauman (2000), for instance, this would include one-dimensional freedom of the marketplace, matched by a withering of real or imagined capacities to act as citizens, along with drastically reduced freedoms for the poor. By the early years of the twenty-first century, and accentuated by 9/11, the imperative to maintain global trade while simultaneously closing borders to all who might be considered terrorists or their categorical cousins added fear to the framing of "ID needs" such that identification spelled security.

The relationships among identification, citizenship, and democracy deserve to be examined more closely. The call for universal IDs may mask fears about particular groups in the population, groups that have historically been marginalized and disadvantaged. After all, as Valentin Groebner rightly says, "The position of the excluded, of the non-identified, is forever evident in the history of identification. The presence of the excluded actually frames identification ..." (Groebner, 2007: 255). The technical trends—inseparable from the corporate trends that support and promote them—have already been shown to lend themselves to a new actuarialism that fosters social sorting, a process which itself leaves much to be desired from a democratic viewpoint. The current context of the security state, already growing but significantly reinforced after 9/11, serves to indicate what sorts of political and policy priorities guide the emergence of systems such as ID cards.

Democracy, citizenship and identification

In democratic societies, the commitment to citizenship has generally meant something like this. Rather than suffering from the vagaries of arbitrary rule, in which citizens may have demands made of them at any time, citizens have—in the right to assemble, in elections, and in the opportunity to run for office—the means to hold government accountable. So, do the new "cyber citizens" find in the new, biometric-based ID systems the chance to hold government to account, or is the balance tilting the other way, so that they are increasingly held to account by government? The e-government opportunities seem to favor the former; the potential for demanding verification in data and documents appears to weight things towards the latter.

Advocates of e-government and "digital democracy" argue for national ID systems on the grounds that the unique ID number will facilitate communication from citizens to government, permitting increasing ease of access to government information. This would include both data held on individuals and policy or regulative information that might be useful to citizens. The fact remains, however, that it is still very difficult for ordinary citizens to obtain access to particularly sensitive information. In many countries of the global North, the only recourse is the time-consuming, and sometimes costly, route of Freedom of Information requests.

Seen from the perspective of ID card holders, the prospects of greater democracy may seem slim—that, at least, is the impression one receives from reading the extensive oppositional material in countries like the United Kingdom, the United States, Australia, and even Japan in recent times. The fear is that government will use the ID card as a pretext for making "legitimate" demands on citizens that place the burden of accountability more and more on their shoulders. Citizens will need to be protected *from* government—there is a fear of fascism or some other kind of authoritarianism—rather than being protected *by* government, as in the democratic dream. Given the relative infancy of new ID card systems, however, it is hard to produce persuasive evidence that these fears are justified.

Citizenship is constantly redefined, especially in these liquid and uncertain times, and it is important to consider how citizenship is currently understood and to compare and contrast this with earlier formulations and experiences. This is the "history question." How do digital media, and especially the increasingly important electronic and database modes of identification, affect our understanding and practices of citizenship? More specifically, how do national ID card systems contribute to the experiences and parameters of citizenship? New identification processes, including national ones, may turn out to be the most significant developments of information systems for governance, globally and locally.

As far as the technical trends are concerned, today's ID systems are electronic, which makes them qualitatively different from earlier systems based on filing cabinets and cards. When seen through the prism of identification systems, the "cyber" terminology is associated with "governing by identity," the process whereby identification systems become the nexus of control mechanisms. One also has to bear in mind that although new IDs are often called "national" they appear in a globalizing world, which further modifies their meaning. The original sense of "cybernetics" had to do with control through feedback loops, and while the idea of governing by identity recalls some aspects of this, it also indicates potential new openings for participation. That is, the democratic potential of "cyber citizenship" is not annulled through governing by identity. However, the modes through which citizenship are exercised will have to alter if this potential is to be realized. This, as I suggest below, brings in a fourth dimension: how can citizenship criteria guide the development of ID cards rather than vice-versa?

The current context is one in which new ID card systems are appearing in countries around the world, based on biometrics, accessed by RFID, and using searchable databases. High-technology companies promote these and governments seek them for administrative efficiency. Crime control and post-9/11 demands for national security provide a rationale for their introduction. Recall that the surveillance issue is not so much the cards themselves as the national registries that process the personal data. Yet it is exactly this fact that is routinely underplayed.

Once established, however, the national registries are likely to foster an amplified "culture of control" whose reach also expands geographically as identification measures are harmonized and integrated across national borders. Arguably, they also encourage less inclusive notions of citizenship, and facilitate the sorting of "desirable" and "undesirable" mobilities, based on the criteria of "identity management." The social sorting capacities of new IDs tend to be underplayed in their promotion, as are the implications for governance of "multiple function" ID systems, which have consequences for social justice.

Changes in citizenship and identification

As noted above, the advent of modern forms of citizenship assumes identification. This was, more patchily, the case with some antique civilizations, too. Citizenship was often linked with city-states from ancient Athens onwards. Western notions of citizenship are associated with status and city membership—the French word *citoyen* expresses this neatly—and sums up the ways that protection and entitlements are available in the autonomous city. The growth of citizenship in the West depended on the cultures of Abrahamic faiths, with their characteristic values relating to the person, universal social membership, and history understood as social change (see Turner, 1993:12). Roman law in European city states added a secular dimension, so that citizenship became secular solidarity where nationalism replaced religious symbolism and solidarity.

Citizenship expanded to nation-states as they developed over the past 200 years, but now global cities and globalization in general create new challenges. While nation-state citizenship will likely continue to be the most prominent type, the emergence of global cities like New York, Shanghai, Tokyo, London, Singapore, and Hong Kong makes for some interesting connections of past and future. Indeed, Singapore and Hong Kong are among the first places in the world to use electronic ID card systems. And while Shanghai is part of a much larger country, it is much more likely that citizens in that city will rely on new IDs in everyday life than would be the case in the rest of the country. Globalization adds further dimensions. Predicated on the movement of people, goods, and information in particular, globalization means that sizeable proportions of some populations within the territorial borders of a given nation-state are actually members of different nations and states. Are they full citizens, and what marks them as one thing or the other? People occupying such contradictory roles may find increasingly that those roles are noted in their identification documents.

New national ID card systems are appearing at a time when notions of national citizenship have attracted considerable criticism. Citizenship has always been a contested concept but there are significant ways in which new IDs reflect some important dimensions of today's world that challenge older views of citizenship. In particular, many have observed how the figure of the consumer has become more salient to social life than citizenship; at the same time, globalism has thrown doubt on the category of "national" citizenship. New ID card systems reflect these emphases on consumption and on globalism and may well stimulate fresh thinking on citizenship in some contexts.

There are some obvious ways in which new IDs reflect consumer and global conditions. Many new national ID systems are designed for multi-purpose use, in commercial and public-services settings, as well as in association with government departments and agencies. It is no accident that they resemble not the booklet-style passport but the ubiquitous plastic credit card. The intention of several powerful lobbies in Europe and North America is to ensure some degree of interoperability between ID card systems. In Europe, new ID cards are already machine-readable in countries geographically remote from the one in which they were issued. They may relate to nationality but also go beyond it. However, it could also be argued that new IDs speak to issues of the displacement of active citizenship by consumer behavior and to the fragmentation of national identity by the forces of globalization. If so, and if this prompts doubts about how positive this may be for the life-chances of citizens and the prospects for democratic participation, one might also ask if IDs may be used in the service of responsible citizenship and cosmopolitanism.

These two dimensions of debates over citizenship may be seen in the work of Zygmunt Bauman, whose evocative designation "liquid" may be applied to many contemporary social situations. The picture painted by Bauman is of an emerging world where what he sees as the one-dimensional freedom of the consumer marketplace eclipses any notion of active citizenship. Having redefined freedom in relation to consumer choice, governments support this shift by restricting the poor, and non-consumers generally, to places and conditions that separate them from the consuming majority. At the same time, global capitalism is in rapid ascendancy, unfettered by the rules and regulations that nation-states were once able to impose. The unpredictable fortunes of such global capitalism affect everyone for better or worse, although consumers enjoy mobility, poorer sections of the populace are trapped by their locality (Bauman, 1998).

Noting the shift away from citizenship to consumer concerns, Bauman also points out that political power "... sails away from the street and the marketplace, from assembly halls and parliaments ... beyond the reach of citizens' control, into the extraterritoriality of electronic networks" (Bauman, 2000:40), which could well be a comment on ID card systems. It undoubtedly permits the discourse around ID cards to be phrased in terms of "identity" rather than "identification" and helps to blur who is included and excluded. In the UK, for example, then Prime Minister Tony Blair claimed that the new ID card would foster a "sense of citizenship and belonging." "Citizenship" seems to connote inclusion while "terrorists" are among the "strangers" and "Others" of whom Bauman writes as potentially excluded categories.

Bauman's comments on citizenship resonate with inclusive ideas about what are citizen's rights (in the tradition of T. H. Marshall, whose ideas are closely related to welfare-state understandings of citizenship; see Turner, 1993), and with a sense of the possibilities for democratic politics, where a concept like "responsibilities" is equally important. Bauman also has much to say about the weakening of social bonds under the pressure of individualism, taking the view that recovering some meaningful modes of citizenship is the only way to recover a sense of common, public, and private good (Bauman, 2000:40). Whether such citizenship could be expressed by, or symbolized in, new ID card systems is doubtful at best.

In fact, it is difficult to see what contribution new IDs could make to the "solidarity" aspect of citizenship, or, for that matter, to democratic participation. Indeed, if the British case is anything to go by, the new ID was introduced despite efforts to involve ordinary citizens in informed debate (the London School of Economics' [LSE] report on the UK ID Card was simply sidelined, for example), which augurs badly for future democratic participation in relation to the system. New IDs seem to have more in common with what David Garland calls the "culture of control" that falls back on technical means of organizing societies in a context of broadly neoliberal anti-welfare policies. Such outlooks are "... more exclusionary than solidaristic, more committed to social control than to social provision and more attuned to the private freedoms of the market than the public freedoms of universal citizenship." (Garland, 2001:193).

We shall return to the question of inclusion and exclusion. First it is worth pausing to consider not only the broader context within which new ID cards are being introduced, which affects the meanings attached to them, but also the possible effects of the new IDs themselves. There are at least two more specific ways in which new electronic IDs are likely to affect the experiences and processes of citizenship.

First, as well as multi-purpose IDs being useful for commercial exchanges, entitlement, and access to government services (whether this is deliberately intended or an "unanticipated" consequence of their use), it is important to recall that they are the product of more than one sector. I refer to this as the "card cartel" (see Lyon and Bennett, 2008, Bennett and Lyon, 2008, Lyon 2008) in which not only government departments but also technology corporations and even the standards and protocols themselves are involved in the emergence of new ID systems. What this means is that "governing by identity" is a process that may be stretched across different institutional areas—not just government administration and crime control—and is symbolized and made operational by those new IDs. Governmentality is thus given a technological frame that facilitates what has been evident to political theorists for some time, that governing occurs in realms well beyond formal government.

Secondly, if new IDs grant a new kind of universality of governance across once-discrete institutional areas, they also encourage a new spatial reach. Those ID cards and documents as markers of citizenship are not only available at borders. Their use encourages the notion that the border is everywhere, including—echoing but not embracing older versions of citizenship—in the city. For many who will be negatively affected by ID cards, this will occur in urban areas, not necessarily at physical borders. This is also true of those advantaged by ID cards. In China, for instance, ID cards really act as badges of urban citizenship, the privileges of which far outstrip the expectations of rural dwellers. And in other countries, especially in the global North, where residents with ambiguous loyalties and origins—immigrants and migrant workers especially—make up significant proportions of urban dwellers, this sense of the border being "everywhere" is likely to be accentuated by the use of new IDs, particularly when they have multiple purposes. This brings us to the question of how new IDs relate to social sorting and to Otherness.

Citizenship, social sorting, and the other

The reasons commonly given for establishing new IDs suggest how the Other features in administrative, policing, and security plans. "Eliminating terrorism," "combating fraud," and "controlling immigration" all depend on setting up categories of terrorist/non-terrorist; non/fraudulent claimants; and il/legal immigrants. In each area, highly sensitive matters are at stake in the determination of the categories and, of course, the software codes by which they will be recognized. Further, the social categories in question all contain a high degree of vulnerability. Those suspected of terrorist activities or proclivities are by definition likely to be members of minority groups; claimants of government benefits and services are likely to be already disadvantaged; and immigrants, whether legal or not, tend to be in positions of relative powerlessness. The social sorting of new IDs touches the lives of the weakest and most marginalized members of the population. Yet the stated purpose is to overcome certain intractable social and political problems by using universal registry and card systems.

While the attacks of 9/11 were a significant factor in promoting the idea of the UK ID cards, it was "asylum abuses" that gave the initial impetus to the political promotional campaign. Then Home Secretary David Blunkett said that he wanted the ID cards because "I do want to know who is here ... I want to know whether they're working legally. I want to know whether they are drawing on services legally" (Travis, 2003). Indeed, at the time, the proposed cards were referred to as "Entitlement Cards" with the express purpose of permitting checks on employment, health, and education to ascertain who was and who was not benefiting legally. The promotional emphasis was on reducing the number of asylum cases rather than on checking the stories of those applying for that status from situations of persecution or torture.

The question of how Others are treated within any ID system is critical. The old welfare-state model, often associated with T. H. Marshall's sociology of citizenship, had everything to do with citizen entitlement. The idea was that citizenship ensured for the worker at least a minimum protection against the vicissitudes of life in the form of sickness, accident, or unemployment. This commitment grew out of the earlier securing of civil rights—common law, *habeus corpus*, and the jury system—political rights in parliament, and an extended franchise. Issues of gender, race, and ethnicity have challenged some of Marshall's tenets by raising the question of rapidly changing identities (Isin and Turner, 2007).

Although there are ongoing debates over the modes of verification in new ID systems, contemporary emphases placed on biometrics could deepen the difficulties of groups that are already marginalized. One reason for this, among many, is the downplaying of verbal evidence from those whose cases are deemed questionable. Again, this is not a new issue, but one that has been exacerbated by the dependence on electronic databases, which tends to diminish the opportunities for discussion and discretion (Groebner, 2001:258). Apart from the questions about how well biometrics systems perform, it is important to note that an individual's category is determined by codes related to bodily and behavioral characteristics. This means that decisions about the prospects for individuals in questionable categories are further abstracted from the struggles and stories of everyday life, of which vulnerable people are likely to be most acutely aware.

At the same time, the biometric and information technology systems that support them enable borders to be redefined in some interesting ways. As Irma van der Ploeg suggests, especially when using biometrics, the border becomes "... part of the embodied identity of certain groups of people, verifiable at any of the many points of access to increasingly interconnected databases ..." (van der Ploeg, 2005:133). Some identities thus produced, she goes on, are more habitable than others, which is why research on IDs must always be mindful of ethical and political issues. Beyond this, as biometric standards are adopted, making the body a password, systems may be linked with other identifying technologies such as RFID, location technologies, and Ambient Intelligence (see SWAMI Report, 2006).

At the same time, the language of "identity management" seems to offer a neutral approach to identification, especially at national borders. This term is now the mantra of border-controlling authorities, but it is important to note that these strategies emerged not from the task at hand—determining who can legitimately travel within or outside the nation-state—but from the realm of internet security in an era of electronic commerce. "Identity Management" is used to protect online systems from hackers and fraudsters. It represents the search for means to prevent access for some and permit it for others, generally for commercial reasons. Fear of economic loss is the driving force behind identity management, and it is worth exploring what such practices really have in common with the far from merely technical and commercial matter of who is a bona fide citizen or traveler (see also Muller, 2004).

In light of this, it is difficult to disagree with the conclusion of Didier Bigo (2005) that new IDs connect not with a surveillance *pan*opticon but with a *ban*opticon. Unlike rights-based notions of citizenship, in which all find a place and at the very least a social safety net, or its related panopticon that includes everyone in the gaze, new IDs seem to be geared to singling out exceptions— those to be excluded or sequestered as undesirable—as quickly and efficiently as possible. Once again, this is not a novel situation, but accentuated by the electronic database and global dimensions of new ID systems. Moreover, if many post-9/11 events are anything to go by, this occurs with relatively little concern about which innocent individuals might be negatively affected. The concern with national security (often translated into simpler terms of personal safety), in particular, trumps civil liberties and privacy concerns, especially in the United States.

The new modes of citizenship emerging at the same time as, and to some extent aligned with, national and other ID systems exhibit characteristics quite at odds with the inclusionary models of citizenship that welfare states aspired to in the post-war period. However one examines them, their exclusionary features stand out. Of course, there are also continuities with previous systems which, despite their apparent inclusionary spirit, were in practice negatively disposed towards particular groups. But the new modes, often stripped of their previously discretionary possibilities for compassionate or affirmative action, tend to single out particular groups for less-than-favorable attention.

Such groups may be thought of as Other—those whose existence stands as a warning and as a limit to those currently enjoying full citizenship entitlements, privileges, and rights. They include Bauman's "flawed consumers," would-be immigrants who now seek asylum or refugee status, and of course the stereo-typical "bad guys" of contemporary anti-terrorist and crime-control rhetoric. One difficulty of such Others, in current identification regimes, is that their ranks may expand at will—or whim—through slight statistical adjustments expressed in the algorithms controlling entry or eligibility. Hence the frequently expressed fears, to take one example, that the "war on terror" is really a "war on immigrants."

For Bauman, and anyone who takes seriously the ethical critique of new identification modes, the treatment of the Other raises basic questions of justice and humanity, not merely of citizenship. Following Emmanuel Levinas, Bauman places moral responsibility for the Other at the existential core of the human condition. On this reading, citizenship schemes should take special care with those whose lives are already marginalized by color, gender, religion, or ethnic or national background. It is hard to resist the conclusion that national ID card schemes will effectively entrench existing disadvantage and vulnerability by automating difference and conducting the relevant assessments remotely.

Identification, global governance, and citizenship

New ID card systems affect citizenship both within the territory of a given nation-state and beyond it. Didier Bigo and Elspeth Guild, for instance, high-light the process of "policing at a distance" or remote control (Bigo and Guild, 2005). They describe this phenomenon in the European context but it can also be seen in the efforts to harmonize border controls across the North American countries. In Europe, the Schengen visa policies that began in the 1980s meant that countries both issued and verified passports and travel documents at borders, but also established intergovernmental agreements, common data-bases, good practices, common manuals, and eventually a common visa. This means that the so-called technologies of control are far from the border itself. Who belongs or does not belong is determined not at the border but remotely. Foreign officials at the EU frontier are involved, along with private security firms sometimes charged with checking documents. In so far as the checking is done in embassies and consulates, it also deals in remote time—would-be travelers across borders may be deemed undesirable on the basis of what they *may* do in the future.

It is important to remember, then, that national ID card systems do not necessarily stand alone within the boundaries of a given nation-state. Increas-ingly, they relate both to the corresponding systems in other countries and to the identification systems of other organizations. Put the other way round, ID systems expand governance beyond the nation-state both internationally and organizationally. Interoperability means that common standards and protocols develop that affect all countries that adopt national ID systems, globally. And governing by identity means that all organizations contribute to governance using identification methods, not just organizations associated directly with the nation-state.

In the later twentieth and early twenty-first century, governments with aging populations and low birth rates began to rely more heavily on foreign migrant labor to keep their economies going while at the same time attempting to placate those in their populations who argued that migration should be mini-mized. Add the more recent post-9/11 concerns about state security and the shoring up of borders, and it is not difficult to see how the categories of migrants, refugees, and asylum seekers might be conflated (Isin and Turner, 2007:10). While migrant workers contribute to growth, they are often seen as parasitic on the host society's health and welfare systems. This is a reminder of Hannah Arendt's (1963) argument that the nation can eat up—in practice be stronger than—the state, making those who are not "nationals" feel less than fully part of the state. This is very clear in a country like Japan, but implicitly so in many others.

An example might be the development of "interim" forms of citizenship, such as the Canadian "Maple Leaf" card that defines migrants as less than full citizens, but as entitled to certain rights and freedoms. As Isin and Turner argue, this has further implications when one considers the possibilities for broader conceptions of citizenship, perhaps including a more global dimension. One still requires a more local basis for citizenship because rights and obligations are in a reciprocal relationship and this implies territory. But could there be a "cosmopolitan citizen?" Citizenship is both a legal status that confers an identity—often expressed in an identity card or passport—and a social status that determines the redistribution and recognition of economic and cultural capital. Now that social relations spill over national borders in unprecedented ways in a globalizing world, some rights and responsibilities are respected—or not—in much more international settings.

Writing of the fast-changing world of contemporary claims to membership of nation-states, Gerard Delanty concludes that citizenship is no longer defined only by nationality and the nation state, but is increasingly de-territorialized and fragmented into separate discourses of rights, participation, responsibility, and identity (Delanty, 2000). Equally, citizenship is no longer exclusively about the struggle for social equality—the dominant post-war mode of struggle—but has become a major site of battles over cultural identity and demands for the recognition of group difference. This cannot fail to be evident in current debates over ID systems.

The fact that new IDs may be internationally interoperable does not indicate that some cosmopolitan globalism is informing the concept of citizenship. On the contrary, the idea of interoperability is generally taken to be a device for strengthening security—policing, border controls, and military intelligence— on an international level. The idea is to be able to respond more efficiently to security threats. This may have some beneficial effects, at least in principle. In practice, however, such interoperable systems tend to reproduce the distinctions and divisions between what Bauman calls "globals" and "locals" that are now overlaid with the "trusted traveler" and "suspected terrorist" categories generated by the backlash of 9/11 responses.

IDs and prospects for citizenship

Much of our discussion thus far has centered on the negative consequences for citizenship of developing new ID systems. While acknowledging that new ID systems do not bear the blame alone for this situation—they are being developed in contexts where "national identity" and identification are already problematic and controversial—it is worth turning the question around to ask whether some less circumscribed modes of citizenship could positively affect the development of new ID systems. The question was raised, earlier, of whether there may be scope for developing ID schemes that avoid some of the negative consequences mentioned here. What effect do forms of organized opposition have on the progress of new ID card systems? Is it possible to engage with forms of "participatory design" in planning ID systems?

It is salutary to note that, in some major cases, the implementation of new ID schemes has been thwarted or at least slowed down by means of organized opinion and informed opposition. The proposed "Access Card" in Australia became the focus of bitter political wrangling during 2007 and was eventually shelved after Kevin Rudd replaced John Howard as Prime Minister following the general election at the end of the year. The appearance of the INES (*identité nationale eléctronique sécurisée*) in France has been put back indefinitely (at the time of writing, early 2008) by the efforts of a coalition of groups opposed to the scheme, who produced a report and petition that both questioned its details and suggested that the social pact between citizen and state in France would be shattered by the new card (Piazza and Laniel, 2008).

In, Japan, the Juki-Net system of national registration was vigorously opposed by many municipalities both before it was launched in 1999 and since. When the corresponding Juki-Card was issued in 2003, further opposition surfaced, which ensured, up to 2007, that less than 1 percent of the Japanese population actually used the ID card (see Ogasawara 2008; Murakami Wood et al. 2007). Similarly, in the USA, a number of states have refused to comply with the requirements of the REAL ID for data-sharing. Various ultimatums have been issued—the latest giving a compliance deadline of May 11, 2008—to pull the recalcitrant states into line. Since several states have actually passed legislation underscoring their non-compliance it appears that the impasse will continue for some time to come (Single, 2008).

Less dramatically, a number of proposals have been made by those working on the design of ID card systems. In 2006, the LSE produced a report on the proposed UK ID card system which, though roundly attacked as flawed, actually made a number of constructive proposals as to how an ID card system might be set up in more secure and less contentious ways than the one legislated. Equally, in Canada, concrete suggestions have been made about developing ID systems in ways that preserve anonymity and avoid the risks associated with a single unique identifier (Clement et al., 2008). Both cases show how, for example, "participatory design" processes could contribute to a more democratically accountable mode of creating ID card systems.

Electronic and biometric identification systems are increasingly a part of everyday life in many countries around the world. The idea that we are "governed by identity" actually means that many other agencies than the nation-state are involved in governance and this has implications for the kinds of citizenship that are now possible and, for that matter, desirable. The debates over ID card systems cannot be understood without considering the broader context of controversies over citizenship and democracy, but equally those questions themselves raise identification issues. In a globalizing world with high mobility rates, more and more people are associated with "states" but not necessarily with "nations"—and it is just this ambiguity that "national" ID cards address. Does this migrant worker qualify for state health benefits? Might this international student have ties to proscribed organizations and thus be a threat to state security? Could this tourist intend to stay beyond the date specified in her visa? These sorts of questions speak to the matter of today's ambiguous identities, which ID cards can attempt to encompass.

New IDs may be considered as a stand-in (see Barney, 2000: Chapter 7) for the kinds of political identities that are important in the twenty-first century. The sorts of characteristics exhibited by new IDs make it clear that citizenship is generally circumscribed, related to nationality but also to country of origin, ethnicity, gender, and even religion. The politics of identity is obscured by or at best subsumed under new regimes of identity management.

The very production of new IDs tends to restrict political dissent and the efforts of those who propose modifications in the kinds of functions such cards have. This is certainly true in major cases such as that of the United Kingdom, the United States, and Japan. ID card systems are the product of a growing coalition between various groups; high-technology hardware and software providers, corporations such as banks for whom the card may also have benefits, and government departments.[1] Their effects tend to be felt most strongly and most negatively among the most vulnerable sectors of the population—immigrants, suspected "terrorists," and welfare claimants. If the measure of good government is the extent to which the weakest are protected from the worst eventualities, then ID cards can hardly be said to enhance such government.

New IDs do what computer networks (on which they depend) generally do best; they contribute to a culture of control. The nature of this control is interesting. It is by definition digital (Jones, 2000) and relates to governance in general, across a range of social realms. It is the product of a long-term historical shift that is visible in the rise of management approaches and neoliberal political economies (Garland, 2001). In utilizing computer networks, it supports a move away from conventional disciplines associated with modernity and (as analyzed by Foucault) towards mere control. These audio-visual protocols, as Gilles Deleuze calls them, deflect attention from the demands of morality and democracy to the calculable, to relations determined by computer codes that express social categories. New IDs "sort things out" (Bowker and Star, 1999) in new ways, the full consequences of which have yet to be seen. Moreover, they do this remotely—at a distance—and using biometric measures, thus removing these markers of identity even further from the struggles of daily life and the sphere of political debate.

That the securitizing of identity is occurring at a juncture when conventional rule of (international) law is being set aside in favor of states of emergency within the so-called war on terror increases the likelihood that new IDs may be used to categorize and disadvantage certain vulnerable groups even further (Wilson, 2006). Add to this the evident power of high-technology corporations and the apparent willingness of governments to embrace the "solutions" they proffer and the situation seems still gloomier, at least from the perspective of the politics of recognition and of human rights. None of this is inevitable, of course, and the development of electronic-based ID card systems is still in its relative infancy. Yet if the current trends are to be questioned or even redirected, not only will clear, critical scholarship be required, but also the political will to put first the interests of citizens and would-be citizens who are registered in ID systems. The abstraction of personal data and the emphasis on precautionary measures within security-obsessed regimes create considerable obstacles to such hopes.

Note

1 I discuss this elsewhere as the "oligopolization of the means of identification."

References

Arendt, Hannah. 1963. *Eichmann in Jerusalem: A Report on the Banality of Evil.* New York: Rowman and Littlefield.
Abercrombie, N., S. Hill, and B. Turner. 1986. *Sovereign Individuals of Capitalism.* London: Allen and Unwin.
Barney, Darin. 2000. *Prometheus Wired: The Hope for Democracy in the Age of Network Technology.* Chicago: University of Chicago Press.
Bauman, Zygmunt. 1998. *Globalization: The Human Consequences.* Cambridge: Polity; New York: Columbia University Press.
———. 2000. *Liquid Modernity.* Cambridge: Polity.
Bigo, Didier. 2005. "Global (in)security: The field of the professionals of unease management and the ban-opticon." *Traces: A Multilingual Series of Cultural Theory* 4:34–87.
Bigo, Didier and Elspeth Guild, Ed. 2005. *Controlling Frontiers: Free Movement into and within Europe.* Ashgate: London.
Bowker, G. and Susan Leigh Star. 1999. *Sorting Things Out: Classification and its Consequences.* Cambridge, MA: MIT Press.
Clement, Andrew, Krista Boa, Simon Davies and Gus Hosein. 2008. "Towards a national ID card for Canada? External drivers and internal complexities." In *Playing the Identity Card: Surveillance, Security and Identification in Global Perspective*, edited by Colin J. Bennett and David Lyon, 233–50. Routledge: London and New York.
Delanty, Gerard. 2000. *Citizenship in a Global Age.* Buckingham: Open University Press.
Garland, D. 2001. *The Culture of Control: Crime and Social Order in Contemporary Society.* Chicago: University of Chicago Press.
Groebner, Valentin. 2001. "Describing the person, reading the signs in late medieval and renaissance Europe: Identity papers, vested figures, and the limits of Identification." In *Documenting Individual Identity*, edited by Jane Caplan and John Torpey, pp. 15–27. Princeton University Press: Princeton New Jersey.
———. 2007. *Who Are You? Identification, Deception, and Surveillance in Early Modern Europe.* Translated by Mark Kyburz and John Peck Cloth, Zone Books: New York.

Hague, Barry N. and Brian D. Loader, Ed. 1999. *Digital Democracy*. London: Routledge.

Isin, Engin F. and Brian S. Turner. 2007. "Investigating citizenship: An agenda for citizenship studies." *Citizenship Studies* 11 (1):5–17.

Jones, R. 2000. Digital rule. *Punishment and Society* 2 (1):5–22.

Levinas, R. 1990. *The Concept of Utopia*. Syracuse, NY: Syracuse University Press.

Lyon, David, 2009. Identifying Citizens: ID cards as surveillance. Cambridge: Polity.

Lyon, David and Colin J. Bennett. 2008. "Playing the ID card: Understanding the significance of identity card systems." In *Playing the Identity Card: Surveillance, Security and Identification in Global Perspective*, edited by Colin J. Bennett and David Lyon, 3–20. Routledge: London and New York.

Muller, Benjamin. 2004. "(Dis)qualified bodies: Securitization, citizenship and 'identity Management.'" *Citizenship Studies* 8 (3):279–94.

Murakami Wood, David, David Lyon and Kyoshi Abe. 2007. "Surveillance in urban Japan: An introduction." *Urban Studies* 43 (3):551–68.

Ng, Wendy. 2002. *Japanese American Internment During World War II: A History and Reference Guide*. Westport, CN: Greenwood Press.

Ogasawara, Midori. 2008. "A tale of the colonial age, or the banner of new tyranny? National identification card systems in Japan." In *Playing the Identity Card: Surveillance, Security and Identification in Global Perspective*, edited by Colin J. Bennett and David Lyon, 93–111. Routledge: London and New York.

Piazza, Pierre and Laniel, Laurent. 2008. "The INES biometric card and the politics of national identity assignment in France." In *Playing the Identity Card: Surveillance, Security and Identification in Global Persepctive*, edited by Colin J. Bennett and David Lyon, 198–217. Routledge: London and New York.

Single, Ran. 2008. "New Real ID rules to shut down nation's airports in May?" *Wired* January 11, 2008.

SWAMI Report. 2006. *Safeguards in a World of Ambient Intelligence* March 2006, European Commission, DG Information Society.

Travis, Alan. 2003. "ID cards to cut asylum abuses." *The Guardian* May 23, 2003.

Turner, Bryan. 1993. *Citizenship and Social Theory*. London: Sage.

van der Ploeg, Irma. 2005. *The Machine-Readable Body*. Maastricht: Shaker.

Wilson, Dean. 2006. "Biometrics, borders and the ideal suspect." In *Borders, Mobility and Technologies of Control*, edited by S. Pickering and L. Weber. pp. 87–109. Springer: Dordrecht.

Zureik, Elia. 2001. "Constructing Palestine through surveillance practices." *British Journal of Middle Eastern Studies* 28 (2):205–27.

Chapter 3

Democracy and its visibilities

Andrea Mubi Brighenti

Democracy and the public

In recent years, critics have raised well-founded concerns about the extent to which surveillance is affecting the health of democratic life. Practices of data collection and retention, as well as the unprecedented development of trace-ability through digital relational databases, have recently been addressed as sensitive topics in surveillance studies (Lyon, 2001; 2007). Even without resort-ing to conspiracy theories or "Big Brotherist" visions, which have already been effectively criticized by various scholars (see, in particular, Lianos, 2003), concerns about a growing tension between the requirements of democratic life and the surveillance activity carried out by governmental agencies appear to be well founded. It is especially so if one takes into account the larger picture, which also includes the rise of "securitarian" and "dangerization" versions of the law-and-order ideology. Waves of securitarian panic stirred up by moral entrepreneurs in Becker's sense and mirrored by the media have led to racial targeting and racial profiling of groups seen to "pose a threat" to public safety (for the Italian case, see for example De Giorgi, 2008). Concurrently, the growing motivational deficit at the heart of contemporary democratic regimes (Critchley, 2007) and the rise of economic inequalities are likely to multiply anti-democratic tendencies.

The public appears as a crucial dimension in the relationship between surveillance and democracy. However, a problem arises when, on the basis of an assumption grounded in political liberalism, the private is simply opposed to the public in a dichotomous way. Concerns about the political effects of surveillance are often interpreted as the task of protecting private life against surveillance. Throughout this chapter, I show the limitations of this view of the private/public divide. We need to replace the false dichotomy of surveil-lance and privacy with a more nuanced and pluralist understanding of the social working of surveillance. Three main concepts will be at the center of my discussion: *visibility regimes*, *technologies of power*, and the *public domain*. Visibility regimes are constitutive of political regimes and as fundamentally interwoven with technologies of power. Because of this interplay, the idea of retreat into the private domain as a means of avoiding surveillance is chimerical. Rather, the real challenge posed by surveillance is the re-articulation of the public domain. An Arendtian conception of democracy, as I argue below, best captures this process, revealing the delusion inherent in the idea of being "free at one's own place." Here again technology plays a crucial role, not simply because power deploys a set of technologies but, more radically, because—following a Foucauldian insight—power itself *is* a technology, it is one among the specific techniques that human beings use to understand themselves (Foucault, 1982).

To begin with, it should be specified that in this context visibility cannot be reduced to a mere visual issue. Visibility is a symbolic field of social meaning: seeing and being seen do not simply correspond to given power positions. Visibility relationships are also constituted by many other, not directly perceptual, forms of noticing, managing attention, and determining the significance of events and subjects. In short, visibility lies at the intersection of aesthetics (relations of perception) and politics (relations of power).

From this perspective, to describe visibility as symbolic does not equate it to a matter of cultural repertoire. Culture is indeed symbolic, but in the case of the visible the symbolic perspective should be taken and turned upside down, so to speak. Images and gestures do not so much constitute the perceptible symbols of some intangible meaning, but rather symbols *are* images and gestures, in the sense that they have the same structure and the same way of functioning. Symbols are nothing more and nothing less than what *is made* visible, and, complementarily, what *makes* the visible. Thus, symbols are the material element of the visible as well as the identifiable *Gestalten* that are drawn in the field. The visible is not only the field where broad cultural meanings are worked out, but also a much more compelling material and strategic field. Visibility is not free-floating meaning, but meaning inscribed in material processes and constraints (see also Brighenti, 2007). Visibility is a domain that is crucially located at the interface between the domains of the technical and the social. Contemporary *sociotechnological complexes* are intimately linked to the forms and features of social visibility and intervisibility, as, for instance, mass media as collective apparatuses of social networking clearly reveal.

Social and political theorists have provided important conceptualizations of the public domain. Hannah Arendt (1958:50) insisted on the existence of a "world in common" among humans as the pivotal condition for politics. In Greek and Roman culture, Arendt argued, it is the experience of the *common* that defines the public sphere as the place where "everything that appears ... can be seen and heard by everybody and has the widest possible publicity ... [and] appearance—something that is being seen and heard by others as well as by ourselves—[is what] constitutes reality" (Arendt, 1958:50). The public sphere is defined by its publicity and commonality, in contrast to the private sphere, which is characterized by deprivation: "To live an entirely private life means above all to be deprived of things essential to a truly human life: to be deprived of the reality that comes from being seen and heard by others" (Arendt, 1958:58). The existence of the public sphere as a world-in-common which joins and separates is, for Arendt, threatened by mass society, which undermines the capacity of the public to articulate meaningful relationships and separations among people. Such "meaningful separation" speaks to the Hegelian theme of recognition, which has been taken up, for instance, by Charles Taylor since the 1970s (see Taylor, 1989). In particular, Taylor argued that the sources of the subject in Western political thought should be conceived by taking into account not merely large-scale social projects (such as theories of justice etc.), but especially the personal desire for recognition as constitutive of life in common.

While disagreeing with Arendt's thesis that modernity is a time of decline for the public sphere, Jürgen Habermas (1982 [1962]) similarly defined the public sphere as a realm of social life that provides a forum for the articulation of common issues. The public sphere emerged in modern society over the period from the seventeenth century to the early nineteenth century, as a third domain, distinct from both private household and public power. The public sphere is the space of civil society, as distinct from private association on the one hand, and institutionalized political society on the other. Its specificity consists in providing the infrastructure for the elaboration of public opinion through public debate—that is, debate on matters of general interest and issues of common concern. Such debate is joined by all those citizens potentially affected by the outcomes of political decisions on the issues at stake. Participation and deliberation are the crucial aspects of this sphere of social action. Linked to institutions such as coffee houses, public libraries, and, above all, modern mass media such as the press, the history of the public sphere is the history of the consolidation of bourgeois society. The defining features of the public sphere are its essential accessibility to all citizens and the principle of the public availability of proceedings (*Publizitätsvorschriften*). Habermas also diagnosed a crisis of the public sphere during the course of the twentieth century, in the form of a "refeudalization." On the one hand, new powerful private actors, such as large corporations, started to undertake direct political action through control and manipulation of communication and the media, thus promoting their private interests in a way that is at odds with the original logic of the public sphere. On the other hand, the Keynesian configuration of the Western welfare state corresponded to a more active engagement of the state in the private sphere and everyday life, leading to an erosion of the distinction between political and civil society which was itself the object of criticism (see e.g. Young, 1990). Following the Frankfurt School's line of analysis, Habermas described the decline of the public sphere as a process of transforming citizens into consumers, which eventually leads to a decline of interest in the common good and in direct participation.

In his theorization of politics, Norberto Bobbio (1999) identified democracy as a type of power that poses a specific challenge to the older elitist tradition of the *arcana imperii* (literally, the secrets of power). The elitist tradition is grounded in a negative anthropology maintaining that there is no cure from the evil of power. In this view history is reduced to a contingent series of facts that do not alter the human being's thrust towards power. Power is believed to have been, and necessarily always bound to be, in the hands of a minority, an elite which is not legitimated from below but rather legitimizes itself. Understandably, this bitter reality of power is often kept hidden to avoid contention and political turmoil. Arguably, conspiracy theories are an offspring of elitist theories, insofar as they extend the elitist belief in the—at least partial—invisibility of power to the idea of the invisibility of power-holders themselves, organized in an invisible ruling synarchy. By contrast, Bobbio defines democracy as "power in public," i.e. power the inner mechanisms of which are made visible and therefore controllable. Modern democracy was born in opposition to medieval and early-modern treatises on the art of government, such as the Machiavellian-style "advices to the Prince." Whereas the precepts-to-the-Prince literature looked at power *ex parte principis*, from the point of view of the prince, modern democracy begins when one begins to look at power *ex parte populi*, from the point of view of the people. The gaze from below amounts to a vigorous call for the openness, visibility and accountability of power. Whereas all autocratic regimes are founded upon the conservation of secrecy in proceedings, the crucial democratic challenge is to achieve a deployment of power that is ideally without secrets. The device of political representation is necessarily public, as recognized even by opponents of this view, such as Carl Schmitt.

For his part, Max Weber (1978[1922]: I, §III, 3–5) saw quite clearly that modern bureaucracy is an ambivalent institution. On the one hand, bureaucracy is necessary to achieve the legal-rational form of power, based on the specialization of competences and the standardization of procedures. Bureaucratic apparatuses can attain the highest degrees of efficiency and are the most rational way to control people because they guarantee highly calculable outcomes. On the other hand, however, not only does bureaucracy produce conformity and uniform technical competence, but it also tends to breed plutocracy and dominance of formalistic impersonality, and, above all, it is constantly tempted to restrict open access to government records, through the production of "classified" documents ("*Amtsgeheimnisse*") and other inaccessible technicalities. These perils of technocracy have also been analyzed by other democratic theorists, such as Robert Dahl (1989). Bobbio himself remarked that "the resistance and the persistence of invisible power become stronger and stronger, even in democratic States, the more one considers issues such as international relations," (1999:365) which often include secret consultations and secret treaties.

In spite of their differences, most social theorists share some concern for the transformations of the public sphere during the twentieth century. The shrinkage of the public sphere—which, as mentioned above, Habermas dubbed "refeudalization"—is regarded as threatening for democracy. In this respect, Craig Calhoun (2005) has observed that democracy requires both inclusion and connection among citizens; in other words, citizens should be able to access relevant information and communicate with each other in a common world extending beyond primary, private associations. This is why the public sphere materialized first of all in urban environments, and was later extended by the media: "Publics connect people who are not in the same families, communities, and clubs; people who are not the same as each other. Urban life is public, thus, in a way village life is not. Modern media amplify this capacity to communicate with strangers" (Calhoun, 2005:5). Hence, the importance of transparent and symmetric communication as constitutive of the public sphere. For Calhoun, indeed, the public sphere cannot be conceived of as the mere "sum" of a set of separate private opinions, for this deletes the fundamental process of the formation of public opinion itself, which takes place through discussion and deliberation.

Overall, these theorizations point to the fact that the public sphere is a sphere of *visibility*. But whereas political philosophers insist in particular on the procedural and deliberative dimension associated with communicative action, sociologists must also study the specificities of public space and the types and modalities of interaction in public. Richard Sennett (1978), for instance, focused on Western urban space in order to locate the public sphere. He argued that it was the very transformation of modern city life that caused a crisis in the public realm. The construction of the public sphere was the construction of an impersonal, role-based model of interaction, which enabled people to deal with complex and disordered situations. The fall of this model is marked by the rise of a new emotivism and the thirst for authenticity, community, and the expression of feelings and desires. Indifference, concerns for personal safety, fear of victimization, and a whole ideology of the "coldness" of public space caused a general retreat into the private, in search of the "warm" human relations supposed to be found in the family and community. Emotivism and communitarianism thus induced a crisis in the dynamism of the public sphere as well as a decrease in "civility," understood as the capacity to relate positively to strangers—"the activity which protects people from each other and yet allows them to enjoy each other's company" (Sennett, 1978:264). In other words, the fall of the public man corresponded to an increasing fear of strangers. Such incapacity to live with strangers, Sennett observed, is deeply problematic, because intimate relations cannot be successfully projected as a basis for social relations at large. Accepting the other as unknown is a crucial component of civility, which is an essential democratic capacity, similar to what Castoriadis (1997) used to call *paideia*. Castoriadis stressed that there is no ultimate guarantee for democracy, but only contingent guarantees. *Paideia*, or "education" in a very broad sense of the term, is one such guarantee that consists in the creation of political subjects aware of both the necessity of regulation and the possibility of discussing, criticizing, and changing the rules of coexistence:

> Rotation in office, sortition, decision-making after deliberation by the entire body politic, elections, and popular courts did not rest solely on a postulate that everyone has an equal capacity to assume public responsibilities: these procedures were themselves pieces of a political educational process, of an active paideia, which aimed at exercising—and, therefore, at developing in all—the corresponding abilities and, thereby, at rendering the postulate of political equality as close to the effective reality of that society as possible.
>
> (Castoriadis, 1997:11)

Sennett's view of the public sphere shares some similarities with ideas emerging from interactionist sociology. Erving Goffman (1963, 1971) approached public space from the perspective of the specific type of interaction that goes on in public, made of fleeting encounters among strangers and small-scale sociality. Working within a Goffmanian framework, Lyn Lofland (1998) insists on the elements of urban environments and stranger interaction as constitutive of the public realm at large. The public realm can be conceived of primarily as a type of register of human interaction that differs from other registers, specifically from the private one. Lofland contends that the realms she describes are social-psychological rather than spatial. The type of realm, in other words, is not defined by the physical space in which it is located but by its predominant relational form. Whereas the private realm is "characterized by ties of intimacy among primary group members who are located within households and personal networks," and the parochial realm is "characterized by a sense of commonality among acquaintances and neighbors who are involved in interpersonal networks that are located within communities," the public realm can be described as "the non-private sectors of urban areas in which individuals in copresence tend to be personally unknown or only categorically known to one another" (Lofland, 1998:9–10).

Consequently, whereas in the private realm the dominant relational form is intimate, and in the parochial or communal realm it is communitarian, in the public realm the dominant form is essentially categorical. A categorical form of relation, which corresponds to the capacity to deal with biographic strangers, stems mainly from the experience of urban life and is based on the only apparently thin capacity to coexist in a civil manner, accepting the existence of social diversity. Thus, Lofland's analysis advances a defense of the public realm on the basis of its social value as an environment for active learning, a site for relief from sometimes oppressive strong ties, a place where both social cooperation and social conflict can be acted out, and, ultimately, the only true place for social communication and the practice of politics.

The public as visibility and territory

Research on the public sphere and the public realm is greatly valuable for the study of the contemporary interplay between democracy and surveillance. But a further key element must be considered: that is, the *interweaving of material and immaterial* dimensions of the social sphere. Both political philosophers and interaction sociologists tend to somewhat downplay the importance and scope of the materiality of the public, and, more precisely, the interweaving and constant *prolongations* of materialities and immaterialities. Indeed, political philosophical reflection on the public sphere is almost exclusively focused on the dimension of political participation and deliberative procedures, while interactionist studies of the public realm are mainly concerned with the cognitive frameworks and registers of interpersonal interaction. However, both approaches miss the spatial and material constraints that constitute the public.

In an attempt to overcome the limitations inherent in such a selective and partial outlook on the part of political philosophers and interactionist sociologists, I adopt the label "public domain" as the most encompassing and general term to address issues traditionally associated in various ways with the public sphere, public realm, and public space. Here, I argue, visibility and territoriality emerge as key analytical points. First of all because, as we have seen, the public domain is itself open and visible; but accessing the public domain also means agreeing to become a *subject* of visibility, someone who is, in his or her turn, visible to others. Secondly, because the practical working of intervisibilities amounts to introducing and managing qualitative thresholds between different types of events going on in the social sphere. The public domain, thus, can be fully appreciated only if we take into account the double articulation of the social sphere, as "matter of the cosmos" and "image of thought" (Deleuze and Guattari, 1980) at the same time.

The public domain has both a material side—defined by bodily experience; density; circulation; and urban dromology—and a social-relational, affective side, referring to the capacity of actors to affect each other. Consequently, we can conceive of the public domain properly as a *territory* (Brighenti, 2006), that is, a specific modalization of situated and materially constrained interaction. Territories are relational, processual and directional phenomena, which always exist in the tension between the material and the immaterial. They are like acts or events that unfold in time, creating determinations, trajectories, and rhythms on the basis of threshold-making, or boundary-drawing acts. Not simply spatial regions, but all types of relational topologies can be appreciated as territorial formations, such as, for instance, the internet. Contrary to what has sometimes been superficially said about media without a sense of place, experiencing the internet is a deeply territorial process, insofar as browsing constantly involves the experience of crossing boundaries and entering new territories made of relational fields defined by domains, access points, protocols, and then inclusion and exclusion, elicitation, participation, banning, and so on. Adopting a distinction first introduced by Michel de Certeau (1984), Mattias Kärrholm (2007) has recently remarked that territorial complexity is due to the balancing of the double process of territorial production and territorial stabilization. Production and stabilization can be either strategic or tactical in nature:

> [t]erritorial strategies represent impersonal, planned, and, to some extent, mediated control, and often involve the delegation of control to things, rules, and so forth. Territorial strategies are (to a degree) always planned at a distance in time and/or space from the territory produced, whereas territorial tactics involve claims made in the midst of a situation and as part of an ongoing sequence (in daily life). Territorial tactics thus often refer to a personal relationship between the territory and the person or group who mark it as theirs.
>
> (Kärrholm, 2007:441)

The territorializing process can be described as a way of carving the environment through boundary-drawing acts that concurrently help to stabilize the set of relationships that take place in that environment.

Recognizing boundaries as a type of operation, or "act," leads to an initial definition of the trajectories and boundaries within and around territories as complementary rather than conflicting elements, or, in other words, as two elements that constantly act upon each other. Like every other territory, the public domain is bounded, but its boundaries are constantly worked upon by actors. One of the crucial processes that is currently reshaping the boundaries of the public domain in significant ways is the emergence of visibility asymmetries fostered by contemporary surveillance practices. Not only is access to many spaces more and more restricted through the use of checkpoints and passwords, but the very type of categories produced by professional surveillance knowledge is intersecting with and even colonizing lay knowledge in the public domain.

Visibility contributes crucially to the demarcation of the public domain. Specifically, the social configurations emerging from new surveillant visibility regimes are leading to a profound transformation of the public. Visibility is not merely a free-floating aspect of social interaction. Rather, it is structured as the result of the activities and practices of all the different actors who aim to plan it or, on the contrary, to resist such planning. Visibility asymmetries are arranged into structured complexes, which we call *regimes*. Contemporary society is organized around regimes of visibility that contribute to the definition and management of power, representations, public opinion, conflict, and social control. Whereas potential ambivalences are inherent to all visibility effects, actual regimes specify and activate contextual determinations of the visible. Thus, the actual effects of visibility are selected by the whole territorial arrangement in which social relationships are embedded.

The threat surveillance poses to democracy today can be related to the fact that the contract of visibility in the public domain is being increasingly blurred and ultimately rendered fictional: the normal and the abnormal, norm and exception cannot be disentangled. This fact, which we are going to discuss in more depth below, reminds us that the study of the public domain itself can be undertaken from at least two complementary if not opposing perspectives: the perspective, already considered, of democracy, on the one hand, and the perspective of government on the other. The governmental perspective has been developed in the most original way by Michel Foucault. Government includes what is commonly referred to as policy and regulation, but is not limited to that. Foucault described the activity of government in these terms: "[w]ith government it is a question not of imposing law on men, but of disposing things" (1991[1978]:95). Governmental activity thus works by defining subject positions inside a field made of strategically "disposed things." It is important to notice that, with this definition, Foucault completely severs the activity of government from state apparatuses. What characterizes the period from the sixteenth to the twentieth century it is not so much the subordination of society to a central state apparatus (*étatisation de la société*), as it is a governmentalization of the state itself (*gouvernementalisation de l'État*). More generally, the governmental field is essentially a relational and, in the terms proposed above, a *territorial* field, which can be sustained by very different types of institutional bonds. The materiality of things and spaces is essential for the exercise of this type of power.

Foucault's interest in government emerged in the context of his study of the genealogy of modern power. Foucault, it is said, diagnosed a *shift* from sovereignty to disciplinary society, and, later, revealed the crisis of disciplinary society, which was the prelude to new forms of control such as security. This view has sometimes been supported with reference to Deleuze's *Postscript* (1992 [1990]), which, however, only describes the crisis of the disciplinary model and the main features of the control model of power. But, in fact, in the period from the mid to the late 1970s, Foucault (1976, 1977 [1975], 1997 [1975–76], 1991 [1978], 2007 [1978]) elaborated a more complex and nuanced quadripartite image of power, where the different forms of power do not simply rule each other out, but rather *co-exist* in subtle ways. In other words, his analysis should not be interpreted as a stage theory (first sovereignty, then discipline, then security) but rather a *pluralist analytics of power forms*. At the most general level, Foucault's analysis is grounded in the idea that modern power is not simply a negative, repressive power, but rather a positive power that assumes the function of "taking care" of human life as a whole: "the modern human being is an animal whose politics puts into question his own life as a living being" (Foucault, 1976:188).

Four major technologies of power are identified by Foucault, corresponding to four types of regulation and four ways of organizing social space. The first technology is *sovereignty*. It aims to guarantee the certainty of a territory, which is a juridical and jurisdictional bounded space. Sovereignty establishes hegemonic control over a spatial territory. Its infrastructure is *law*, a discursive device that works essentially through prohibition (legal philosophers confirm that *forbidding* is the original deontic form). Foucault explored the technology of sovereignty to a lesser extent, since he regarded it as the classic model of power, which had already been conceptualized by classic theorists and was in fact being increasingly infiltrated by the second and third types of technology. What is interesting in the sovereign technology is the specific type of spectacle of power it sets up, especially in the form of parades, triumphal marches, and so on. As Tony Bennett glosses in the case of museums, "the people, so far as their relations to high cultural forms were concerned, were merely the witnesses of a power that was paraded before them" (1995:22).

The second technology is *discipline*. Discipline is a modern creation, whose aim is to cultivate, engender, and "orthopaedically" correct individual habits. It is a form of "microphysical" power in the sense that it is exercised directly upon individual bodies. The major disciplinary tool is the *norm*. The norm proposes a positive ideal, enforced within a clearly delimited institutional space, which separates normal and abnormal subjects. Discipline thus follows the maxim of *divide et impera*: it divides up both subjects and space, it introduces boundaries and establishes enclosed institutions. Discipline acts upon confused multiplicities in an attempt to eliminate confusion, categorize subjects and enhance their conformity to the norm. Famously, discipline aims to produce "docile bodies."

The third type of technology is *security*. Security is not a single apparatus but comprises a set of technologies whose general aim is to govern multiplicities in open spaces on the basis of actuarial devices. Such multiplicities cannot be pinned down to the individual level, so security cannot be applied to individuals. Rather, security organizes space according to a series of *possible events* that are to be managed and kept under control. Security aims to control events that are temporary and even aleatory to a degree. In order to do so, it conceives and organizes the space as an *environment,* a system of possibilities, of virtualities that do or do not become actual. Whereas discipline aims to govern a multiplicity of subjects by impacting directly, *singulatim,* upon individual bodies—in order to control them, train them, or get them accustomed to the norm—security governs the multiplicity as an *omnes*, an undivided whole. Whereas the norm works by "normation," security works by "normalization." In other words, within the disciplinarian framework people are classified by reference to a norm, setting apart the normal from the abnormal; in the securitarian framework people are treated as an undivided whole and the issue becomes one of operating an aggregate, statistical, or average normalized management of biological processes such as nutrition, health, and so on. Consequently, if the object of the application of discipline is the body, the object upon which security is exercised is an entity called *population*. Population is not an individual but a global mass, a collective and statistical concept. It exists only as a pattern within a grid of dimensions and variables, which include "impersonal" events such as birth, death, production, reproduction, and illness. The population has no will, it is neither "a people" in the classical political-philosophical meaning, nor an actor in the sociological sense of the word. It just shows certain *tendencies* that must be normalized. From this point of view, technologies of security define *biopolitics*, which is different from *anatomopolitics*, the technology of disciplinary power exercised on individual bodies. If the latter aims to shape an individual's habits and drives, the former can "only" control aggregate tendencies, without shaping them from within. Discipline individualizes; biopolitics massifies. Biopolitics is a politics of life, but not of individuals; rather, it addresses "the multiplicity of humans as a global mass that is affected by overall processes that characterize its life" (Foucault, 1997 [1975–76]:216).

The fourth set of technologies of power analyzed by Foucault is the set of technologies of the Self (Foucault, 1982). Despite the fact that Foucault ultimately concluded that his major interest throughout his career was the exploration of the emergence of the subject, for the purposes of our present discussion on surveillance and democracy we will take into consideration only the first three types of technologies.

Visibility management and surveillance

Shaping and managing visibility is a huge task that human beings perform tirelessly. The management of visibility is embedded in sociotechnological complexes through which the phenomenological here-and-now of the local *Umwelt* is prolonged by means of activities of import/export. In other words, the media are devices for establishing connections between different *Umwelten*. Clearly, from such a McLuhanian perspective (McLuhan, 1964), the media cover a much broader category than *mass* media. Indeed, the mass media correspond to only one among the many configurations or patterns of visibility, i.e broadcast, or one-to-many communication. More broadly, following Régis Debray (2000), the mediation process can be described as a technosocial "middle realm" in which the social and the technical meet and mix. Frédéric Vandenberghe (2007:26) has summarized this mixing as the process through which "the spirit gets materialized into technology at the same time as the social gets organized into society and reproduced through history." Democracy is one such sociotechnological complex. Ideals and discourses about equality and freedom are not just abstract philosophical amusements, but are fixed in very intricate and often twisted ways into the material aspects of the social, down to the most concrete and apparently dull details of an office, its furniture, its application forms, and the bureaucratic jargon spoken by its employees. Hence, the importance of the dimension of (in)visibility in the social field.

Every time the mass media and new communication technologies enlarge or reshape the field of the socially visible, visibility turns into a supply-and-demand market. At any change in the field, the question arises of what is being seen, and at what price—along with the normative question of what should and should not be seen. These questions are never simply a technical matter: they are inherently practical and political. This means that, at every change in the field, the practice, the rationale and the scope of intervisibilities is going to be problematized and the specific parameters, delimitations, and dynamics of visibility are renegotiated. Therefore, to understand the real stake of the management of visibilities we need to adopt and confront those two opposing, or at least complementary, points of view on the public domain, which are the democratic and the governmental.

Another crucial aspect is connected to the fact that mediation can enhance asymmetries in visibility. Surveillance comprises all those processes through which a target population is kept under scrutiny. Surveillance can be described as specific management of the relative visibilities and visibility asymmetries among people. Within the framework of the thesis of a passage from disciplinary societies to societies of control, it has been argued that contemporary society is characterized by the fact that surveillance becomes methodical, systematic, and automatic (Virilio, 1994), rather than discontinuous, as was the case with the disciplinary technology of power. We no longer have *virtual* control—which was made possible by the internalization of the gaze on the part of the disciplined subject—but rather *actual* control, made possible by new technologies and the availability of new types of high-tech "unsleeping eyes." Information and communication technologies have multiplied the range and scope of surveillance processes and have made these processes routine, rather than techniques applied in exceptional circumstances.

More nuanced surveillance studies, however, have revealed that surveillance itself is not monolithic (Lyon, 2007). Rather, it comprises a set of activities promoted by different agencies for different purposes. In this vein, Lianos (2001, 2003) has argued that contemporary institutional control is acentric and acephalic, perioptical rather than panoptical. In this hypothesis, post-industrial social control is aimed not at surveillance on the part of a single central authority but rather at the creation of differential individual positions of inclusion/exclusion as well as the promotion of individualist competition for inclusion. However, it is still possible to say, whether it is exercised by a single or by multiple agencies, that what remains common to all surveillance activities is a selectively focused attention paid to personal details that are monitored, recorded, checked, archived, and retrieved. The traceability of acts and events is enhanced by information storage and data retention, which are enacted for the most diverse institutional aims and crucially create the possibility of *retrospective* investigation. A single surveillance process thus consists in the effort to achieve and subsequently manage the visibility of people's identities and behaviors to the advantage of the specific agency promoting that surveillance activity, but the overall interconnections among the many surveillance systems generate outcomes that are often unpredictable in terms of the extent and the precision of tracking. In any case, it is clear that visibility is to be understood not merely as a visual condition but, in a broader sense, as the availability of personal data useful to compile general behavioral profiles. New surveillance technologies lead to a widespread diffusion of often uncoordinated control practices and systematically activate contextual visibility asymmetries among those who scrutinize and those who are scrutinized both at the material-sensorial and the immaterial level.

Inside a visibility regime, it is necessary to explain how the classification (and territorialization) of surveilled people takes place in practice, understanding how relations of perception (the visual) and relations of power (the visible) prolong and constantly flow into each other. To identify the visual and bodily features that are employed for the categorical identification and profiling of people entails explaining the whole social organization of visual perception inside a sociotechnical diagram or apparatus. Professional *savoirs* are deployed in the perception of images, and surveillance is usually a professional activity. This fact holds crucial consequences for surveillance practices. One of the most striking characteristics of contemporary surveillant visibility regimes seems to be their *uncertainty*. It becomes more and more difficult for lay people to know the specific knowledge that will be applied to scrutinize them. Sometimes it may even be hard to determine which types of behavior would cause one to be profiled as posing a threat.

In order to stress the complex functioning of surveillance that exceeds the process of the norm, Haggerty and Ericson (2000) described the "surveillant assemblage" as a mechanism of transposition of surveillance from the material to the immaterial level, which operates as flows:

> [t]he surveillant assemblage does not approach the body in the first instance as a single entity to be molded, punished, or controlled. First it must be known, and to do so it is broken down into a series of discrete signifying flows. Surveillance commences with the creation of a space of comparison and the introduction of breaks in the flows that emanate from, or circulate within, the human body.
>
> (Haggerty and Ericson; 2000:612)

Just like the technologies of security, the surveillant assemblage addresses a type of control upon open space qualitatively different from that adopted for enclosed spaces. The surveillant assemblage is a visibility regime. Similarly, Lianos has described contemporary institutional control as based on routine and even unintentional processes of de-subjectification: "institutional control is about the 'de-subjectification' of the individual, who is being largely transformed into a fragmented user, since the object of control is to regulate exclusively the specific institutional shell of activity concerned each time" (2003:423).

The de-subjectified individual, though, is only part of a wider picture. Space can be controlled dividually, for instance, through boundary policing. But whenever some redrawing of boundaries takes place, other technologies will eventually intervene, leading to re-subjectification and re-individualization. These could be, for instance, repressive measures against single trespassers, but also, at the same time, work as orthopaedic and even exemplary demonstration for non-trespassers, for the law-abiding majority. In these cases, the institutional, the administrative, the sovereign, and the expressive intermingle. The threat to democracy in this case comes from the rise of arbitrary and capricious forms of governance.[1] Surveillance regimes make more things more visible, and bring more practices to the attention of surveillance agencies, but they do so in ways that are not openly accountable, based as they are on professional *savoirs* who are themselves invisible. There exists a greater threat than the fact that people are profiled by (relatively) invisible agencies: it is the fact that profiling criteria themselves are invisible. Such criteria may not necessarily be designed for evil purposes, such as overt racial discrimination; on the contrary, they may simply mirror pragmatic short-term concerns that are linked to the organizational logic of the surveillance agency. But their unintended consequences can nonetheless be quite harmful to people, and even fatal at times. Whether we decide to call these outcomes errors or not, whether we decide to locate them in an Orwellian or Kafkaesque atmosphere, we should not be blind to the fact that they draw a bleak picture for democracy.

A pluralist analytics of the technologies of power that could foster research on surveillance should recognize that surveillance comprises different types of processes at once. Rather than understanding sovereignty, panopticism, and security as historical, overarching models that are subsequent to each other, whereby the newer replaces the older, we should regard them as analytical dimensions of power, visibility, control, and surveillance. More specifically, the contemporary surveillant visibility regime seems to lie somewhere in between *juridical*, *anatomopolitical*, and *biopolitical* technologies. Different regimes selectively activate one or more of these three sets of technologies, which have different objects, different methods, and different rationales, but always determine and subsequently manage visibility asymmetries.

The concept of visibility regime allows us to explain surveillant practices not as mere *external* intrusions into privacy, but rather, more radically, as the emergent *internal* organization of social relations by means of visibility arrangements. The notion of privacy inherits the same old problems as the classic liberal concept of social contract: both concepts presuppose a state of nature where property and/or privacy should exist before any subsequently intervening political dimension and social restraint. This view does not hold, given that social restraints are not subsequent but rather inherent to the concepts of property and privacy. The usual liberal dichotomy of private as opposed to public cannot explain the fact that visibility relationships effectively shape the domains of both the private and the public.

To fully understand the relationship between democracy and surveillance, then, we must complement the democratic perspective with the governmental perspective, and, more specifically, take into account all three technologies of power identified by Foucault: the juridical, the disciplinary (or anatomopolitical) and the biopolitical. As for the juridical technology, while surveillance studies rightly focus on the technological aspects of surveillance practices, the legal processes inherent in surveillance should always be clearly borne in mind, given that the law inherently territorializes subjects and their relations. But not all can be captured through the juridical lens: disciplinary technology works in localized, enclosed institutions and exercises a direct grip on bodies. Some surveillant practices, such as the famous panoptic device, work in this way. But the picture would once again be incomplete without taking into account the third layer, i.e. biopolitical technologies of security. Surveillance is exercised in the open space of the public domain and is focused on a "population" which is regarded and scrutinized *qua* "dividual" information flows. What matters, in the latter case, is control through exclusion and selective access. However, if security is de-subjectified, subjectification is provided, in two different guises, by law and norms. If, in the case of the law, the subject is addressed mainly in order to be restrained, in the case of norms s/he is addressed in order to be shaped and "educated." In short, the three linguistic devices that correspond to law, norm, and security are, respectively, *prohibition, slogan,* and *password.* Whereas the first is based on negative, directly repressive command, the second corresponds to a type of power that is positive in the disciplinarian sense, a power that wants to create unanimity among people around a norm that classifies them; finally, the third designates a situation in which classification is done not so much in order to correct deviants but to exclude them, establishing a selective procedure of access to safe and wealthy territories. It is not difficult to see these devices at play in contemporary surveillance practices, and it is hoped that empirical research may document them in detail.

Ultimately, the outcome of this process is not easy to foresee because of the many different forces at stake. Neither as recognition nor as control is visibility linearly associated with empowerment or disempowerment. In fact, sociotechnological complexes open up a range of possibilities for resistance, too. Resistance itself can be conceptualized as a visibility strategy. At times, resistance may aim to bring back into visibility (the political) what receded into invisibility (the economic), as the struggle for the democratization of the media and, more broadly, of global institutions reveals. In many other instances, though, resistance takes the path towards hidden practices. Secrecy lies not only at the core of power, but also at the core of the possibility of escaping and opposing it. James Scott's (1990) work reminds us that many forms of resistance actually avoid open confrontation with the structures and the official organization being resisted, but can, nonetheless, be quite effective. Resistance to surveillant visibility regimes is not confined to being reactive or merely oppositional. Resistance is not simply a struggle against visibility *per se.* On the contrary, resistance involves a transformative drive that actively re-articulates sociotechnological complexes and their respective visibility regimes.

From this point of view, resistance is much akin to democracy as conceptualized by agonist theorists Cornelius Castoriadis, Claude Lefort, and Jacques Rancière. The latter, in particular, has argued that democracy is formed by all those practices that constantly oppose themselves to the shrinkage of the public *qua* common that is inherently brought about by government:

> The spontaneous practice of all government tends to shrink this public sphere, to make it into its private affair and, for that purpose, to consign the interventions and the places of intervention of non-state actors to the side of private life. Democracy, then, far from being the form of life of individuals dedicated to their private happiness, is the process of struggle against this privatization, the process of enlarging the public sphere.
>
> (Rancière, 2006:299)

To conclude, some crucial dynamics in contemporary society, ranging from the most immediate micro-interaction in the public domain to the very redefinition of the boundaries of the public in sociotechnological complexes, can be explained as concerning, and fundamentally consisting of, visibility and territorial relations. In this context, a Foucauldian analytics of power forms can be quite important. Once again, it is important to stress that sovereignty, discipline, and security do not represent successive historic eras. To think so is to make the mistake of taking the part for the whole. We do not live in a post-panoptic society. Discipline has not disappeared from our political horizon because of a new emphasis on security, just as sovereignty and law have not disappeared because of the appearance of disciplinary power during the eighteenth and nineteenth centuries. Power formations such as sovereignty, discipline, and control constantly interact with each other and the relative balance of emphasis in a contingent situation should not lead us to overlook the compound nature of sociotechnological complexes and the plurality of power forms they entail. It is hoped that a theoretical contribution that takes into account all these elements may foster further empirical research into the processes of management, struggle, and resistance in the field of the visible as the ground for any sociological analysis of democratic social life in the public domain.

Acknowledgements

I wish to thank all the people who were most helpful in improving earlier versions of this text, in particular Cécile Brich, David Lyon, Kevin Haggerty, and Minas Samatas.

Note

1 Thanks to Kevin Haggerty for suggesting this notion of "capricious governance."

References

Arendt, Hannah. 1958. *The Human Condition*. Chicago: University of Chicago Press.

Bennett, Tony. 1995. *The Birth of the Museum: History, Theory, Politics*. New York: Routledge.

Bobbio, Norberto. 1999. *Teoria generale della politica*. Torino: Einaudi.

Brighenti, Andrea Mubi. 2006. "On territory as relationship and law as territory." *Canadian Journal of Law and Society / Revue Canadienne Droit et Société* 21 (2):65–86.

——. 2007. "Visibility: A category for the social sciences." *Current Sociology* 55 (3):323–42.

Calhoun, Craig. 2005. *Rethinking the Public Sphere*. Presentation to the Ford Foundation, February 7.

Castoriadis, Cornelius. 1997. "Democracy as procedure and democracy as regime." *Constellations* 4(1):1–18.

Critchley, Simon. 2007. *Infinitely Demanding. Ethics of Commitment, Politics of Resistance*. London: Verso.

Dahl, Robert A. 1989. *Democracy and Its Critics*. New Haven, CT: Yale University Press.

De Giorgi, Alessandro. 2008. "Policing the crisis—Italian style." *Lo Squaderno* 9:18–27.

de Certeau, Michel. 1984. *The Practice of Everyday Life*. Berkeley: University of California Press.

Debray, Régis. 2000. *Introduction à la Médiologie*. Paris: P.U.F.

Deleuze, Gilles. 1992 [1990]. "Postscript on the societies of control." *October* 59:3–7.

Deleuze, Gilles and Félix Guattari. 1980. *Mille Plateaux*. Paris: Minuit.

Foucault, Michel. 1976. *La volonté de savoir*. Paris: Gallimard.

——. 1977 [1975]. *Discipline and Punish: The Birth of the Prison*. London: Penguin Books.

——. 1991 [1978]. "Governmentality." In *The Foucault Effect. Studies in Governmentality*, edited by Graham Burchell, Colin Gordon, and Peter Miller. pp. 87–104. London: Harvester Wheatsheaf.

——. 1997 [1975–76]. *Il faut défendre la société: cours au Collège de France, 1975–1976*. Paris: Gallimard, Seuil.

——. 1982. "Technologies of the self." In *Technologies of the Self. A Seminar with Michel Foucault* edited by Luther H. Martin, Huck Gutman, and Patrick H. Hutton. pp. 16–49. London: Tavistock, 1988.

——. 2007 [1978]. *Security, Territory, Population: Lectures at the Collège de France, 1977–1978*. Basingstoke: Palgrave Macmillan.

Goffman, Erving. 1963. *Behavior in Public Places: Notes on the Social Organization of Gatherings*. New York: Free Press of Glencoe.

——. 1971. *Relations in Public: Microstudies of the Public Order*. New York: Basic Books.

Habermas, Jürgen. 1982 [1962]. *The Structural Transformation of the Public Sphere*. Cambridge: Polity Press.

Haggerty, Kevin and Richard Ericson. 2000. "The surveillant assemblage." *British Journal of Sociology* 51(4):605–22.

Kärrholm, Mattias. 2007. "The materiality of territorial production." *Space and Culture* 10(4):437–53.

Lianos, Michalis. 2001. *Le nouveau contrôle social: toile institutionnelle, normative et lien social*. Paris: L'Harmattan.

——. 2003. "Social control after Foucault." *Surveillance and Society* 1(3):412–30.

Lofland, Lyn H. 1998. *The Public Realm. Exploring the City's Quintessential Social Territory*. New York: De Gruyter.

Lyon, David. 2001. *Surveillance Society. Monitoring Everyday Life*. Buckingham: Open University Press.

——. 2007. *Surveillance Studies: An Overview*. Cambridge: Polity Press.

McLuhan, Marshall. 1964. *Understanding Media: The Extension of Man*. New York: McGraw-Hill.

Rancière, Jacques. 2006. "Democracy, republic, representation." *Constellations* 13 (3):297–307.

Scott, James C. 1990. *Domination and the Arts of Resistance: Hidden Transcripts*. New Haven, CT: Yale University Press.

Sennett, Richard. 1978. *The Fall of Public Man*. New York: Vintage Books.

Taylor, Charles. 1989. *Sources of the Self*. Cambridge MA: Harvard University Press.

Vandenberghe, Frédéric. 2007. "Régis Debray and mediation studies, or How does an idea become a material force?" *Thesis Eleven* 89:23–42.

Virilio, Paul. 1994. *The Vision Machine*. Indiana: Indiana University Press.

Young, Iris M. 1990. *Justice and the Politics of Difference*. Princeton NJ: Princeton University Press.

Weber, Max. 1978[1922]. *Economy and Society*. Berkeley: University of California Press.

Chapter 4

Perioptic on: control beyond freedom and coercion – and two possible advancements in the social sciences

Michalis Lianos

Post-industrial societies largely experience freedom as competitive individual participation in work and consumption. In many ways, security inevitably becomes the most indispensable part of freedom when freedom is exerted via capitalist competition. Surveillance presents itself then as a precondition rather than an antagonist of democracy, a necessary precaution for governing a society where individuals combine available ready-made options in their effort to distinguish themselves from others. Paradoxically, the question to ask in this context is if we can have a democratic society without some form of control that homogenises collective behaviour and, to the same extent, makes formal surveillance redundant.

The link between democracy and freedom is a product of history. Since modernity, we understand this link as the association between majority voting and individual liberties. This is how the private sphere was established as the fulcrum of sovereign bourgeois identity, a sphere that no one is entitled to enter except when the justice system authorises it on grounds of serious criminal suspicion. From this angle, privacy, and the consequent lack of surveillance, is the historical assertion of an ascending class and its priorities and interests, as Elias has shown (Perrot, 1990: 89, 473; Ronnes, 2004; Delzescaux, 2002). Conversely, freedom for the lower classes is rarely associated with the lack of social control and an impenetrable individual sphere. It is primarily a matter of having the means to be free in practice, that is, a matter of equality. Post-industrial democracies are caught in this transitional trap between the rise of the mass society and the decline of the bourgeois subject as a hegemonic citizen. As a result, the opposition between control and democracy is increasingly defused as we move towards Automated Socio-Technical Environments (Lianos and Douglas, 2000; Lianos, 2003). In fact, the very meaning of democracy changes as such environments deliver to the post-industrial citizens the efficient outcomes of a dense web of institutions and organisations which shape both the market and the state.

Dystopias of social control

Understandings of control based on discipline and surveillance were faced with a minor challenge during the 1990s. Dangerousness was quickly being recognised as the fulcrum of understanding and criminalising deviance. As a result, dangerousness had to be integrated into the critique of panoptical dystopias and disciplinary nightmares. There was an obvious match to make between the understanding of control in terms of discipline and the rise of dangerousness, since only that match would allow criminology to joyfully continue on the well-trodden path of critiquing an omnipresent, restrictive, disciplinary and pervasive control, exerted by powerful state institutions that stand sovereign and overlook individuals, groups and societies. A long series of works has integrated dangerousness into the understanding of social control, which remains focused on coercion and discipline (for an overview, see Coaffee, 2005).

All evidence that nuances or abates that perspective (see for example Alford, 2000; Walby, 2005, 2006) is happily bypassed by the critical ardour of arguments defending liberty, emancipation, identity and a series of other instances of collective and individual freedom. The issue is not of course whether that defence is well intended, for few of us would doubt that. The issue is rather whether critique has instrumentalised reality to the point of abandoning serious analysis of it.

A shortlist of the counter-evidence that I mentioned would certainly include the following points and developments:

- Disciplinary control is neither an exclusive form of control nor its most representative form. Foucault's argument is in fact that it is a specific shaping of control, peculiar to the shaping of the modern subject. In that sense, disciplinary control is a historical outcome of the limits imposed on centralised political power in its post-feudal forms. The obvious doubt that arises is that contemporary conditions are rather different and, in that sense, it would be ahistorical to believe that the same model of control would apply to current conditions. In fact, the more one projects Foucault's historically specific conclusions onto the present the more one betrays Foucault's method and theoretical legacy. Foucault himself cautioned against such indiscriminate projections even for the historical period that he discussed in *Discipline and Punish*:

  > The Panoptic system was not so much confiscated by the State apparatuses, rather it was these apparatuses which rested on the basis of small scale, regional dispersed Panopticims. In consequence one cannot confine oneself to analysing the State apparatus alone if one wants to grasp the mechanisms of power in their detail and complexity. There is a sort of schematism that needs to be avoided here—and which incidentally is not to be found in Marx—that consists of locating power in the State apparatus, making this into the major, privileged, capital and almost unique instrument of the power of one

class over another. In reality, power in this exercise goes much
further, passes through much finer channels, and is much more
ambiguous, since each individual has at his disposal a certain power,
and for that very reason can also act as the vehicle for transmitting
a wider power.

(Foucault, 1972: 72)

- State institutions that remain sovereign over individuals and societies are
  linked to pacified societies and non-violent forms of control which are,
  again, historically specific. This is why notions such as biopower or
  govermentality and their derivatives (e.g. biopolitics) denote a large spectrum of involvement with shaping collective organisation, socioculture and
  behaviour; they indicate a general mode rather than a concrete form of
  control. In that sense, it is again the specifics of applied forms of control
  that can inform us on the nature of relations between institutions and
  society, not the fact that a broad conceptual label may apply to such
  relations. Stating that video surveillance or stored health-related data are
  part of some type of post-industrial governmentality or biopower is not a
  discovery, much less a critique. It is a *mere fact* that does not advance our
  understanding of contemporary forms of control.
- Post-industrial capitalism is driven by a new equilibrium between the
  market and the state. Simply put, the market is today the motor of social
  and political existence to the point of underlying the entire range of
  human coexistence, from political legitimacy to individual identity. Control, as an expression of power relations, *cannot but serve* that market/
  state equilibrium. Therefore, control delivers to all actors the priorities of
  that hegemonic equilibrium in the form that corresponds to the respective
  role of each actor in maintaining it. Contemporary control must therefore
  be as flexible and differentiated as the modes of post-industrial stratification and the multiple structures that support post-industrial capitalist
  interaction; it must be as flexible and differentiated as the techno-
  institutional networks that deliver all forms of management, from
  distribution of goods to political governance and from mobility of capital
  to personal entertainment (Castells, 2000: 18ff).
- Finally, an obvious point: there is no intentional, unified or even conscious
  socio-cultural project in post-industrial societies, much less an overarching
  ideological framework that disciplinary control presupposes. There are
  few prescriptive values and practically no institutions that would be
  inclined to promote specific values as prescriptive. None of the institutional actors that are powerful in post-industrial societies seek to impose
  such values via control practices. In fact, it is a precondition of dominance
  that actors defend their legitimacy on grounds of utility—economic, social
  or geopolitical—not on grounds of prescriptive values and normative
  practices.

This is also the consequence of what Robins and Webster propose in their analysis:

> What we have is an ever more extensive information apparatus—propaganda, censorship, advertising, public relations, surveillance, etc.—through which opinion management has become not only authoritarian, but also routine and normative. Our argument is that the totalitarian aspect of this process is to be found in its increasingly systematic (totalising), integrated and 'scientific' ambitions and tendencies. Now, we must emphasise that this argument does not presume the existence of a manipulative and conspirational élite of mind managers. The logic of information control and management is, rather, an integral and systemic aspect of the modern nation state.
>
> (Robins and Webster, 1999: 142)

In a nutshell, it seems that fascination with Big Brother has overshadowed the premises of its very critique. Big Brother is not totalitarian *because* he holds information on individuals and on society as a whole, but he seeks to hold information because he is totalitarian. Control in this case is used to enforce values that are minutely laid down on an ideological map, but it is not control as such that generates such values. Totalitarianism, or for that matter any form of direct coercion, is not the only motive for gathering information; management, coordination or mere financial gain are frequent causes too (Lyon, 2003: 14). Although control is by definition associated with power, it is perhaps time to face the possibility that accumulated data do not necessarily amount to a plan and even less so to a totalitarian plan.

The fact that information can be used to several ends, sometimes subsequent to its gathering, is well known. Nowhere is that more frequent than in 'traditional' societies where all information on each other is a powerful resource used to generate the highest degree of conformity. This is also why authoritarian or totalitarian regimes prefer that form of 'community' control. (See for example Zhong and Broadhurst, 2007 on China and Pfaff, 2001 on Eastern Germany, where centralised surveillance was really much less effective than 'community' control; see also a plea for resorting to the power of community control today in Hirst, 2000). To those who study social control these are banal statements, not critical findings; for these, one would more usefully turn to the fundamental questions that in my view underlie the critical understanding of social control in any society, independently of time:

> *What are the mechanisms that explain conformity within a society and how do they deliver in practice the priorities imposed by that society's model of socio-economic organisation?*
>
> *How do dominant socio-economic actors shape the socioculture that tends to use social control to maintain their influence?*

Control and the institutional web

The market is the obvious point of departure for asking these questions in a post-industrial context. Contemporary capitalism has transformed the very essence of what we understand as an institution. The shaping of an institutional web comprised of private organisations and public institutions is at the origin of a series of transformations in human sociality. That web brings operational efficiency because it fragments the dense social bond of community relations into task-specific roles. As Haesler points out:

> [...] institutions should be understood as obstacles in the first instance. They should be understood as third parties whose role is either to prevent fusion [in human relations] or to perpetuate incomplete relations. This universe of rules and procedures is, however, ambivalent as such; in imposing order on the chaos of relations, institutions display that annoying tendency towards hegemony, which leads to a totalitarian order if pursued to its end.
>
> (Haesler, 2005)

To sum up a long analysis (see Lianos, 2001a), interaction via cultural structures, which was historically the primary form of negotiating human relations, has been largely replaced by interaction via organisational settings. Functional institutional priorities have supplanted values and beliefs as coordinating mental maps. Utilitarian claims on efficiency have drastically limited the capacity of post-industrial societies to interact through cultural systems, i.e. systems that are not controlled by institutional 'third parties' seeking to frame human interaction according to institutional priorities.

The founding 'third party' in this sense was of course the modern state, with its intention and capacity to mediate social interaction towards a specific political project, what we recognise as modernity. The social sciences have been fully aware of this phenomenon and its ramifications,[1] but have refused to look at the continuation of this process, which now involves not only the state and its dependent institutions but all types of institutional actors and, in particular, all private-sector actors. It is in fact the continuing fascination with the state as a sovereign socio-political actor that keeps us from understanding that the establishments that mediate human behaviour, from the local shop to the global conglomerate, are all institutions. I will focus this general problematic on the theme of social control.

Institutions are defined by their capacity to shape mental and physical human interaction, in relatively stable and recognisable forms. Anything that endures and produces normativity is an institution. That is the thread that links entities of very different orders, such as marriage, the army, religion, universal suffrage, the National Museum of Modern Art, potlatch, or social security. Late-modern normativity is produced as part of organisational flows of action which configure individual and social behaviour according to the specific settings of those flows. This is the very meaning of being a 'user' of such settings, i.e. a passenger in a transport system, a spectator in a media system, and—inevitably—a 'client' in almost every system, from the luxury industry to welfare distribution. Some implications of that development are of particular interest here:

i.   Late-modern normativity is mentally fragmented but organisationally convergent. The rules that govern each institutional environment are not meaningful as part of our overall social coexistence but as norms of efficient operation. We move from a *polysemic* normativity, where overall values govern the operation of all specific settings, to a *monosemic* normativity, where there is no link between the different sets of rules that are to be observed as we perpetually traverse successive operational settings.

ii. Accordingly, social control processes are redefined. Conformity is essentially demanded by post-industrial institutions not on the grounds of sovereignty or a value-based culture, but on the grounds of efficient performance that will benefit users and providers alike. As there is no other reason to always drive on one side of the road apart from the fact that it is more efficient to do so, no additional reason is needed to establish, withdraw and modify rules except for the evidence that people, goods and information move faster, easier and safer. The basis of conformity thus shifts towards organisational evidence and efficient competition within the institutional web. *Compliance is efficiency.*

iii. The innumerable and ever expanding uses of the institutional web, of which only a small part will be explored by any one post-industrial citizen during her lifetime, have grown to the point of composing almost all individual and collective experience. 'Direct' social relations cannot compete with the institutional web in terms of reliability, diversity of supply or facility of access. The decline of community and personalised social relations such as friendship, is in fact no more than the outperformance of these relations by institutional efficiency. That decline brings to similar decline the cultural complexities of social control as we knew it. *Instead of enforcing reciprocal conformity to a shared culture, social control is now a matter of optimally exploiting institutional resources.*

iv. Not unlike capitalism, contemporary social control neither constitutes nor reflects a prescriptive project for social behaviour except in as much as it concerns maintaining the conditions of diversity and competition. In this sense *late-modern control is less and less social*, and that is why I provisionally used the term 'new social control' (Lianos, 2001a) until the passage of time allows us to see it more clearly.

v.   The combination of these tendencies forms a context that obliges us to seriously reconsider the very premises of thinking about social control.

a. First, the lack of an overarching social, cultural and political content does not allow for critiques still attached to a model which assumes that control aims to produce a specific social subject. No soul is trained, no moral 'dressage' is intended; *the modern subject is well behind us.*

b. Second, the subject under control needs to ascribe some meaning to the continuum of functions that jointly shape the institutional web into a puzzle of experience. Such interpretive work is required, if only to sustain the degree of coherence that is indispensable to self-conscience and social identity. Beyond its minimal content of ensuring operational efficiency, control *is realised via a paradoxical autonomy of the controlled subject.*

c. Third, the functions that compose the institutional web seek to accelerate flows and make them more reliable. The purpose is activation, autonomy and growth, not hindrance. Late-modern control *can only be justified by its originators as a necessary evil*, not as a properly legitimate social function. This is why it is meaningful to speak of 'unintended' control, in the sense that it is not exerted to deliver conformity to a pre-existing model but to prevent actions that antagonise the optimal function of the specific institutions.

d. Fourth and most significantly, late-modern control *is conceived to enable, to augment, to liberate individual action and desire.* It is a procedural accompaniment to the main theme of fluid capitalism, not a function aimed at preventing activities that might lend themselves to deviance, a function that used to be the essence of social control.

These developments can be organised into three major transitions: *privatisation, dangerisation* and *periopticity.* Privatisation should be understood both in its admitted sense, i.e. that of non-state actors being increasingly at the origin of controlling practices (Bharat Book Bureau, 2008, Avant, 2005, Lock, 1999), but also in the sense that the development of an asocial control via the uninterrupted presence of institutional functions is profoundly atomising. The homogeneity of the mass society is supported by an overwhelming diversity in the minutiae of individual experience that is capable of maintaining the illusion of personal uniqueness. The endless combinations of such minutiae allow for each individual trajectory to be distinct from any other. Control practices and *dispositifs* filter, trace and supervise that trajectory *as a distinct private experience.* Contrary to a panoptical arrangement, CCTV, magnetic gates, RFID tags, turnstiles and biometric access control seek to filter out threatening exceptions without imposing common rules and morals. Traceability and retroactive identification, two of the major logics of contemporary control, are precisely oriented towards reconstituting distinctly unique instances of existence. The tendency toward privatisation is in this sense an approach that governs not only the production but, less obviously, also the delivery of control. We have entered the era of a control *in personam*, which is concerned with all levels of individual existence, public and private, and not any longer meant to address society as such.

Social control has largely become a private affair, and in that sense, it is less and less social. The institutional web applies control as a means to exploit contact with individuals (e.g. as consumers) or to manage and contain that contact (e.g. in traffic flows, crowd control or deviance). Far from being a political and economic conspiracy, this transition represents the exit of sociality from community settings, which is largely due to the very support and efficiency of the institutional web. Mutually enforced cultural values have consequently been replaced with private, individual adherence to specific settings of behaviour that are socially validated by an institutional rubber stamp. The endless and seamless transition from one framework of adherence to another is our new sociality and, like pre-modern and modern sociality, it signifies belonging to a hegemonic socio-economic and cultural model and being controlled for compatibility with that model. Contemporary normativity therefore does not enforce abstract value systems but one unified principle: do not disrupt the efficiency of the institutional web. This is the underlying explanation for the redundancy of grand narratives: society works for you without asking you to hold any specific beliefs or even opinions, just to not hinder how it works. Contemporary control simply delivers the essence of capitalism as the lowest common social denominator. Inevitably, this entails private, albeit massively multiplied, arrangements between institutions and users. When one drives, enters any place except for one's own home, travels by plane or uses a computer programme, one implicitly accepts traffic rules, non-smoking rules, biometric controls and intellectual property rights. Doing these things, using the institutional web, is the current form of social belonging and it should not be surprising that it includes in-built dimensions that enforce the web's hegemony. This is after all what social control is, a framework of preconditions to social belonging. The interesting development is that this framework is now mediated by massive, but private, relations with the institutional web.

In its daily expression, *dangerisation* is the tendency to look at the world from a point of view of threat avoidance with the aggregated effect of increasing the senses of insecurity and the consequent demand for security. The concept of dangerisation is, as such, a critique of the 'risk society' thesis and links the primacy of threat in late-modern culture and governance with the socio-economic premises of social change (Lianos, 1999). Avoiding the pitfall of attributing a risk culture to new, qualitatively different dangers is essential, because doing so would distract us from the interesting processes at work, i.e. the processes that represent socio-economic conditions via a specific culture. I have extensively argued (Lianos, 2001a: 29ff, 194ff; 1999) that risk is nothing but the cultural expression of a social deficit peculiar to contemporary capitalism and that our acutely experienced hegemony of insecurity is a direct and identifiable consequence of specific conjunctures of socio-economic change. Such a thesis both admits the theorisation of the 'risk society' by Beck and Giddens as a descriptive approach, not an explicative one, and diverges from the numerous theoretical comments which have accepted that theorisation as explicative (e.g. Bauman, 2000).

Dangerisation naturally arose in the area of control and deviance much earlier than in many other areas. This is not surprising since the passage from 'direct' to institutionally mediated sociality caused the rapid decline of community-based control mechanisms over non-organised deviance. Developments in fear of crime and bystander behaviour graphically depict that retreat as part of the sense of belonging to a group (Levine et al., 2002). Since the 1970s, dangerousness has increasingly overdetermined the meaning of deviance. That tendency fully imbibed the penal sphere by the late 1980s. Not only did fear become the motor of crime perception and public policy but it also helped spread the dominance of a risk culture within the institutional sphere. Thus rose the continuum that we acknowledge as 'actuarial justice' (Feely and Simon, 1994) and we now take for granted that dangerousness underlies every aspect of dealing with deviance, from the level of concepts (e.g. criminalising behaviour) to that of daily practice (e.g. committing 'incivilities').

Mary Douglas and I have explained in detail (Lianos and Douglas, 2000) the processes that fill the voids opened by the decline of social relations with insecurity. This occurs most conspicuously in what we have called the 'Automated Socio-Technical Environments' (ASTEs) which mediate institutional functions. The efficient performance of the institutional web conveys a culture of insecurity that is now hegemonic. Control mechanisms are part of the vicious circle that fuels demand for institutionally managed and surveyed territories and activities used to distance oneself from threat. The starting point of dangerisation in the area of fear-provoking deviance is generalised suspicion. Suspicion not only allows but obliges the institution to inspect everyone for the 'comfort and security' of everyone else. Within this regime, control performs its traditional function of validating conforming behaviour, with the remarkable difference that this validation does not endorse the collectivity that one belongs to but serves as an institutional guarantee covering the duration of the interaction; this is why we often feel safer in our local shopping mall than in the area in which we live, notwithstanding the fact that in each location we are surrounded by the very same people. The institutional function guarantees operational fluidity and the selective suppression of threats, just like anti-virus software is supposed to do in an IT environment; and like email messages that have been verified as free from viruses, vetted institutional environments confer mutually recognisable guarantees that increasingly amount to social identities.

Dangerisation has de facto transformed late-modern normativity into an order of reciprocal reluctance and continual demand for efficient institutional mediation between social participants. From this angle, dangerisation underlies not only the hegemony of discourses and practices promoting insecurity but also the illusion that these discourses and practices tend to maintain. That is, dangerisation augments *the illusion of a central source of power and coordination* that is capable and willing to assume the overall governance of post-industrial societies, including the normative priorities of social relations. This comforting belief in centralised control, whose locus is often assumed to be the state, constitutes the grand narrative of late-modern societies. Every form of power is consequently obliged to invest itself with a protective, securing function in order to claim social and political legitimacy. Not only are these claims utilitarian in terms of the primary function of each institutional sector, but they must also include an indispensable security dimension. Water companies provide cleaner, safer water; rail companies provide faster, safer travel; IT companies provide more reliable, safer networks; supermarkets provide tastier, cheaper, safer food; states provide wealthier, safer societies.

Grand narratives cannot establish themselves without some degree of internal antagonism, which sustains their discursive framework as the hegemonic framework of reference. Religion is really powerful when there are schisms and marginal heresies; class struggle when minority groups antagonise the revolutionary orthodoxy; nation-states when local idioms are discreetly spoken at home. Critiques that approach control in terms of coercion and discipline supply, in this context, some ground of cultural survival for the state's declining sovereign functions. Alleging that *dispositifs* of surveillance and data gathering offend citizen rights and fundamental liberties amounts to asserting that states and citizens are still in their historically modernist roles. In that context, individual self-realisation and social identities largely depended upon the ground that the sovereign state was willing to cede by awarding guarantees of non-involvement in social interaction, thus offering the individual a framework of certainty in exchange for a degree of conformity (e.g. Kelsen, 1967: 216ff). Such critiques unwittingly reflect a deeply bourgeois conception of control in which the state coordinates a value-based project for society that promotes individual over collective existence, an orientation perfectly represented in the priority awarded to the protection of privacy.

It has perhaps been adequately explained so far that these critiques are profoundly obsolete with regard to late-modern control. During modernity, the state, with its ancillary mechanisms, was the only institutional mediator of social control. All other controlling functions were still performed by direct social relations. The dense institutional web that today mediates all social interaction has not only atrophied such direct social relations but also marginalised the state as an actor that can determine the dynamics and orientation of the entire social system. Except during major crises, the role of the state and other public institutions is limited to encouraging the growth and increasing the performance of this dynamic. For, state legitimacy depends on the efficient performance of the market in particular, and of the institutional web in general. In the area of control, the state is therefore a competitive actor with a disproportionate halo bequeathed by modernity. Casting the critique of late-modern control in disciplinary terms takes this halo at face value.

The third major transition in contemporary control is directly related to the competitive nature of the institutional web. While private and public institutions together mediate and configure all social relations, their roles and influence as isolated actors are not guaranteed. To gain and maintain that influence, institutions constantly compete to attract the broadest spectrum and the highest frequency of interactions. The late-modern subject is at the same time empowered and controlled by the institutions that she increasingly chooses over others; she is therefore coveted as a client that adheres to one institutional environment rather than another. This is why it is more appropriate to think of the controlling dimensions of private and public institutions not as panoptical (with a central outward-looking gaze monitoring everybody) but as *perioptical*, since they build their power by attracting the gaze of individual and institutional actors instead of projecting their own gaze onto these actors. Each individual always resides at the intersection of multiple institutional activities all the time and increasingly comes into social existence via her relation with such institutional activities.

The capitalist periopticon

We have moved from a centralised and distributive understanding of control to a fragmented and contributive one. If this seems paradoxical, it is precisely because the disciplinary aspects of modernity do not allow us to acknowledge that social control processes originate in the fusion between our choices about associating in social relations and the inevitability of making such choices. Contrary to the nostalgic assumptions about our past, relations in 'traditional' societies and 'communities' are not undifferentiated (e.g. Lawson, 1992; Peel, 1980). Although each member of such societies is obliged to socially belong, belonging materialises via preferential relations that entail various degrees of association, ranging from close solidarity to intense antagonism. Social-control processes are therefore geared towards integrating differentiation into an overarching normativity reflected in social belonging. From that point of view, *the centralised panoptical metaphor of social control in modernity is a historical exception, not a rule*. Social control is rather a process that generates conformity and determines deviance via varying degrees of adherence to established frameworks of thought and action. This is precisely what happens in contemporary conditions, but with a major difference. Social relations have been replaced by relations with instances of the institutional web. This specificity has important consequences, some of which need to be accentuated here:

i.   The organised settings of institutional environments generally do not negotiate with their users. Instead, they offer their user a given framework which he can either adhere to, and use the supplied resources, or decline, and reject the contact. The banal omnipresence of this arrangement obscures its significance, for it is constant negotiation between actors that generates social culture; as Mary Douglas graphically put it, when people exchange, they force culture down each others' throats (Douglas, 1978: 6). *Adherence to given institutional settings* is the very source of deculturalised control and the consequent lack of a value-based culture in late modernity. Since normativity becomes an essential binary choice between adhering and refusing, the strategic cultural resources that are mobilised in social negotiation, such as values and beliefs, become redundant because they are inefficient in the new environment (see Lianos, 2001b). As a result, the great majority of interactions in late-modern society are not only institutionally mediated but also institutionally configured in precise ways. Control is consequently a matter of operational compatibility with the structures of late capitalism.

ii.   Adhering to institutional expectations would be a highly coercive process, were it not for capitalism. For the institutional web develops innumerable options to which one can adhere in all sectors of activity, from goods and services to art works and tax regimes. Just as social belonging materialises via differential associations in unmediated social normativity, adherence to monosemic institutional environments materialises via the ceaseless exertion of options in late-modern normativity. One should insist that the multiplicity of options does not amount to choice, for there can be no social integration without exerting such options. *Optionality* is an essential part of late-modern control and it is naturally associated with enabling individuals to compete over necessary adherence to the archipelago of institutional outlets.

iii. In post-industrial capitalism, it is unsurprising that competition should be at the centre of understanding control. Accumulating resources depends on one's capacity to mobilise institutional functions to one's benefit. Education modules, career moves, financial products, real-estate acquisitions, eating preferences, sexual partners and social networks, all come together as part of a competitive condition that is hopefully personally adequate. Via the diversity of private and public institutional performance, late capitalism *amalgamates obligation and empowerment through dynamic control processes which are exerted not via disciplinary coercion but via competition.*

iv.   Late-modern control is not structured around the state, for both are structured around the institutional web where the logic of the capitalist market prevails. As individuals compete by adhering to the options of institutional activity, institutions compete by providing attractive options in a way that captures the highest possible adherence with the lowest possible resources. Public governance and private management converge to espouse a model of efficiency that mediates social activity in their respective areas of competence. Benchmarking performance in welfare systems and hospitals is not different from doing so in supermarkets and banks; institutional functions increasingly move from the public to the private sector according to projections of optimal performance, 'better service' and greater value for money. It is by now clear that control processes are also shaped by this plasticity, because normativity is part of the delivered goods and services. In fact, *control processes are themselves an integral part of competition between institutions, which strive to deliver safety via smooth and undisrupted performance.* Making control easier is fundamental to the performance of all systems, particularly large-scale systems that cannot afford breakdowns. This can take many forms, from remotely debited windscreen tags on road tolls to algorithms that control trade limits in financial markets and from transmitting health histories to surgeons and anaesthetists to technologies that automatically detect people drowning in swimming pools. This is why CCTV *dispositifs*, for example, have spread to an otherwise inexplicable level; no institution can afford not to compete to achieve the best balance between control of its field and fluidity of its operation.

Perioptical control expresses the irresistible annexation of three dimensions of social existence by post-industrial capitalism: the structure of political governance, the relations of social collectivities, and personal existence as such. The historical parenthesis of modern control, inspired by the politics of morality and the schemes of sovereign governance, seems to be closing. While the significance of this transition is undoubted, it is important to look at the continuities that sustain contemporary normativity. Before turning to that question, a comment on the ambiguities and uncertainties of periopticity is in order.

Contemporary control perfectly exemplifies Foucault's conception of power. Although the individual actors involved are not equally powerful, even the weakest possess some ability to circumvent rigid rules and seek alternatives as institutions compete for their attention. It is precisely this competition that makes even the most powerful institutional actors fragile. The less obvious but most significant transition in the late capitalist periopticon is that the influence and position of all actors, far from being taken for granted, depends on constant speculation. Any disruption in institutional performance can seriously damage its influence and in many cases the mere supposition that a problem may arise is enough to expose powerful institutions to an irremediable loss of influence. Billions of dollars in share value disappear rapidly with the slightest dysfunction if financial analysts deem it 'a risk.' Officials are hastily disposed of when public institutions come under media pressure. The mismanagement of an individual case that initially looks insignificant can lead to an entire sector being painfully restructured. Again, this is not to say that perioptical control is unstratified; it is deeply stratified and contains remarkable disproportions that isolated cases do not annul. The difference is that those disproportions in power are not as certain and durable as they used to be. The very structure of the institutional web is such that conjunctural factors may lead to the collapse of the threads spun by institutions facing difficulties. In a competitive context, such gaps serve as opportunities for other institutional actors to rapidly fill the void. Control processes accordingly depend only upon the overall perioptical dynamics, not upon specific institutions, which are increasingly interchangeable. Private policing, for example, replaces functions that were at the heart of the social sovereignty of the state, IT consultants build and manage defence databases, private accountancy firms audit government departments; shopping malls, bus companies and corner shops practice extensive CCTV surveillance and individuals install motion detectors around their houses in a continuum that is essentially concerned with desirable outcomes rather than the symbolic distinction of institutional spheres. Each isolated actor, however powerful, is systemically fragile and cannot aspire to influence late-modern normativity beyond its narrow area of thematic competence and operational efficiency. All actors, taken together as an entire system, provide a very solid basis for perpetuating periopticity because of their competitively generated uncertainty. Individual vulnerability is the cornerstone of collective strength, a condition that invests contemporary control with a distinctive historical role in social organisation. For the first time in human history, social control self-adjusts to organisational priorities and accelerates change rather than delaying it. For over thirty years, perioptical control seems to have been reproducing the effects of the capitalist market in the area of normativity, a tendency that accelerated with the collapse of applied socialism. This facilitation of change by means of control was an unexpected and unplanned development that the studies of control and deviance have yet to acknowledge.

Deviance in perioptical times

We have known control processes as social processes that produce normativity via determining thresholds of deviance. As was pointed out, this configuration is based on socio-cultural negotiation through values, beliefs and other crystallisations of social culture. The involvement of the first institutional actor that aspired to coordinate that negotiation, the modern state, has been extensively studied both in its motives and its intended and unintended consequences (for example, Cohen and Scull, 1983; Garland, 1985; for a less statist perspective, Roodenburg, 2004). Perioptical control has moved a great distance from both these contexts. Its polycentric structure and fragmented, monosemic content poses an obvious challenge to the processes of determining deviance and the various contents that deviance may assume. Criminalised deviance, in particular, is a reliable point of departure. The turn towards risk in criminal legislation and criminal-justice practices is substantiated enough to confirm that *dangerisation has produced a consequential understanding of deviance.*

This can be rendered into a simple axiom according to which any behaviour that causes fear to others should be criminalised. As a result we are faced with a major change in the social classification of crime, which is now de facto divided into fear-provoking and non-fear-provoking offences. Besides relegating most forms of white-collar crime to even more unassailable territory for the criminal law, this bifurcation exemplifies a formidable trend in perceiving deviance not as a social phenomenon but as a personal, intimate threat. Crime has largely become a category of individual vulnerability rather than social acceptability. Of particular interest is the *perceptual proximity* mechanism reinforced by perioptical control. Post-industrial citizens assess information on an offence with regard to the probability of being exposed to a similar act. The middle and lower-middle classes do not worry about being killed by stray bullets on a council estate in a gang-related drive-by shooting. Instead, they are disturbed by unprovoked assaults on people walking their dogs in the park and by children who disappear in 'safe' residential areas. This regression to evading adverse probabilities on an individual level does not only pertain to crime but traverses the whole spectrum of personal existence, including work, health, income and personal relations. Just as happens with institutions, any single individual is by definition interchangeable to the point of being acutely aware of that condition. Competition, in accumulating references for one's CV or in buying houses, has reached the depth of perceived individual exposure to deviance. That convergence is mainly expressed in being able to choose where one lives and the school one's children attend.

Deviance, therefore, follows the pattern of control as deviance is now constituted as a category of defensive, not prescriptive, representations. As the object of control determines the significance of the institutional actor, the perceived victim determines the significance of the offence. Inevitably, the quintessential offence in the perioptical context is what one may term a 'decontextualised' offence, a hazardous act that is not justified by 'normal' circumstances, i.e. a daylight mugging in a 'safe area', or violent bullying in an expensive school. These types of offence cause an entire defensive life plan to collapse, along with its stratified benefits and the institutional guarantees supplied by perioptical control. It is 'the offence that is not meant to happen here, nor to someone like me.'

Expectedly, desocialised, individually oriented control processes entail desocialised constructions of deviance by associating deviance to the disruption of planned activities and trajectories. As normativity and operational efficiency merge under the influence of the institutional web, disruption and deviance also merge. Entering a road in the lane intended for the opposite direction remains illegal today not because of the evaluative premises of the behaviour, i.e. disrespect for the ethics of the Highway Code, but because of the assumption that disrupting operational organisation is dangerous and that awareness of this fact is ingrained in post-industrial conscience. This shared awareness is the very essence of establishing legal principles that do not associate tort with blame or even wrongdoing (see for example Simester, 2005; Cane, 2002; Watkins, 2006); 'strict liability' is the quintessential normativity and sociality of the institutional web. Beyond traditional forms of penality, this individual and organisational understanding of deviance merges everything that prevents the efficient control of isolated individual trajectories into an increasingly undifferentiated totality of deviant behaviour. A good example of this merger is the UK 'Anti-Social Behaviour Order' whose definition is telling:

An application for an order under this section may be made by a relevant authority if it appears to the authority that the following conditions are fulfilled with respect to any person aged 10 or over, namely—

a. that the person has acted, since the commencement date, in an anti-social manner, that is to say, in a manner that caused or was likely to cause harassment, alarm or distress to one or more persons not of the same household as himself; and
b. that such an order is necessary to protect persons in the local government area in which the harassment, alarm or distress was caused or was likely to be caused from further anti-social acts by him;

(Crime and Disorder Act, 1998, 1.1)

This definition excellently represents the advent of legal measures that deal with deviance in conditions of institutional sociality and perioptical control. The problem can be conceived in simple terms: what is to be done with behaviour that is not attracted by the capitalist periopticon? For, any activity that is not an integral part of the performance of the institutional web is by definition uncontrolled. Those who cannot or, more rarely, do not wish to constantly compete for the benefits of institutional performance become in that sense ipso facto suspicious and potentially deviant because there are no direct sociality environments that can exert more 'traditional' forms of control on their behaviour. What the capitalist periopticon cannot attract is of unknown normative content, therefore outside the limits of established, mutually recognisable conformity. *In perioptical conditions, disenchantment is already deviance.* Distance or abstinence from exploiting institutional mediation may trigger all ills, from 'mucking about' for poor young males to joining a sect for the lower middle classes or becoming a 'martyr' for a religious faith if one's origins allow for radical beliefs. Very few social processes constantly supervise and hinder the rise of alternative socio-cultural environments. Once the post-industrial bird is out of its cage no preset rules direct its flight.

The role of the state, including the justice system, is to integrate behaviour into the institutional web so as to allow each social participant to simultaneously achieve control, self-realisation and autonomy. By the same token, repression represents failure, particularly when it is passive. For example, any admission of resorting to 'warehousing' forms of incarceration would today be an admission of institutional weakness; this is why such admissions are strictly avoided despite the harsh reality of overcrowded prisons. This is also why forms of activating and integrative punishment are so symbolically precious today that great concessions are being made in their direction, to the point of assimilating punishment to the self-management of change (e.g. NC Division of Corrections, 2005). The panoptical institutions of modernity sought to build a morally sound, productive subject by avoiding physical violence as a means of punishment. Perioptical late-modern institutions now need to avoid coercion in all its forms, from ideological promotion to carceral punishment, in order to build a continuously active and collaborative subject. Competition and autonomy are naturally the preferred perioptical ways to ensure collaboration with a type of control that is exerted as a function of capitalist performance.

The force of weakness

Perioptical control represents a new era in the relation between institutions and individuals, an era in which cultural negotiation of social interaction and sovereign governance of society have largely been replaced by a web of competing utilitarian functions. The decline of modern institutions is not only of symbolic change, it is first and foremost the consequence of the development of the market into a fully operational substitute both for direct social relations and for the governance of society by the state or, in fact, by any coordinating power. This condition implies a radically different understanding of all institutional dimensions that deliver control in contemporary society; that understanding could be built around five main principles:

i. *Perioptical control is operationally specific.* As in all times, control is still about achieving optimal conformity to a targeted outcome but this outcome is now limited to purpose-built structures. The main conceptual consequence of this change is that we need to envisage as control the effective sum of the largely unrelated controlling activities which support operational functions.

ii. *Perioptical control is of secondary nature.* Such control accompanies the delivery of enabling primary functions and no longer occupies a primary social function to which productive and organisational relations are subordinated. It follows that conceptualising control as a disciplinary aspect of sociality misses this secondary aspect, which is in fact much more difficult to isolate and identify than previous forms of control.

iii. *Perioptical control is reactive, not active,* in the sense that it is constituted as a multitude of solutions to problems and has no independent cause of existence—and no legitimacy—outside of providing adequate solutions. The social subject becomes accessible to control only in terms of an existing or potential problem.

iv. *Perioptical control is both uncoordinated and highly convergent*, just like the market on which it is inevitably modelled. The absence of a homogeneous framework of governance and the lack of any desire for a homogeneous socio-cultural outcome do not necessarily entail incoherence; this is because the market model ensures meaningful communication between its participants.

v. *Perioptical control is born as practice not as discourse*. It becomes a discourse via the solutions that it provides, that is, inevitably, a discourse on efficiency.

A series of other points can be made in the same direction. The overall dynamic is, however, identifiable. Institutional performance has atrophied direct social relations, which can no longer compete with the reliability of organised systems. The ensuing corrosion of socio-cultural negotiation further weakens the links which were until recently the only concrete forms of sociality. The distinctive line between norm and deviance is now controlled by operational organisation and the degree to which each one of us conforms to such organisation. It is obvious that daily organisational performance requires weak forms of sociality which cannot exist without organisational mediation. Perioptical control reflects precisely the immense force of this weakness by demonstrating that it is possible to generate normativity only as an outcome of decentralised, fragmented, utilitarian coordination.

In light of these developments, significant advancements can be made for the social sciences. One such advancement is to *acknowledge that conformity is not necessarily the outcome of control; it can actually be its generating cause*. Post-industrial control, in particular, shows quite clearly that human beings can mutually align their behaviour without any centralised or coercive prescription, thus giving birth to a hegemonic model which will ipso facto become a model of control. It seems that modern social organisation did not need more than two centuries to overtake age-old human sociality as the dominant engine of conformity. This change was realised via the capillary spreading of competitive market dynamics into all social functions, which delivered efficiency to each isolated social participant, thus making him independent from the others.

A second major advancement is that the corrosion of socio-cultural negotiation in human relations does not necessarily entail the decline of socio-culture as such. In particular, *the existence of norms does not depend upon the existence of values or belief systems*. Once again, post-industrial control shows that meaning arises as a mental picture of an established concrete reality, so long as that reality is binding. Simply put, *what works in terms of motivating behaviour generates conformity to the point of becoming practically binding. When this point is reached, social meaning will ensue and new norms will painfully organise themselves into a total that finally appears coherent.* It is therefore by adapting to the constraints of a fragmented practical world that we generate social coherence and the normativity that goes with it.

Such conclusions update our premises for understanding social control and question well-established perspectives in the social sciences. The Pax Mercatoria (Lianos, 1999) of post-industrial capitalism, a peace justified on grounds of promoting trade and prosperity, and the reconfiguring impact that such commercial peace has on human sociality, is a splendid opportunity to capture normativity as a fundamental dimension of individual existence, in which society originates.

Note

1 From that angle, there is a continuous line linking early legal and socio-legal theory (e.g. the works of Max Weber); state socialism (e.g. Pashukanis's work); Carl Schmitt's exceptionalist legal theory, which was oriented towards institutional efficiency; the nascent economics of late modernity culminating in Keynesianism; and the social critique of the institutional and ideological ramifications of the state, from Rusche and Kirchheimer (1939) to Foucault and Althusser; and to contemporary critiques of control.

References

Avant, D. 2005. *The Market for Force: The Consequences of Privatizing Security*. New York: Cambridge University Press.

Bauman, Z. 2000. *Liquid Modernity*. Cambridge: Polity.

Alford, C. F. 2000. 'What would it matter if everything Foucault said about prison were wrong? Discipline and Punish after twenty years.' *Theory & Society* 29 (1): 125–46.

Bharat Book Bureau. 2008. *World Security Equipment Forecasts for 2012 & 2017*. Mumbai.

Cane, P. 2002. *Responsibility in Law and Morality*. Oxford: Hart Publishing.

Castells, M. 2000. *The Rise of the Network Society*, 2nd edition. Oxford: Blackwell.

Coaffee, J. 2005. 'Urban renaissance in the age of terrorism: Revanchism, automated social control or the end of reflection?' *International Journal of Urban and Regional Research* 29 (2).

Cohen, S., and A. Scull. 1983. *Social Control and the State*. New York: St. Martin Press.

Delzescaux, S. 2002. *Norbert Elias: Une sociologie des processus*. Paris: L'Harmattan.

Douglas, M. 1978. 'Cultural bias.' Occ. Paper No. 35, *Anthropological Institute of Great Britain and Northern Ireland*, London.

Feely, M., and J. Simon. 1994. 'Actuarial justice: The emerging new criminal law.' pp. 193–201. In *The Futures of Criminology*, edited by D. Nelken,. London: Sage.

Foucault, M. 1972. 'Questions on Geography', in *Power/Knowledge: Selected Interviews and Other Writings, 1972–1977*. pp. 63–77. New York: Pantheon.

Garland, D. 1985. *Punishment and Welfare: A History of Penal Strategies*. Aldershot: Gower.

Haesler, A. 2005. 'Penser l'individu? Sur un nécessaire changement de paradigme, 1. Les impasses du néo-individualisme sociologique.' *EspacesTemps.net*, Available at http://espacestemps.net.

Hirst, P. 2000. 'Statism, pluralism and social control.' *British Journal of Criminology* 40 (2): 279–95.

Kelsen, Hans. 1967. *Pure Theory of Law*. Berkeley: University of California Press.

Lawson, B. E. 1992. 'Uplifting the race: Middle-class blacks and the truly disadvantaged.' pp. 90–113. In *The Underclass Question*, edited by B. E. Lawson., Philadelphia: Temple University Press.

Levine, M., S. Reicher, C. Cassidy, and K. Harrison. 2002. *Promoting Intervention Against Violent Crime: A Social Identity Approach*. ESRC report.

Lianos, M., and M. Douglas. 2000. 'Dangerization and the end of deviance: The institutional environment.' *British Journal of Criminology* 40: 261–78.

Lianos, M. 1999. 'Point de vue sur l'acceptabilité sociale du discours du risque.' *Les cahiers de la sécurité intérieure*. IHESI, Vol. Risque et démocratie n. 38.

——. 2001a. *Le nouveau contrôle social & toile institutionnelle, normativité et lien social*. L'Harmattan. Paris: Logiques Sociales.

——. 2001b. 'Safety, deviance and control: The postindustrial transition from values to results.' *Sciences Sociales et Entreprises* 1 (3): 127–44.

——. 2003. 'Social control after Foucault.' *Surveillance and Society* 1 (3): 412–30. http://www.surveillance-and-society.org.

Lock, P. 1999. 'Africa, military downsizing and the growth in the security industry.' In *Peace, Profit or Plunder? The Privatisation of Security in War-Torn African Societies*, ed.J. Cilliers and P. Mason, Cape Town: Institute for Security Studies.

Lyon, D. 2003. 'Surveillance as social sorting: Computer codes and mobile bodies.' pp. 13–30. In *Surveillance as Social Sorting: Privacy, Risk and Digital Discrimination*, edited by D. Lyon, London: Routledge.

North Carolina Division of Community Corrections. 2005. *Guide to Offender Management: Engaging the Offender in the Change Process*. Raleigh.

Peel, J. D. Y. 1980. 'Inequality and action: The forms of Ijesha social conflict.' *Canadian Journal of African Studies* 14 (3): 473–502.

Perrot, M., ed. 1990. *A History of Private Life, Volume IV: From the Fires of Revolution to the Great War*. Cambridge: Harvard University Press.

Pfaff, S. 2001. 'The limits of coercive surveillance: Social and penal control in the German Democratic Republic.' *Punishment & Society* 3 (3): 381–407.

Ronnes, H. 2004. 'A solitary place of retreat: Renaissance privacy and Irish architecture.' *International Journal of Historical Archaeology* 8 (2): 101–17.

Roodenburg, H. 2004. 'Social control viewed from below: New perspectives.' pp. 145–58. In *Social Control in Europe*, edited by H. Roodenburg, Ohio State University Press.

Rusche, G., and O. Kirchheimer. 1939. *Punishment and Social Structure*. New Brunswick: Transaction Publishers.

Simester, A. P. ed. 2005. *Appraising Strict Liability*. Oxford: Oxford University Press.

Walby, K. 2005. 'How closed-circuit television surveillance organizes the social: An institutional ethnography.' *Canadian Journal of Sociology* 30 (2): 189–214.

——. 2006. 'Locating televisual and non-televisual textual sequences with institutional ethnography: A study of campus and apartment CCTV security work.' *Culture and Organization* 12 (2): 153–68.

Watkins, J. 2006. 'Responsibility in context.' *Oxford Journal of Legal Studies* 26 (3): 593–608.

Zhong, L. Y., and R. G. Broadhurst. 2007. 'Building little safe and civilized communities: Community crime prevention with Chinese characteristics?' *International Journal of Offender Therapy and Comparative Criminology* 51 (1): 52–67.

Part II

Surveillance policies and practices of democratic governance

Chapter 5

Surveillance as governance

Social inequality and the pursuit of democratic surveillance

Torin Monahan

Technological surveillance is often criticized as being antithetical to democratic principles, and with good reason. At its core, surveillance is about control; it tends to produce conditions of constraint, wherein human and technical action is regulated and limited. The degree and kind of constraint vary according to the values and assumptions that are embedded in respective surveillance apparatuses and generated by surveillance practices. Although control could be exercised with surveillance systems for purposes of care or protection, such systems are most often characterized by coercion and repression, and offer few avenues for accountability or oversight. Airport security systems, for example, require people to submit to elaborate surveillance rituals of conformity and exposure, making people more open to external scrutiny and manipulation even while the rights of citizens and others are left intentionally vague. Commercial surveillance of people for marketing purposes betrays a similar trend: it encourages (or requires) people to reveal their shopping preferences and habits so that companies can target their products more profitably or sell their customer data to others; meanwhile, individuals know little about what data are being collected about them, by whom, or for what purposes. Similarly, state surveillance of those accessing social services, such as welfare, has become much more fine-grained since automated data systems have been implemented to distribute and manage "benefits;" at the same time, the disclosure of information to welfare recipients about how their data are used or even about policies for disciplining or rewarding recipients based on their spending habits has been restricted.

These disparate examples, which represent commonplace rather than exceptional surveillance practices, share a set of characteristics that are clearly non-democratic. They each open people up to examination and control, while constraining individual autonomy. They each rely upon opacity instead of transparency; most people under surveillance have little knowledge of the inner workings of the systems or their rights as citizens, consumers, or others. Finally, because these systems are closed, they resist opportunities for democratic participation in how they are designed, used, critiqued or regulated.

In this paper, I argue that the underlying conditions of most contemporary surveillance systems run counter to principles of democratic governance. First, I draw upon writings from the field of technology studies that deal with democracy and technology to frame technologies, including those of surveillance, as political in their own right, apart from how they are used by government agencies, corporations, or others. Second, I analyze the dominant functions of surveillance today with regard to the differential treatment and automated control of populations, functions which both produce marginal identities and resist democratic participation or oversight. Finally, to avoid deterministic conclusions about surveillance, I explore several examples of democratically empowering surveillance systems that encourage openness, transparency, accountability, participation, and power equalization among social groups and institutions.

Technology and democracy

Inquiry into the relationship between surveillance and democracy can fruitfully begin by recognizing the non-democratic character of most technological systems. Following from John Dewey, I understand democracy to be much "more than a form of government"—as a mode of associated living predicated upon conditions of *social equality*, along lines of race, class, gender, and other categories of difference (Dewey, 1916:87). At least since the Enlightenment, technologies have been wrapped up in a mythology of social progress, which frames any new advancement as an unqualified good (Adas, 1989). Seldom have people stopped to ask the crucial question of what *kind* of progress is being achieved by new technological systems (Marx, 1997). Social progress *could* be measured in terms of personal satisfaction, educational achievement, environmental sustainability, access to health care, strong community ties, reduced economic inequality, and so on. Instead, in most circles progress has come to be synonymous with greater technical efficiency or economic gain.

Science and technology studies (STS) scholars, at least those in the normative branch of this field, have argued that democratic design processes and outcomes should be the primary criteria for evaluating technological systems and deciding upon their social worth (Winner, 1986; Sclove, 1995; Martin, 1999; Woodhouse et al., 2002). The rationale for this position is that because of the exclusionary nature of the design of most technologies, technological systems tend to overlook the needs of diverse populations, force homogenization and adaption, and produce a series of so-called externalities—from toxic waste to energy dependency—for which people and institutions must take responsibility. By increasing public participation in the process of technology design and evaluation, we could at the very least circumvent some of the most destructive outcomes of new systems. Even better, such systems could empower citizens by including them in the process, recognizing their tacit expertise, and cultivating new knowledge about the merits of some technologies over others. Finally, involving more people in what is typically seen as the domain of technical experts could speed up feedback loops so that problems could be identified and corrected sooner, preferably before large-scale infrastructural investments have been made (Woodhouse and Nieusma, 2001).

The democratization of technology sounds radical, in part, because of the presumed impracticality of public involvement. It is probably not a coincidence that as the scale and scope of technological mediation increases, meaningful democratic participation in most aspects of governance decreases (Winner, 1977). There are productive counter-examples to this trend, of course, as with the formation of new social movements (Juris, 2008; Hess, 2007) or participation in formal politics over the internet (Ratcliffe and Lebkowsky, 2005). Nonetheless, the public is generally excluded from active participation in *most* matters considered technical, from transportation to city planning, from energy resources to military weaponry, from food production to communication networks. At least in the United States, public involvement in decisions about technological systems has been restricted to consumer choices, occasional ballot measures, and infrequent—and largely symbolic—public meetings. The infeasibility of public involvement has been partially conditioned by the closed technological systems upon which people depend. If democratic participation is an unfamiliar and unsupported activity throughout most aspects of people's everyday lives, it should not be surprising that the prospect of greater participation in decisions about technology might sound absurd.

An important analytical step toward democratizing technology is recognizing the political nature and social agency of all technologies. As Langdon Winner writes: "Far from being merely neutral, our technologies provide a positive content to the arena of life in which they are applied, enhancing certain ends, denying or even destroying others" (Winner, 1977: 29). Much like legislation, technological systems provide a set of rules, or scripts, encouraging certain uses or interactions and discouraging others (Winner, 1986; Akrich, 1992; Lessig, 1999). For example, video cameras lend themselves to the remote observation of others; highways lend themselves to vehicular transportation; walls and gates lend themselves to the regulation of belonging. The scripts of technological systems *partially* determine social practices by exerting agential force upon people and contexts. Moreover, technological systems introduce a series of dependencies—such as those upon electricity, data networks, or security systems—that require institutional commitments for the systems to continue to operate. Because technologies frame what is possible and practical for people and organizations, they can be said to be "political," even though decisions about them are seldom made through democratic processes. This neither denies the agency of people nor depends upon a simplistic belief in technological determinism. Instead, it sets the stage for a critical reading of technology in society, including an analysis of the role of technology in instituting and maintaining non-democratic practices and social inequalities.

By pulling technologies into the realm of the political, one can subject them to critical analysis and debate. Richard Sclove proposes, for example, that all technological systems be assessed with strong democratic principles in mind in order to mitigate the dominant non-democratic trajectory of most systems. He explains this position with a simple but persuasive syllogism:

> Insofar as (1) citizens ought to be empowered to participate in shaping their society's basic circumstances and (2) technologies profoundly affect and partly constitute those circumstances, it follows that (3) technological design and practice should be democratized.
>
> (Sclove, 1995:ix)

To the extent that people value ideals of democratic governance, it is logical that they should embrace the democratization of the technological systems that increasingly shape all aspects of life and act as social structures in their own right. It is important to note, however, that this does not imply eliminating technical experts or political representatives but instead further including technological decisions in policy-making processes. Sclove elaborates:

> The strong democratic ideal envisions extensive opportunities for citizens to participate in important decisions that affect them. A decision qualifies as important particularly insofar as it bears on a society's basic organization or structure. The commitment to egalitarian participation does not preclude continued reliance on some representative institutions, but these should be designed to support and incorporate, rather than to replace, participatory processes.
>
> (Sclove, 1995: 26)

The mechanisms for such participation can vary, from full-scale participatory design processes—where citizens collectively decide what kind of technologies they need and involve themselves in their production—to citizen consensus conferences or review panels for evaluating proposed or existing technologies. These processes can accommodate either direct or representative forms of democratic participation. Participatory design has proven to be a successful approach for designing spaces, technologies, and systems in meaningful collaboration with occupants or users (Schuler and Namioka, 1993). A key tenet of participatory design is that all users are experts in what they do, and designers can tap this expertise to generate better and more democratic outcomes (Howard, 2004). A less robust but more prevalent form of public involvement in technology design is the practice of "user-centered design" (Nieusma, 2004; Norman, 1988), which focuses on the needs or preferences of users and can be seen, for instance, with the widespread practice of beta-testing for computer software. At the very least, regulatory boards or government agencies could be established to investigate the social, environmental, and economic impacts (or implications) of new technologies and make those findings available to policy-makers and the public. The United States Office of Technology Assessment, which was dissolved in 1995, serves as an important precedent and a possible form for establishing future governmental bodies devoted to technology assessment.

Apart from this focus on the largely absent but necessary democratic *processes* for technology production and evaluation, there remains the question of what kinds of technological systems are inherently more democratic by design. Ivan Illich (1973) introduces the generative concept of *conviviality* to describe technologies of community and self-empowerment that exist in opposition to the hegemony of industrial modes of production, which he perceives to be anti-democratic in nature. Convivial technologies are those that encourage self-sufficiency, local autonomy, community building, and self-actualization. Possible examples might be community-based solar power systems (Nieusma, 2007) or water pumps that are easy to install, operate, and fix (de Laet and Mol, 2000). By definition, convivial technologies are small-scale, transparent, accessible, and easy to use and/or modify.

Whereas most large-scale technological systems, including those for surveillance, are relatively closed and difficult to alter, convivial technologies possess a property that might be called *structural flexibility*, meaning that they not only afford but also invite modification on the part of users, support diverse modes of expression, and enable power equalization among people (Monahan, 2005). For instance, elements of structural flexibility can be seen with internet sites such as Indymedia, which allows users to post their own news stories, or with certain decentralized educational settings that support student exploration and collaboration on inquiry-driven projects (Monahan, 2005). Structural flexibility, as an ideal, does not deny the value of standardization but instead encourages continually revisiting categories and standards to determine which are most appropriate and least exclusionary for any given situation. Although such technological systems are all too rare, their presence provides a valuable alternative position from which to probe the democratic potentials and threats of contemporary technological surveillance.

Surveillance as control

It is now widely recognized that the emergence of information systems and shifts in modes of capital accumulation, especially since the 1970s, have brought about an increasingly globalized information or network society (Harvey, 1990; Castells, 1996; Hardt and Negri, 2000). Information and communication technologies now mediate and govern most domains of life, especially in industrialized countries. What is seldom noted, however, is that information societies are perforce surveillance societies (Giddens, 1990; Lyon, 2001). The orientation of information systems is toward data creation, collection, and analysis for the purposes of intervention and control. Surveillance societies have deep roots in the modern bureaucratic project of rational, scientific management of organizations and populations, which is itself a powerful iteration of the Enlightenment belief in scientific and technological progress (Porter 1995). The popular motif of Big Brother, or state-run surveillance operations, however, fails to account for the almost complete integration of information systems, and therefore surveillance functions. David Lyon elucidates:

> surveillance societies are such in the sense that surveillance is pervasive in every sector of societal life, courtesy of an integrated information infrastructure. Far from state surveillance being predominate, surveillance activities may now be found in work situations and consumer contexts as well. ... Moreover, surveillance data is networked between these different sectors, to create degrees of integration of surveillance systems undreamed of in the worst Orwellian nightmare, but with actual social effects that are far more ambiguous and complex.
>
> (Lyon, 2001:34–35)

Concern for democracy, therefore, must attend to the state but also extend beyond it to question all the modes of information-facilitated control— it must look to the extreme and the mundane, from state spying programs to targeted consumer marketing, for instance. Whereas the previous section of this paper stressed non-democratic trends in relation to technologies more generally, this section concentrates on surveillance systems in particular, with specific attention paid to the types of control they exercise and enable.

As a starting point, I define surveillance systems as those that enable control of people through the identification, tracking, monitoring, and/or analysis of individuals, data, or systems. Although surveillance hinges upon control, it must be recognized that control is a loaded term that deserves to be unpacked. The term *control* stands in, usually, as shorthand for "social control," meaning the mechanisms for ordering society through the regulation of individual and group behavior. Manifestations of social control can be informal, such as cultural norms and sanctions for improper behavior, or formal, such as laws and state policing of deviance. Social control is usually perceived unfavorably by critical social scientists because of the negative connotations associated with hard forms of coercion and police discipline, which have been applied in highly particularistic and discriminatory ways. Nonetheless, some form of social control is necessary, and indeed inevitable, in societies, so the question should be about what forms of control are more equitable, just, and democratic. With surveillance, such analysis should begin by identifying the de facto control regimes enforced by surveillance systems, whether intentionally or not, and then move toward recommendations for control systems that are more democratic in their design and effect.

Two types of surveillance in particular directly challenge ideals of democratic governance. These are systems of *differential control* and *automated control*, the effects of which are most egregious when the systems coexist or are one and the same. Differential control can be witnessed first with the "social sorting" functions of surveillance systems (Lyon, 2003, 2007). Surveillance, in this regard, operates as a mechanism for societal differentiation; it assists with discerning or actively constructing differences among populations and then regulating those populations according to their assigned status (Gandy, 2006; Haggerty and Ericson, 2006). The most obvious example of this might be airport screening systems or "watchlists" for targeting people who are thought to represent a higher risk of being terrorists and then subjecting them to additional searches and interrogation, or simply precluding them from flying altogether.

Because information technologies imbricate with most aspects of life and all information technologies possess a surveillance modality, such practices of social sorting manifest in many less obvious ways as well. For example, surveillance-facilitated social sorting occurs with all kinds of status assignments for access to basic services or needs, including transportation systems that provide dedicated automobile lanes for those who can afford to pay while the commuting needs of others are neglected (Graham and Marvin, 2001); energy-provision services that offer convenient budget plans for "low-risk" groups while others must contend with unforgiving pay-as-you-go plans with hefty surcharges and penalties (Drakeford, 1995; Graham and Marvin, 2001); preferred-shopper programs that give elite shoppers handsome discounts based on past purchases or preferences while intentionally overcharging for basic staple goods more likely to be consumed by the poor (Albrecht and McIntyre, 2006; Turow, 2006); and so on. As Minas Samatas aptly observes:

> Political surveillance is not only that which is conducted by the state for directly sociopolitical control purposes, but also the private, commercial, consumer surveillance, which can sort individuals accordingly, by including or excluding them, and affecting their life chances.
>
> (Samatas, 2004:150)

If social equality and equal participation (or representation) in governance processes are necessary conditions for strong democracy, then systems that perpetuate social inequalities are antidemocratic. Whereas social sorting typically works through the differential application of *the same* technological systems to the governance of different populations, there are other ways that surveillance can produce unequal outcomes. What I refer to as "marginalizing surveillance" entails unequal exposure to *different* surveillance systems based on one's social address. More often than not, this means that some of the most invasive systems of scrutiny and control are disproportionately applied to the poor, to ethnic minorities, or to women. Mandatory drug testing for minimum-wage service employees or welfare recipients are particularly egregious examples of marginalizing surveillance (Staples, 2000; Campbell, 2006). Another example might be the surveillance of low-level employees with keystroke-tracking software, global positioning systems, or radio-frequency identification badges (EPIC and PI, 2000; Lyon, 2006). Rituals of extreme technological and police surveillance of public-school students, especially in lower-class minority neighborhoods, could be interpreted as another example of marginalizing surveillance (Monahan and Torres, 2010). Those with alternative social addresses, especially the relatively affluent, are largely insulated from the degree and kind of surveillance represented by these cases. Such surveillance does not simply regulate marginalized groups—it actively produces both identities and conditions of marginality. These marginalizing effects might be more pronounced, in the eyes of subjects and objects of surveillance, given the universalist and objective mythology surrounding all technological systems, because discrimination can be masked behind the supposedly impartial functions of "the system."

The forms of differential control engendered by social sorting and marginalizing surveillance are both compounded and insulated by the automation of surveillance functions. Automated control depends predominately upon algorithmic surveillance systems, which take empirical phenomena—translated into data—as their raw material, ranging from commercial purchases to mobility flows to crime rates to insurance claims to personal identifiers. Spaces, activities, people, and systems are then managed through automated analysis of data and socio-technical intervention (Norris, Moran, and Armstrong, 1998; Thrift and French, 2002; Graham and Wood, 2003). Examples could include real-time management of traffic flows through the identification and prioritization (and/or penalization) of some drivers, or modes of transport, over others; integration of face-recognition software with video surveillance systems so that positive "matches" with faces of suspected terrorists, for instance, generate automatic alerts for security personnel; geo-demographic mapping of reported crime incidents by neighborhood to create risk-based response protocols for police; or automatic exclusion of individuals from medical insurance coverage based on their genetic predisposition to acquiring debilitating diseases.

Automated control systems share a predictive orientation toward people; individual or group dispositions are rendered into statistical probabilities that can be acted on in advance or in real time, usually for the sake of institutional efficiency and commercial profit rather than social wellbeing. The systems seek to fix identities in advance for more effective control, regardless of the questionable ethics associated with acting on predictions, or actualizing such predictions. Thus, an important ontological shift accompanies the transition to automated surveillance practices. Whereas non-automated systems of social control seek to identify and *eliminate exceptions* (i.e. to keep everyone in line to ensure social cohesion), automated systems seek to *verify conformity* through processes of anticipatory inspection (Lianos and Douglas, 2000:269). Everyone is presumed guilty, in a sense, until they pass preprogrammed expectations for acceptable data. Of course, one should bear in mind that such systems can be differentially applied as well; an added layer of automated control can exist for "high risk" groups while "low risk" groups might bypass such verification tests altogether.

It may be tempting to ascribe a totalizing force to automated systems and make radical claims about the gradual elimination of trust relations, ethics, and even culture under such systems (see, e.g., Lianos and Douglas, 2000). Taking a cue from other STS scholars (e.g. Bijker and Law, 1992; Bowker and Star, 1999), I find it more productive—and empirically accurate—to see such systems as socially constructed, as embodying the values and cultural logics of their contexts of production, as being thoroughly social even in their cold technical rigidity. Moreover, while the systems may be increasingly automated, that does not preclude the necessity of their ongoing maintenance by engineers, operators, programmers, and others; nor does it preclude active negotiation, appropriation, and resistance by the targets of such surveillance. Nonetheless, automated systems do resist participation, challenges, or alteration. As with other non-democratic technological systems, exclusionary politics are encoded in their design, enforced by bureaucratic structures of technical experts, and propagated through the application of such systems to social settings.

These surveillance systems absorb and reproduce the dominant cultural values of the contemporary political economy, most especially those associated with neoliberalism. Neoliberalism is generally understood as an orientation toward governance that emphasizes the privatization of public institutions and the deregulation of industry (Harvey, 2005). Beyond that, however, neoliberalism is a market rationale that colonizes most spheres of public life and transforms their functions to prioritize economic gain over all other measures of quality or success. From education, to health care, to transportation, to public safety, neoliberal policies and practices have come to dominate public institutions over the past few decades, in the United States and beyond (Duggan, 2003; Giroux, 2004). This shift in governance predictably pushes responsibility onto individuals for what used to be the purview of the state, effectively depoliticizing social problems and normalizing social inequalities (Brown, 2006). For example, if access to health care is seen as something that can be chosen and purchased on the open market, instead of something that is a right, then this relieves the state of responsibility for providing health care and legitimates conditions of unequal access (Fisher, 2009). Moreover, there is a disciplinary dimension to neoliberalism, whereby those who fail—or are unable—to comply with the now-pervasive market logics are excluded or criminalized in Darwinian fashion (Bourdieu, 1998; Garland, 2001; Simon, 2007). Therefore, existing social services, such as welfare programs, adopt policing functions to spy on, punish, and exclude those who are already presumed guilty because they are poor (Gilliom, 2001; Eubanks, 2006). Conditions of economic insecurity, or the inability to meet one's needs through consumption, are suspect in this brave new neoliberal world.

Differential and automated control systems fuse with neoliberal rationalities to further normalize conditions of social inequality and civic passivity, both of which are antithetical to democratic principles. Social-sorting surveillance systems may have begun by separating out those who could pay for augmented services from those receiving basic services, but they have quickly mutated into schemes to reduce or eliminate basic services altogether, as evinced by the reduction in staffed airport screening stations for non-elite travelers, the reduction in lanes for cash-paying travelers at toll-road stations, or the reduction of public spaces and services more generally in lieu of surveillance-controlled private zones for housing, commerce, education, health care, and so on. If social sorting lends the appearance of providing *incentives* for differential treatment based on economic or other status or risk indicators, marginalizing surveillance threatens with disciplinary *disincentives* for those unable or unwilling to compete in the neoliberal world. This helps to explain why the most invasive and discriminatory forms of marginalizing surveillance focus almost exclusively on the economically or politically disenfranchised, including those who depend on state-supported health care, welfare, public education, public transportation, and even those trying to access polling places in communities with a preponderance of ethnic minorities. The automation of these, and other, forms of differential surveillance depersonalizes instances of discrimination and masks the exclusionary trends of neoliberalism more generally. Most concerning, perhaps, for this discussion about democracy is how these systems might be contributing to the production of neoliberal subjects who approach the world through the eyes of consumers rather than those of citizens entitled to rights (Rose, 1999; Brown, 2006). Because the marketization of public and private sectors eviscerates spaces for political debate, critique, or action, it should not be much of a stretch to say that it similarly deflects and delegitimizes any kind of critical democratic engagement with the mechanisms of neoliberal control, including those of surveillance.

This section has revealed some of the technological politics behind modern surveillance systems. Surveillance is predicated upon control. The dominant manifestations of surveillance-based control today are disturbingly anti-democratic because of the way they sort populations unequally, produce conditions and identities of marginality, impinge upon the life chances of marginalized populations, and normalize and fortify neoliberal world orders. There are two main reasons to perceive such surveillance systems as anti-democratic. First, surveillance technologies, like other technologies, act as forms of legislation without much—if any—democratic participation or representation. Second, perhaps as a direct result of the absence of democratic processes with technology design and evaluation, social inequalities are aggravated rather than ameliorated, which hinders the actualization of democratic modes of associated living. Given the structural forces and constraints commented on in this section, even the apparent decentralization and diffusion of surveillance systems, such as peer-to-peer surveillance, cannot be viewed as democratizing because they do not in any way challenge structural inequalities (Andrejevic, 2005). As with most technological systems, surveillance resists public participation or critique by means of its opaque design and management by technical experts, people who often prefer to hide or deny the surveillance functions of the systems they oversee (Monahan, 2007). The question remains as to whether surveillance could foster democracy rather than undermine it.

Democratic surveillance

What manifestations of surveillance support democracy? Control may be a necessary and inevitable function of social regulation, but how can its enforcement by surveillance technologies be more democratic and empowering for more people? For the purpose of this inquiry, urban theorist Kevin Lynch provides an instructive view of spatial control, which he posits as one of the key criteria for good city design:

> Control will sometimes enter a self-destructive spiral: perhaps downward—as when behavior begins to escape any regulation and control groups lose their confidence—or perhaps upward—as when a threatened control progressively rigidifies, prescribing actions and rights more and more minutely. These instabilities will also require intervention. Once again, the ideal state of congruence must be balanced by external regulation.
>
> (Lynch, 1984: 212)

Critical social scientists, who usually write about the negative dimensions of surveillance (and I include myself in this camp), may be doing a disservice to progressive social change when they quickly equate social control with disempowerment or oppression. What Kevin Lynch reminds us is that social and spatial control require constant monitoring and regulation in order to minimize oppressive tendencies and maximize empowering ones.

Perhaps it is obvious, but individually empowering, participatory, community-based control mechanisms—the likes of which might be called strongly democratic—flourish in small decentralized societies but are suppressed in large centralized ones (Lynch, 1984:234; Illich, 1973). The same might be said of technological systems: those that are locally based, small-scale, open-ended, transparent, and participatory will be inherently more democratic and less prone to abuse. Elsewhere I developed a parallel argument that surveillance systems should be designed and regulated along these lines, to cultivate local expertise and minimize problematic uses through transparent design, public involvement, and local accountability (Monahan, 2006). Several problems introduce themselves at this point, however. The first is that even strong democratic processes do not always produce democratic outcomes, so firm criteria for evaluating new technological systems and preserving future democratic involvement must be included in any deliberation about or evaluation of technology (Sclove, 1995). Legal scholar Lawrence Lessig compares such criteria for technology infrastructure design to a constitutional framework. A constitution—or information architecture, as the case may be—cannot hope to stipulate all the rules for preserving democratic governance or predict in advance the host of future threats it might face. What a constitution can do is provide a set of guiding principles against which cases can be evaluated and decisions can be made. Lessig writes:

> We build a world where freedom can flourish not by removing society from any self-conscious control; we build a world where freedom can flourish by setting it in a place where a particular kind of self-conscious control survives ... I mean an *architecture*—not just a legal text but a way of life—that structures and constrains social and legal power, to the end of protecting fundamental *values*—principles and ideals that reach beyond the compromises of ordinary politics.
>
> (Lessig, 1999:5)

Because technology is most often perceived as political in its application but apolitical in its design, and because technology production is most firmly rooted in capitalist, free-market systems, the self-conscious establishment and preservation of such democratic architectures will probably continue to encounter serious resistance until such time as justice arguments can be merged with capitalist imperatives. That said, the current popularity of open-source software and growing interest in universal design may be harbingers of a phase shift, or at least a moment of opportunity to move in this direction.

The second problem that must be addressed, or at least acknowledged, concerns the influence of neoliberal structures and cultural logics upon the social field for technological development and engagement. In this context, even if transparency were achieved with the operation of surveillance systems, it could easily be appropriated to support a highly limited, consumerist orientation toward market "choices" instead of socially beneficial or community empowering outcomes. One can see this clearly in the domain of pharmaceutical drug marketing, for instance. A certain form of transparency is actualized through direct-to-consumer advertising, allowing consumers to obtain knowledge about drugs without having that information mediated by medical professionals (Fisher and Ronald, forthcoming). In such situations, transparency can actually reinforce a consumerist and individualist logic, which has little room for democratic control, by implying that with adequate information, consumers can make choices and vote with their dollars. A related problem can be seen with the provision of information in the name of transparency without accountability or any obvious mechanism to alter what is transparently extractive, exploitative, or otherwise problematic. Physician conflict-of-interest statements or bank privacy statements (which might be more accurately called "lack of privacy statements") function in this way by disclosing something that is unsavory without offering effective steps to mitigate it or real options to choose something different. In sum, transparency is no substitute for deeper structural changes that include real power equalization and serious accountability mechanisms.

At this stage, I would like to bracket these persistent (and important) structural problems in order to discuss some concrete possibilities for democratic surveillance. Thus far, the argument has been that we need democratic design processes and democratic criteria to regulate surveillance and other technological systems (e.g. egalitarian participation, conviviality, structural flexibility, and accountability). In addition to this, I would like to pursue the idea that the most democratic and socially empowering designs (of spaces, products, or technological systems) are those that work to correct power asymmetries. Often these are designs that are explicitly intended to include social groups that have been historically marginalized or discriminated against by the built world, including women, the elderly, the young, the visually impaired, the mobility impaired, and so on. It turns out that design for marginalized populations often produces designs that are better for most populations. For example, curb cuts in sidewalks or ramps up to buildings may be intended for people in wheelchairs, but most people benefit from them: people pushing strollers, people with canes or walkers, people on bicycles, and so on. The same insight could be applied to the design of surveillance infrastructures—to produce technological sensing and control devices that minimize power asymmetries to the benefit of individuals and the empowerment of a democratic citizenry.

The website Scorecard.org offers a compelling example of a surveillance system with impressive democratic potential. This site serves as a clearing house for information about releases of toxic chemicals and other contaminants in local neighborhoods (Fortun, 2004). It synthesizes "toxic release inventory" data compiled by the United States federal government, along with maps of "superfund sites," lists of likely polluters in one's neighborhood, comparisons with pollution in other cities, and action items for direct public involvement. It is a surveillance system in the sense that it manipulates data for purposes of control, meaning, ideally, the policing of potential and actual industrial polluters and the cleanup of toxic materials in one's community. While this is not a completely transparent, open, or participatory form of surveillance, it is democratic in that it invites participation, fosters learning, and affords a degree of power equalization among local communities and institutions, be they industry or government.[1]

Related surveillance systems might actively monitor air, water, or noise pollution and alert officials and communities to dangerous conditions. Artist Tad Hirsch, for example, has implemented a system called "Tripwire" for sensing spikes in noise pollution in communities around airports and then generating automated (and individualized) complaint messages to local government hotlines.[2] The idea behind such complaint messages is that they must be accounted for as "data" in official government documents and that a preponderance of them may require some kind of regulatory action. While this system is even less participatory than Scorecard.org, it does represent another qualified form of democratic surveillance because of its attention to power equalization. It also points to opportunities for similar systems that could be more democratic in their design, such as ones that disseminated the data directly to the public or taught community members how to document environmental problems in a more scientific way (see, e.g., Ottinger, 2005).

In a different vein, the development of pervasive computing environments introduces other possibilities for democratic surveillance. For instance, in collaboration with design schools, companies like Intel are sponsoring experimental design projects for elderly care, with the idea of making older people less dependent on (and controlled by) caregivers. Pervasive sensing systems might assist with daily functions like food preparation, communication, entertainment, or health monitoring. Whereas most of today's technologies for elderly care seem to stress disciplinary forms of surveillance, such as the use of wander guards and boundary alert units (which are systems designed to prevent movement by the elderly beyond certain perimeters), by shifting the user focus from caregivers to elderly populations, it is possible that more liberating and demarginalizing designs might emerge (Kenner, 2008). Designs *for* the elderly will likely be far more profitable for companies like Intel too, especially given the growth in senior populations in countries like the United States.

Obviously, such pervasive computing systems could be used by caregivers or others to further reduce the agency of the elderly by better controlling their daily activities, such as medication compliance or coffee consumption, for instance. Pervasive computing systems could also easily become information-extraction devices for marketing purposes. Therefore, in order for these systems to maintain their democratic orientation, safeguards would have to be implemented to protect the privacy of the elderly, and to place control of the technology in their hands. The risks for abuse may be high, but they do not erase the potential for empowerment, which may best be preserved though the active and ongoing negotiation of "shared protocols" by the primary stakeholders (Galloway, 2004; Murakami Wood, 2007). Additionally, reflexive design criteria could guide the design of pervasive environments to minimize their repressive qualities and maximize their empowering ones (Phillips, 2005). These might include basic tenets such as that the systems must be self-disclosing, default to harmlessness, preserve privacy, conserve time, and be deniable by users without any penalty (Greenfield, 2006).

It is important to recognize that in each of these examples democratic surveillance relies on the work of technical experts, even as in its ideal form it encourages the development of technical literacy on the part of citizens. Technical expertise, however, is reoriented—or appropriated, as the case may be—away from instrumental logics of technical efficiency and toward broader social goals. According to the philosopher of technology Andrew Feenberg (1999), this reorientation is necessary in order to change the codes or architectures that shape technological practice over time, which is part of the process toward that he calls "deep democracy." Feenberg writes:

> I will call a movement for democratization "deep" where it includes a strategy combining the democratic rationalization of technical codes with electoral controls on technical institutions ... Deep democratization promises an alternative to technocracy. Instead of popular agency appearing as an anomaly and an interference, it would be normalized and incorporated into the standard procedures of technical design.
>
> (Feenberg, 1999:147)

Whether one calls them codes, infrastructures, protocols, or something else, democratic technologies, including those of surveillance, hinge upon the intentional harnessing of control to structure environments for empowerment. Democratic codes are directed at achieving and preserving social goods beyond the technocratic or capitalistic ones of efficiency and profitability.

Conclusion

This paper has explored some of the democratic pitfalls and potentials of surveillance technologies. As a rule, contemporary surveillance systems are antithetical to democratic ideals both in their design and application. They individualize, objectify, and control people—often through their use of data—in ways that perpetuate social inequalities; they obfuscate social contexts through their lack of transparency; people are largely unaware of the functioning of their systems, or of their rights; and they resist intervention through their closed technical designs and management by technical experts or institutional agents. Especially by shutting down avenues for meaningful participation (or representation) in design processes that affect most people's lives and by aggravating social inequalities, surveillance systems threaten democracy. That said, most large-scale technological systems are anti-democratic in their design and effects, so surveillance technologies should not necessarily be viewed as exceptional in this regard. What is important to note, however, is the pervasiveness of surveillance systems and the intensification of their social-control functions.

In theory, social control by technological means is desirable in advanced industrialized societies because it actively reproduces values and norms necessary for social cohesion but which are difficult to achieve in contexts of intense geographical dispersion, cultural diversity, and social stratification. In practice, the surveillance functions of information systems tend to create and sustain conditions of inequality and identities of marginality through their differential application. For instance, surveillance as social sorting does not just discover and act upon differences; it manufactures *meaningful* differences based on particularistic indicators, such as wealth or skin color, and then excludes or includes populations accordingly, thereby shaping individual experiences and life-chances. David Lyon relates: "When people's life-chances depend upon what category they have been placed in, it is very important to know who designed the categories, who defines their significance and who decides the circumstances under which those categories will be decisive" (Lyon, 2007:186). In spite of the proliferation of social sorting and marginalizing technologies, most decisions about important categories or protocols are made by people far removed from any formal mechanisms of democratic control, ranging from city engineers to computer programmers to corporate managers.

What I call "marginalizing surveillance" takes social sorting to a more explicit level of discrimination by selectively targeting those of lower social status, usually the poor, for the most invasive forms of scrutiny and control. The converse of this holds true as well. For instance, whereas the spending habits of people on welfare might be tracked so that punitive measures can be taken for any deviation from the rules, the spending habits of the relatively affluent are tracked so that they can be rewarded for expensive purchases with further discounts or special offers. The automation of surveillance then serves to aggravate social inequalities by encoding into the systems neoliberal values of institutional efficiency and commercial profit, often to the exclusion of the social good. In addition to minimizing opportunities for democratic participation, or even inquiry into surveillance practices, automated surveillance destabilizes traditionally democratic beliefs in the possibility of achieving social status; instead one's value or risk is assigned in advance based on statistical probabilities.

Democratic surveillance implies intentionally harnessing the control functions of surveillance for social ends of fairness, justice, and equality. First, more than simply using surveillance systems in different ways, democratic surveillance involves reprogramming socio-technical codes to encourage transparency, openness, participation, and accountability to produce new systems and new configurations of experts and users, subjects and objects. Second, because neither participation nor transparency is enough (for example, one can willingly participate in one's disempowerment, and exploitation can be made transparent without allowing for change), democratic surveillance requires a set of protocols or criteria against which to measure social value. The shorthand that I offered is that democratic surveillance should lead to the correction of power asymmetries. Because surveillance societies appear to be here to stay, democratic ways of life may depend on tempering the growing hegemony of differential and automated control with alternative, power-equalizing forms of surveillance.

Notes

1 Similar systems for disseminating information and inviting action might not necessarily achieve democratic outcomes. For instance, one can imagine mapping systems
that alerted residents to "undesirable" people, such as registered sex offenders, living
in their neighborhoods. It is easy to imagine that such systems would be employed
to further marginalize or harass those people considered undesirable rather than
work to include them safely in community life.

2 http://web.media.mit.edu (accessed September 16, 2008).

References

Adas, Michael. 1989. *Machines as the Measure of Men: Science, Technology, and Ideologies of Western Dominance*. Ithaca, NY: Cornell University Press.

Akrich, Madeleine. 1992. "The De-scription of technological objects." In *Shaping Technology / Building Society: Studies in Sociotechnical Change*, pp. 205–24. ed. W. E. Bijker, and John Law. Cambridge, MA: The MIT Press.

Albrecht, Katherine, and Liz McIntyre. 2006. *The Spychips Threat: Why Christians Should Resist RFID and Electronic Surveillance*. Nashville, Tenn.: Nelson Current.

Andrejevic, Mark. 2005. "The work of watching one another: Lateral surveillance, risk, and governance." *Surveillance & Society* 2 (4):479–97.

Bijker, Wiebe E., and John Law. 1992. *Shaping Technology / Building Society: Studies in Sociotechnical Change*. Cambridge, MA: MIT Press.

Bourdieu, Pierre. 1998. "The essence of Neoliberalism." *Le Monde Diplomatique* December. http://mondediplo.com.

Bowker, Geoffrey C., and Susan Leigh Star. 1999. *Sorting Things Out: Classification and Its Consequences*. Cambridge, MA: MIT Press.

Brown, Wendy. 2006. "American nightmare: Neoliberalism, Neoconservatism, and de-democratization." *Political Theory* 34 (6):690–714.

Campbell, Nancy D. 2006. "Everyday insecurities: The micro-behavioral politics of intrusive surveillance." In *Surveillance and Security: Technological Politics and Power in Everyday Life*, edited by T. Monahan, 57–75. New York: Routledge.

Castells, Manuel. 1996. *The Rise of the Network Society*. Cambridge, MA: Blackwell Publishers.

de Laet, Marianne, and Annemarie Mol. 2000. "The Zimbabwe bush pump: Mechanics of a fluid technology." *Social Studies of Science* 30 (2):225–63.

Dewey, John. 1916. *Democracy and Education: An Introduction to the Philosophy of Education*. New York: Free Press.

Drakeford, M. 1995. *Token Gesture: A Report on the Use of Token Meters by the Gas, Electricity and Water Companies*. London: National Local Government Forum against Poverty.

Duggan, Lisa. 2003. *The Twilight of Equality? Neoliberalism, Cultural Politics, and the Attack on Democracy*. Boston: Beacon Press.

EPIC (Electronic Privacy Information Center), and PI (Privacy International). 2000. *Threats to Privacy* [Website]. http://www.privacyinternational.org (accessed July 9, 2007.

Eubanks, Virginia. 2006. "Technologies of citizenship: Surveillance and political learning in the welfare system." In *Surveillance and Security: Technological Politics and Power in Everyday Life*, edited by T. Monahan, 89–107. New York: Routledge.

Feenberg, Andrew. 1999. *Questioning Technology*. New York: Routledge.

Fisher, Jill A. 2009. *Medical Research for Hire*. Brunswick, N.J: Rutgers University Press.

Fisher, Jill A., and Lorna Ronald. 2008. "Direct-to-consumer responsibility: Medical Neoliberalism in pharmaceutical advertising and drug development." *Advances in Medical Sociology* 10:29–51.

Fortun, Kim. 2004. "Environmental information systems as appropriate technology." *Design Issues* 20 (3):54–65.

Galloway, Alexander R. 2004. *Protocol: How Control Exists after Decentralization*. Cambridge, Mass.: MIT Press.

Gandy Jr., Oscar. 2006. "Data mining, surveillance, and discrimination in the post-9/11 environment." In *The New Politics of Surveillance and Visibility*, edited by Kevin D. Haggerty and Richard V. Ericson, 363–84. Toronto: University of Toronto Press.

Garland, David. 2001. *The Culture of Control: Crime and Social Order in Contemporary Society*. Chicago: University of Chicago Press.

Giddens, Anthony. 1990. *The Consequences of Modernity*. Stanford: Stanford University Press.

Gilliom, John. 2001. *Overseers of the Poor: Surveillance, Resistance, and the Limits of Privacy*. Chicago: University of Chicago Press.

Giroux, Henry A. 2004. *The Terror of Neoliberalism: Authoritarianism and the Eclipse of Democracy*. Boulder, CO: Paradigm Publishers.

Graham, Stephen, and Simon Marvin. 2001. *Splintering Urbanism: Networked Infrastructures, Technological Mobilities and the Urban Condition*. New York: Routledge.

Graham, Stephen, and David Wood. 2003. "Digitizing surveillance: Categorization, space, inequality." *Critical Social Policy* 23 (2):227–48.

Greenfield, Adam. 2006. *Everyware: The Dawning Age of Ubiquitous Computing*. Berkeley, CA: New Riders.

Haggerty, Kevin D., and Richard V. Ericson. 2006. "The new politics of surveillance and visibility." In *The New Politics of Surveillance and Visibility*, edited by Kevin D. Haggerty and Richard V. Ericson, 3–25. Toronto: University of Toronto Press.

Hardt, Michael, and Antonio Negri. 2000. *Empire*. Cambridge, MA: Harvard University Press.

Harvey, David. 1990. *The Condition of Postmodernity: An Enquiry into the Origins of Cultural Change*. Cambridge, MA: Blackwell.

———. 2005. *A Brief History of Neoliberalism*. Oxford: Oxford University Press.

Hess, David J. 2007. *Alternative Pathways in Science and Industry: Activism, Innovation, and the Environment in an Era of Globalization*. Cambridge, MA: MIT Press.

Howard, Jeff. 2004. "Toward participatory ecological design of technological systems." *Design Issues* 20 (3):40–53.

Illich, Ivan. 1973. *Tools for Conviviality*. New York: Harper & Row.

Juris, Jeffrey S. 2008. *Networking Futures: The Movements Against Corporate Globalization*. Durham: Duke University Press.

Kenner, Alison Marie. 2008. "Securing the elderly body: Dementia, surveillance, and the politics of 'Aging in Place.'" *Surveillance & Society* 5 (3):252–69.

Lessig, Lawrence. 1999. *Code: And Other Laws of Cyberspace*. New York: Basic Books.

Lianos, M., and M. Douglas. 2000. "Dangerization and the end of deviance." *British Journal of Criminology* 40 (2):261–78.

Lynch, Kevin. 1984. *Good City Form*. Cambridge, MA: MIT Press.

Lyon, David. 2001. *Surveillance Society: Monitoring Everyday Life*. Buckingham England: Open University.

———, ed. 2003. *Surveillance as Social Sorting: Privacy, Risk, and Digital Discrimination*. New York: Routledge.

———. 2006. "Why where you are matters: Mundane mobilities, transparent technologies, and digital discrimination." In *Surveillance and Security: Technological Politics and Power in Everyday Life*, edited by T. Monahan, 209–24. New York: Routledge.

———. 2007. *Surveillance Studies: An Overview*. Cambridge: Polity Press.

Martin, Brian, ed. 1999. *Technology and Public Participation*. Wollongong: Science and Technology Studies, University of Wollongong.

Marx, Leo. 1997. "Does improved technology mean progress?" In *Technology and the Future*, edited by A. H. Teich, 3–14. New York: St. Martin's Press.

Monahan, Torin. 2005. *Globalization, Technological Change, and Public Education*. New York: Routledge.

———. 2006. "Questioning surveillance and security." In *Surveillance and Security: Technological Politics and Power in Everyday Life*, edited by T. Monahan, 1–23. New York: Routledge.

———. 2007. " 'War Rooms' of the street: Surveillance practices in transportation control centers." *The Communication Review* 10 (4):367–89.

Monahan, Torin, and Rodolfo D. Torres, eds. 2010. *Schools under Surveillance: Cultures of Control in Public Education*. New Brunswick: Rutgers University Press.

Murakami Wood, David. 2007. "Pervasive surveillance: Enabling environments or embedding inequalities." Paper read at Workshop on Surveillance and Inequality, March 16–18, at Arizona State University.

Nieusma, Dean. 2004. "Alternative design scholarship: Working toward appropriate design." *Design Issues* 20 (3):13–24.

———. 2007. "Challenging knowledge hierarchies: Working toward sustainable development in Sri Lanka's energy sector." *Sustainability: Science, Practice, & Policy* 3 (1):32–44.

Norman, Donald A. 1988. *The Design of Everyday Things*. New York: Doubleday.

Norris, Clive, Jade Moran, and Gary Armstrong. 1998. "Algorithmic surveillance: The future of automated visual surveillance." In *Surveillance, Closed Circuit Television and Social Control*, ed. C. Norris, J. Moran and G. Armstrong, 255–67. Aldershot: Ashgate.

Ottinger, Gwen. 2005. "Grounds for action: Community and science in environmental justice controversy." Doctoral dissertation, Energy and Resources Group, University of California, Berkeley, Berkeley.

Phillips, David J. 2005. "From privacy to visibility. Context, identity, and power in ubiquitous computing environments." *Social Text* 23 (2):95–108.

Porter, Theodore M. 1995. *Trust in Numbers: The Pursuit of Objectivity in Science and Public Life*. Princeton, NJ: Princeton University Press.

Ratcliffe, Mitch and Jon Lebkowsky. 2005. *Extreme Democracy*. Lulu.com.

Rose, Nikolas S. 1999. *Powers of Freedom: Reframing Political Thought*. New York, NY: Cambridge University Press.

Samatas, Minas. 2004. *Surveillance in Greece: From Anticommunist to Consumer Surveillance*. New York: Pella Publishing Company.

Schuler, Douglas, and Aki Namioka. 1993. *Participatory Design: Principles and Practices*. Hillsdale, NJ: Lawrence Erlbaum Associates.

Sclove, Richard E. 1995. *Democracy and Technology*. New York: The Guilford Press.

Simon, Jonathan. 2007. *Governing through Crime: How the War on Crime Transformed American Democracy and Created a Culture of Fear*. Oxford: Oxford University Press.

Staples, William G. 2000. *Everyday Surveillance: Vigilance and Visibility in Postmodern Life*. Lanham, Md.: Rowman & Littlefield Publishers.

Thrift, Nigel, and Shaun French. 2002. "The automatic production of space." *Transactions of the Institute of British Geographers* 27 (4):309–35.

Turow, Joseph. 2006. *Niche Envy: Marketing Discrimination in the Digital Age*. Cambridge, Mass.: MIT Press.

Winner, Langdon. 1977. *Autonomous Technology: Technics-out-of-control as a Theme in Political Thought*. Cambridge, MA: MIT Press.

———. 1986. *The Whale and the Reactor: A Search for Limits in an Age of High Technology*. Chicago: University of Chicago Press.

Woodhouse, Edward, David Hess, Steve Breyman, and Brian Martin. 2002. "Science studies and activism: Possibilities and problems for reconstructivist agendas." *Social Studies of Science* 32 (2):297–319.

Woodhouse, Edward J., and Dean Nieusma. 2001. "Democratic expertise: Integrating knowledge, power, and participation." In *Knowledge, Power and Participation in Environmental Policy Analysis*, edited by M. Hisschemöller, R. Hoppe, W. N. Dunn and J. R. Ravetz, 73–96. New Brunswick, NJ: Transaction Publishers.

Chapter 6

Democracy, surveillance and "knowing what's good for you"

The private sector origins of profiling and the birth of "Citizen Relationship Management"

Kirstie Ball, Elizabeth Daniel, Sally Dibb and Maureen Meadows

Introduction

Using critiques developed in surveillance studies, this chapter examines some of the key issues that arise in using Customer Relationship Management (CRM) techniques for governmental purposes, paying particular attention to its implications for democratic forms of governance. One of the earliest critiques of CRM was that it was an undemocratic mode of social ordering (Lyon, 1994), and its application in governmental contexts challenges democratic principles. This chapter explores this issue in more detail. We begin by giving a brief introduction to the surveillance society, of which CRM is an important facet. The extension of CRM into governmental contexts is examined and critiqued using democratic principles. This raises three questions which need to be addressed in future research. First, given that CRM is predicated on the differential treatment of groups or individuals, how does it interact with the democratic notion that all citizens are equal? Second, by virtue of its focus on predicting and shaping consumer tastes, could CRM also undermine democratic notions of participation? Third, despite claiming to create unique customer "knowledge" and focusing on "relationships," questions remain about the role of accountability and control in such "relationships." We conclude by calling for greater reflexivity about applying CRM in the public sector. This includes a need for research to examine the potential impacts of CRM on democratic rights, individual citizens, and wider population groups.

The surveillance society

This chapter commences from the notion that CRM is a central element of "the surveillance society." Put briefly, in a surveillance society one of the dominant organizing principles is the collection, recording, storage, analysis and application of information on individuals as they go about their daily lives. Surveillance, in this context, refers to the purposeful, systematic, routine, and focused attention to electronic personal information (Surveillance Studies Network, 2006). Personal information can include CCTV images, iris scans, communication records, and data about the person held in numerous private and public-sector databases, such as the United Kingdom's children's database, corporate marketing databases, and so on. To say that surveillance is systematic, purposeful, focused, and routine implies that the scrutiny of personal details is linked to an overarching goal or strategy, is supported by an organizational and governing infrastructure, is woven into the fabric of everyday life, and is concerned with the minutiae of people's lives. As people's daily lives have many different aspects—for example, work, consumption, travel, citizenship, and so on—these form different "domains of surveillance." Within these domains there are different kinds of actors: institutions, business organizations, governments, regulators, individuals, and groups of individuals within a population who are subject to different kinds of data collection, classification, and so on. The surveillance society is not, therefore, a monolith: it is a complex, multi-layered stratification and interrelation of people, communities of practice, organizations, governments, cultures, and systems linked by a common principle—that of surveillance.

From the outset it is important to note that the surveillance we are referring to is not a malign plot hatched by evil powers designed to oppress people. It is also not solely the product of new technologies, nor is it conceptualized by the unidirectional gaze of Big Brother or the inertia of the panopticon. It is intimately connected to a long-term shaping of modern society. As large bureaucracies emerged to manage local areas, business dealings, and governments, the rational bureaucratic ethos, based on the impersonal holding of vast amounts of filed information, meant that people could be dealt with in a standardized fashion. Manipulating and understanding the content of these files became a central part of bureaucratic activity. With information systems enhancing processing power, electronic surveillance was born. Parallel developments in the military regarding tracking and identification techniques made surveillance on a grand scale a real possibility.

In many senses, surveillance bestows benefits and entitlements. It is a normal and often prosaic characteristic of modern life. However, there are various pitfalls in surveillance systems which deserve comment. First of all, being in charge of a surveillance technique or practice bestows power, and it is important that power is wielded fairly, with due respect for human rights, civil liberties, and the law. Wielding surveillance power can have undesirable consequences: for example, leaders appeal to some supposed greater good such as "the war on terror" to justify unusual, draconian, or warlike surveillance tactics directed at citizens which are normally only applied in situations of open conflict. Sifting through consumer records to create a profitable clientele means that certain groups obtain special treatment based on their ability to pay, whereas others fall by the wayside. The form that surveillance takes also conveys a strong message about what is valued and important: it meta-communicates. Surveillance fosters suspicion in those who wield it; it focuses on correcting the abnormal and communicates a message that those who are watched are not to be trusted. Crucial questions arise about the nature of the social worlds created in a surveillance society, pertaining to: accountability, trust, discrimination, participation, and other ethical matters that relate to mass data collection, processing, and application.

CRM and surveillance

Customer Relationship Management (CRM) involves capturing and managing data generated by consumers as they select, purchase, and use products. This, in turn, enables organizations to select, attract, and retain high-value custo-mers. Databases of customer characteristics and buying behavior are used to produce statistical consumer profiles. These profiles can identify the current attractiveness (Zeithaml et al., 2001), value and relative "lifetime value" of customers to the organization (Reichheld, 1996; Reinartz and Kumar, 2003). Such practices, developed originally in the private sector, have now been adopted by public-sector agencies in both central and local government (Cabinet Office, 2000), where CRM now forms a major component of mod-ernization efforts (Cabinet Office, 2005). This widespread use of CRM means that virtually every person in the United Kingdom has a "data double" (Clarke, 1988) stored in one or more databases, even if they did not explicitly elect to join a marketing or loyalty scheme. As CRM uses personal information to differentiate between individuals in their lives as consumers, and is associated with established corporate infrastructures and strategies, it is one manifesta-tion of the wider emergence of a surveillance society (Danna and Gandy, 2002; Graham, 2005; Burrows and Gane, 2006).

According to Ryals and Knox (2001) the CRM philosophy has four elements. First, an orientation towards fostering a long-term relationship with the customer based on their personal preferences in relation to a particular product or service (Gummesson, 1999). Second, a focus on retaining customers and finer definition of customer preferences in order to secure repeat purchases of an organization's products (Verhoef, 2003). Third, that this long-term, focused relationship creates a better and more valuable experience for the customer (Reinartz et al., 2004) and fourth, that the relationship is managed using information technology, typically by holding data about consumer pre-ferences within a database and mining the data for new patterns, profiles, and relationships.(Swift, 2001). Definitions of CRM reflect these different compo-nents. Yuan and Chang (2001) describe CRM as a three-part technological life cycle consisting of: (i) collecting and integrating customer data from a range of sources; (ii) analyzing the data to gain deeper knowledge of customers; and (iii) taking action which will positively shape customer relationships. As Karakostas et al. (2005: 854) explain, implementing CRM involves every aspect of the organization's contact with its customers: "From receiving an order through the delivery of the products and services, CRM aims to co-ordinate all business processes that deal with customers ..."

CRM is much vaunted as a way to enhance business performance (Knox et al., 2003; De Wulf et al., 2001; Galbreath, 1998), and organizations, unsurprisingly, are attracted by its promise of greater profitability. For customers, the benefits include more responsive suppliers, better-tailored products, and enhanced service. CRM is particularly important in the service sector, where the intangible character of products increases the importance of service as a source of competitive advantage (Perrien and Ricard, 1995). Deregulation in some United Kingdom service sectors has also raised the competitive stakes, making protection of the customer base a much higher priority (Reichheld and Sasser, 1990).

The emergence of CRM also reflects the progression from database and niche marketing to relationship management (Peppers and Rogers, 1993). With marketers seeking increasingly detailed customer profiles, CRM capitalizes on IT developments to capture and manage desired customer information. CRM also supports the kind of ongoing customer and supplier conversation which Peppers and Rogers (1993; 1997; 1999) refer to as a "learning relationship," something which is now sought by many service organizations. By combining superior customer information and database marketing capabilities with a commitment to long-term relationships, businesses can better tailor their customer offerings. The use of technology to implement CRM and enhance customer relationships has never been more extensive (Thurston, 2000; Sievewright, 2001).

CRM in the public sector

A number of drivers encourage the uptake of CRM in the public sector. The extensive privatization of public-sector services, which took place in the United Kingdom from the 1980s onwards, produced a concomitant emphasis on the consumption and marketing of government services. The alleged superiority of providing services through the market rather than the public sector established the idea that the "citizen-consumer" is the recipient of public services. Public bodies that serve the "needs" of their relevant populations now contend with market-driven issues such as price and customer choice, retention and relationships. Moreover, consumption now has new political meanings as individuals express their political values through consumption choices (Parker, 1999).

Conceptually, the consumer, as opposed to the citizen, marks a strong distinction between the state and the market. This rise in the figure of the consumer seems to downplay notions of community, collective interest, and social development in favor of a singular fixation on financial efficiency. According to Clarke and Newman (2008), the notion that the "consumer" is the target of government services dates back to critiques of the public sector developed in the 1970s (Nisnaken, 1971). Since then, we have seen the dominance of quasi-market-based approaches to governance, most familiar in citizens' "right to buy" their council homes, "parental choice" in secondary-school selection, and "patient choice" in health services. The current government in the United Kingdom has since committed to the further modernization of public services, something it equates with a greater consumer ethos:

> more markets; more competition between "competing providers"; more devolved management; more governance systems for "managing at a distance"; and a conception of services as being more centred on the needs or wants of their "customers."
>
> (Clarke and Newman, 2008:739)

As a consequence of this approach to public services, marketing has taken a more prominent role in public-sector organizations. Under the rubric of "New Public Management" (Aberbach and Christensen, 2005) the main developments in management practice in the last twenty years have concerned analyzing the quality of services provided, customer relations, market research, public relations, advertising, and promotion. The development of the "internal market" for governmental services has resulted in services being outsourced to the private sector, along with more charging and competitive tendering for service contracts. Public-sector organizations now try to develop corporate images, logos, and identities while customer-care training has become prominent in many front-line roles. Implementing CRM is the latest frontier in the public sector's attempt to target service provision, give citizens more choice, and make them aware of relevant or attractive services. As such, citizen-consumers, who have had their service expectations set by encounters with large private-sector organizations, now seem to expect more personalized and efficient public services that can ostensibly be provided by CRM. Greater focus on citizen-consumer needs may also result in cost reduction, the better targeting of resources, and anticipating emerging needs. The ability of CRM to produce profiles is also cited as a key weapon to counter fraud, particularly benefit fraud, and is already being used for that purpose in the Department of Work and Pensions. Significantly, Hewson et al. (2003) also argue that CRM can be used in election campaigns, particularly to target people who traditionally do not vote. When these factors are coupled with strong overtures from technology companies eager to win lucrative government contracts, the vision of deploying CRM in "joined-up government" and e-government to effectively deliver public services becomes ever more likely.

However, there are also several disincentives to implementing CRM in the public realm. CRM segments the market, but, unlike private-sector organizations, the public sector cannot choose which people they want to serve, or target those who offer the best "lifetime value." In fact, government often has to target people who qualify for a service or benefit, but actively resist approaches from public service organizations. Technology vendors have little experience reaching those who are not already connected to the "consumption infrastructure" through previous purchases, credit-card or internet use. It will therefore likely be hard to use CRM to provide services to difficult-to-reach groups, such as the elderly or learning disabled. There are high political disadvantages of not reaching those groups. Developing and implementing effective CRM strategies may also prove difficult in the public sector because of resource limitations, and the fact that many talented managers are enticed to the private sector by higher salaries. As well as being technology-centered, CRM also involves reconceptualizing how service is delivered, which will involve major organizational changes, including cultural shifts. Actively managing and updating the consumer information database, while maintaining data protection and privacy, will likely be another challenge, as will identifying which measures to use in evaluating service delivery. CRM is therefore not a quick-fix or short-term solution to problems with effectively delivering government services.

Governmental applications of CRM

As is the case with many other surveillance technologies, CRM has already been used for a range of purposes in contexts of both care and control (Lyon, 2001). In each scenario, its appeal has been based on the predictive and pre-emptive possibilities of mining data for patterns and relationships, which can then be used to focus the deployment of organizational resources and accrue benefits. In the public sector, one example is provided by Sussman and Galizio (2003). Their extensive research demonstrates that CRM is used in electoral campaigns all over the world. They argue that the growing use of political consultants to conduct electoral campaigns has resulted in targeting votes through an expansive use of marketing techniques. The consultants who manage such campaigns are skilled in modern fundraising techniques, knowledgeable about the use of ICTs, and are well connected in the media. As Sussman and Galizio (2003:314) note:

> ... media consultants draw on the success of modern commodity advertising to *sell* [their emphasis] candidates, emphasising not so much their content (issues) as their image, employing the constant use of focus groups and polling not to incorporate public demand as much as to hone a saleable message and test the effectiveness of their political propaganda. The information base developed in electronic consumer surveillance for marketing products and brands is appropriated for marketing candidates. Voters are seen by consultants not as citizens but as political consumers.

Alternatively, CRM has also been used in the United Kingdom to target health-care advice and treatment to "at risk" groups, such as smokers and the obese. Even more prominently, CRM has been used in national-security applications. This is most apparent in how profiling and the pre-emptive screening of potential "terrorists" draws upon CRM techniques. Since 9/11, counter-terrorism measures in the United Kingdom and United States have relied upon CRM practices conducted by private financial and travel organizations. With governments attempting to stem the international flow of terrorist funds, financial services institutions in G7 countries must now monitor their customers' accounts for suspicious transactions and are also subject to a range of international financial governance measures. The premise is that terrorist networks can be detected before any terrorism occurs, and to that end institutions are now using techniques to profile the predictability of their customers' financial behavior (Vlcek, 2008; Canhoto and Backhouse, 2007; Amoore and DeGoede, 2005). The same is true in the travel industry, which was initially the hardest hit by 9/11 as air travel declined and customer service levels decreased due to long waits at airport security checks. The government in the United Kingdom is currently implementing a comprehensive e-Borders program, which features, among other things, detailed risk profiling of travelers. Both airlines and travel operators acknowledge that they use CRM to profile individuals before they travel. If such profiles are combined with judgments about likely criminality, numerous ethical issues arise as to how this could affect individual liberty (Turow 2006, Elmer 2004). Given these developments, it is timely to consider the desirability of expanding to governmental contexts this avowedly private-sector and market-based approach to selling products.

Ultimately, different assumptions underpin marketing in the private as opposed to the public sector. In the private sector, the consumer is said to be "sovereign," and winning their business is paramount. Corporations see it as crucial to provide suitable goods or services at the right price and distribute those through appropriate channels to encourage repeat business. It is also vital to ensure customer satisfaction and prevent people from exiting a particular marketplace, while also ensuring that goods and services are distributed to geographically dispersed consumers. For services in the public sector, the assumptions are somewhat different. For example, collective choices are expected to dominate when implementing policy. Public services also need to be resourced effectively, regardless of fluctuations in demand. Because public resources are scarce, it is reasonable that resources should be targeted. Services are ideally distributed in a manner promoting fair and just outcomes for citizens, which means that they are assigned according to particular needs, rather than the ability to pay. It is more important in the public sector to encourage wider inclusion and different forms of political participation, rather than repeat purchase and excluding those with a lower "lifetime value" to the organization.

Many of these assumptions affect the degree to which CRM is suitable for use in the public sector. The key question is whether CRM can be used as an appropriate technique to provide social benefits given its individualist ethos and basis in economic transactions. Notwithstanding all of these difficulties, using CRM may present a helpful solution to the problem of targeting scarce resources at the most needy. The remainder of this paper reviews CRM practice in greater detail and highlights some of the conceptual and practical issues involved in applying this technology in the public sector.

Practical issues with CRM

A number of research findings highlight how, even in the private sector, applying CRM can be problematic. Comparable concerns are likely to arise in the public sector. The first set of findings address difficulties with implementing CRM and the varying degrees of sophistication in how it is used. The second set of findings concern the accuracy of profiles, and the third highlight ethical issues surrounding applying such profiles.

Implementation and uptake

In spite of its well-publicized potential, organizations use CRM with varying degrees of sophistication, from using it as a blunt instrument to a finely crafted tool (Dibb and Meadows, 2004). Studies also show that CRM is not uniformly implemented and that its processes and outcomes are not a foregone conclusion (Karakostas et al., 2005). Such variability is partly a result of the many and diverse challenges which can arise when embracing a relationship approach (Dibb and Meadows, 2001; Perrien and Ricard, 1995). Dibb and Meadows (2004) consider progress towards using CRM on the basis of a number of "hard" (the *customers* and *technology* used) and "soft" (the *company* and its *staff*) dimensions and use these factors to classify a financial services firm's progress in implementing relationship management. They find that while investments in appropriate technology and systems can readily alleviate some of the harder barriers, the softer issues pertaining to corporate culture and staff orientation can be much more problematic. This is consistent with the view of other authors who suggest that despite the importance of different roles and perspectives of organizational members for the success of CRM (Srivastava et al. 1999), there continues to be a dearth of empirical research into these factors (Hart et al., 2002; Plakoyiannaki, 2005). Indeed, only one study has been conducted to date examining changes to employment conditions brought about by CRM (Kwakkelstein, 2002). This study of a call center found that using CRM to manage "one to one" relationships with customers meant employees were subject to more rules regarding customer interaction, and found their autonomy, decision latitude, and level of creativity all diminished.

Creating profiles

By its very nature, CRM is a discriminating technology: it seeks ways to make organizations treat their customers differently based upon their personal characteristics or habits. Traditionally, CRM has been used to define customer attractiveness, value, and benefit, and promises organizations a great deal in terms of enhanced profits and customer relationships. However, as most people have a "data double," we are all increasingly scrutinized by algorithms, for all kinds of reasons. This is particularly disconcerting given that CRM may be used to identify and screen out "risky," "undesirable," or "criminal" elements.

As the stakes of using consumer profiles are raised, their accuracy becomes critical. However, research to date accentuates how the techniques used to create profiles consistently produce errors and biases. Errors occur so often that it has been observed that CRM is nearly always "wrong" at the level of the individual (Berry and Linoff, 2000). Such errors occur in many ways, most conspicuously when databases are combined, inaccurate or unrepresentative data are used, and missing data are "filled in" (Danna and Gandy, 2002). Recent evidence (Canhoto, 2007; Beckett and Nayak, 2008) also suggests that producing profiles is a socially embedded practice that replicates the prejudices of CRM experts. Such prejudices can become manifest, for example, in the algorithms used to identify risk, entitlement, and criminality. This is consistent with studies of other surveillance practices which demonstrate how the prejudices of workers become mobilized as surveillance technology is applied (Smith, 2007; Norris and Armstrong, 1998). As a result, data subjects can suffer unjust discrimination, or may be allocated to inappropriate categories. Moreover, such inadequacies tend to perpetuate themselves because it can be both expensive and complicated to replace a legacy system (Head, 2007). Given that being in the "wrong category" can result in having one's assets frozen, being deported, or imprisoned, any shortcomings in creating profiles are critically important.

Applying profiles

Despite being virtual creations, profiles have very real consequences for customers, and the employees who must interact with customers. Profiles are commonly based on geodemographic information and consumption patterns, and seek to ascribe economic worth to different groups of people. When particular consumption patterns or preferences are combined with geographic information such as postcodes, lifestyles and places begin to merge (Burrows and Gane 2006) and neighborhood characteristics come to determine the products and services offered to individuals living in specific areas. Some of these characteristics include discriminatory categories that would be illegal in other settings. For example, in the noteworthy American legal case of *Cherry v Amoco Oil*

Co., it was revealed that a white woman who lived in a predominantly black neighborhood was refused a credit card not because of her personal credit history, but because the credit-checking system considered her residential postcode to be too risky. Profiles can concretize prejudices and link such biases not only to economic opportunity but also to access to public services. Moreover, there is the danger that those with alternative and marginalized lifestyles who do not "register" in the system—for example, if they do not have a passport, do not use mainstream banks, and predominantly use cash—may start to form an excluded underclass (Amoore and DeGoede, 2005).

Surveillance, democracy and CRM: conceptual issues

The issues related to the use of CRM reviewed in the previous sections suggest that there are also conceptual issues relating to whether it is appropriate to use CRM in governmental contexts. In light of such issues, we identify three questions which should be addressed in future critical debates and research studies. First, by virtue of its ability to discriminate between groups or individuals, how does CRM interact with the democratic notion that all citizens are equal? Second, in focusing on predicting and shaping consumer tastes, how does CRM interact with democratic notions of public participation? Third, despite its apparently benign efforts to create unique customer "knowledge" and "relationships," what locus of control and discipline is created in such "relationships?"

CRM and citizen equality

Our first question, linked with the discriminatory consequences of the surveillance society, concerns how CRM interacts with the democratic notions of citizenship: that all citizens are equal and that the citizen is a unified entity. CRM is a technique which discriminates among different groups of consumers in terms of the "value" they offer an organization. Discrimination is based on geographical location, and many other personal characteristics such as race, gender, age, and so on. A CRM approach, which provides different levels of services to different groups of consumers, may not translate well to a public-sector context where equality of access for all is a maxim. Moreover, some citizens receiving a higher standard of service than others is antithetical to the democratic ideal of equal citizens.

As part of this process, the person, as represented in the CRM system, becomes a divided self. It is "split," disaggregated, and appears first as a "consumer of relative value" and then as a series of variables in which the organization has an interest. As Zwick and Dholakia (2004) observe, as mass consumer information becomes aggregated data, the net effect is to disaggregate representations of the consumer from their whole, co-present identity. Instead of "individuals," or sovereign, bounded entities, they become "dividuals" (Deleuze 1990), partial representations of the embodied person. Aberbach and Christensen (2005: 226) argue that viewing sovereign citizens as consumers is akin to adopting a "liberal" and self-interested definition of the citizen, where citizenship is seen as "a set of individual rights, rather than a set of obligations to others in the community or nation." The latter obligations are typical of a "republican" definition of citizenship, where citizens view themselves as part of a community, which itself has interests, as well as being self-interested. As a corollary, Fitchett and McDonagh (2000) comment that CRM's orientation towards "micromarketing," a focus on the profit motive and satisfying individual needs, rather than "macromarketing," which takes in broader societal concerns, may underplay environmental, social-justice, or community issues associated with government. Fitchett and McDonagh (2000: 219) argue that CRM theory "negates the role of the citizenry in its conceptualisation ..." hence ignoring any collective, societal or environmental interests the consumer may have, unless they are relevant to the consumer profile. Instead, the focus is entirely on the individual consumer, their stream of consumption decisions and their individual relationship with a particular organization or set of organizations with interlinked products. Within this view, a singular focus on consumer "satisfaction" is "at best ill conceived and at worst a threat to self government, and, therefore, profoundly undemocratic" (Aberback and Christensen, 2005: 227). A focus on the individual consumer by definition excludes issues of community to concentrate on individual wants and needs. Hence, aspirations towards equality and social justice are in danger of being overtaken by a fixation on customer service.

That said, a sophisticated and reflexive application of CRM in governmental contexts that aims to identify and target resources specifically towards disadvantaged groups may help to redress inequalities. Because of power differentials and differential access to resources, government would still find it easier to serve some groups than others. Hence, for CRM to be used progressively, considerable effort would have to be invested to identify disadvantaged groups. Any consideration of the differential supply of public services to citizens should therefore not rely solely on "customer focused" or private-sector values.

CRM and participation

Our second question, based on the ability of CRM to pre-empt and predict patterns of consumer behavior, concerns how it may negatively affect democratic participation. In the private sector, CRM is used to identify the consumption patterns of assorted groups and to undertake differentiated actions based on these patterns. This includes predicting their future needs and using those predictions as the basis for resource allocation, securing revenues and developing marketing and other communications strategies. The focus of CRM on pre-emption highlights the prescriptive approach that is often taken to consumer demands, as the intent in certain circumstances is to decide what is "best" for a particular consumer group before pitching an offer to the already defined marketplace (Fitchett and McDonagh, 2000). Using CRM within certain governmental contexts to predetermine provisions according to the organization's assessment of "need" may therefore curtail a citizen's right to participate in that process. For example, voting is a fundamental element of political participation. As Sussman and Galizio (2003) point out, using consumer data to target election messages to different sections of the electorate compromises the freedom of information underpinning individual voting decisions.

CRM, accountability and control

Our final point, stemming from issues in the surveillance society relating to accountability, concerns the nature of relationships produced by CRM, something that is significant given that CRM stands for "customer *relationship* management." Proponents of CRM argue that understanding past consumption patterns, and cross-referencing transactional data with all manner of other data relating to individual consumers, presents organizations with an opportunity to "know" and enter into a long term "relationship" with their customers. Managers then decide whether the customer's spending brings sufficient value to the organization to justify holding on to them with offers, superior service, and so on.

However, the resulting relationship is more akin to discipline and control than based on humanitarian principles (see also Murakami Wood and Ball 2008; Fitchett and McDonagh, 2000). An enormous imbalance of power is created by the opacity and commercial sensitivity of data-mining techniques, which are owned by large organizations and applied on large disaggregated consumer populations, sometimes without their knowledge (Ball, 2002). While proponents of CRM say that the relationships created between consumers and organizations are mutually beneficial, they are not mutually determined or negotiated. Indeed, surveillance scholars have long criticized CRM's application of profiles, which subtly restructures society according to economic means and consumption patterns. This is an undemocratic form of social ordering because it is unaccountable to the layperson. Individuals and groups find it difficult to discover what happens to their personal information, who handles it, when, and for what purpose. Most of the time, ordinary citizens and consumers simply do not have the time or the incentive to go in search of such details. Given the emphasis of CRM on a lifetime relationship with the consumer, and the differentiated impact of CRM-fuelled marketing on their lives, it seems fair that the consumer should be able to see the kinds of decisions which are taken by the organizations using their data (Surveillance Studies Network, 2006; Zweick and Dholakia, 2004). No such mechanism exists in relation to consumer data, yet the massive data-power of a Tesco or a

Wal-Mart is almost unparalleled. The emergence of today's surveillance society demands that we shift from self-protection of privacy to the account-ability of data-handlers. Such work parallels the efforts of regulators to enforce controls and to press for minimizing of surveillance. So, in govern-mental contexts, the question concerns how elected representatives can hold CRM accountable, but uncovering the complexities of CRM practice, includ-ing the creation and application of profiles, has proved a very difficult task for researchers to date.

A brief conclusion

Although CRM is not used universally or uniformly, its application is wide-spread and growing in popularity. CRM as it is currently used in the private sector emphasizes some of the problems and concerns inherent in the surveil-lance society, particularly the accountability of surveillance organizations for their data-handling practices, discrimination between sections of the popula-tion, democratic participation, and control over information use. Surveillance scholars have argued that the private-sector use of CRM is an undemocratic mode of social ordering, because the data-mining associated with it presents different opportunities to different sections of society.

In considering the growing application of CRM in the public sector we urge caution. This is because, in many ways, the principles of CRM do not rest well with democratic notions associated with the unity and equality of citizens, open participation in political processes, and transparent and accountable governance. Indeed a key message is that when CRM is used in government extreme reflexivity should be encouraged, particularly because of its surveillant consequences and its potential conflict with democratic values. Research on private-sector uses of CRM so far has shown that it is fraught with pitfalls, and indeed that it is not associated with any singular outcome. The relative "success" of a CRM scheme is tempered by a number of factors. First, orga-nizational heritage and culture shape CRM, something that is exacerbated in the public sector because of traditions which do not prioritize customer ser-vice. Second, the creation and application of profiles has been shown by research to occasionally feature inaccurate and unethical characterizations which are difficult to erase because of legacy systems.

However, because of the contextual differences between private and public-sector applications of CRM, particularly because of the less commercial nature of the public sector, an opportunity is presented to democratize CRM practice in the public sector.

Problems of accountability, which in the private sector are attributed to "commercial sensitivity," could be overcome because of the non-profit nature of service provision in the public sector. Public reporting on data-mining structures, criteria, and decisions would illuminate and remedy some of the less savory, and, indeed, discriminatory bases of the practice, presenting an extension of opportunities for participation in civic decision-making. This is particularly relevant in the context of national security and benefit claims, where the basis of risky categorizations could be more finely honed and less based on blanket categorizations relating to ethnicity or economic position. Moreover, if applied reflexively and openly, CRM could be used proactively to redress inequalities and promote health and other benefits for citizens.

The danger, however, remains that by "reducing" citizens to consumers in different governmental contexts, the presence and exercise of democratic principles could be overlooked or negated.

References

Aberbach, J. D., and T. Christensen. 2005. "Citizens and consumers: An NPM dilemma." *Public Management Review* 7 (2):225–45.

Amoore, L., and M. deGoede. 2005. "Governance, risk and dataveillance in the war on terror." *Crime, Law and Social Change* 43:149–73.

Ball, K., 2002. "Elements of surveillance: A new framework and future directions." *Information, Communication and Society* 5 (4):573–90.

Beckett, A., and A. Nayak. 2008. "Governing the consumer: Every little helps." *Paper presented at the 25th EGOS colloquium.* Amsterdam 10th – 12th July.

Berry, M., and G. Linoff. 2000. *Mastering Data Mining.* New York: Wiley.

Burrows, R., and N. Gane. 2006. "Geodemographics, software and class." *Sociology* 40 (5):793–812.

Cabinet Office. 2005. *Connecting the United Kingdom: The Digital Strategy.* Prime Minister's Strategy Unit and the Department of Trade and Industry.

———. 2000. *eGov – Electronic Government Services for the 21st Century* Performance and Innovation Unit.

Canhoto, A. I. 2007. *Detecting Undesirable Customers: Context and Cognition in Profiling.* Unpublished manuscript.

Canhoto, A., and J. Backhouse. 2007. "Profiling under conditions of ambiguity: An application in the financial services industry." *Journal of Retailing and Consumer Services* 14:408–19.

Cherry vs Amoco Oil Co 490 F Supp 1026 (ND Ga 1980).

Clarke, J., and J. Newman. 2008. "What's in a name?" *Cultural Studies* 21 (4):738–57.

Clarke, R. 1988. "Information technology and dataveillance." *Communications of the ACM* 31 (5):498–512.

Danna, A., and O.H. Gandy. 2002. "All that glitters is not gold: Digging beneath the surface of data mining." *Journal of Business Ethics* 40 (4):373–86.

Deleuze, G. 1990. *Negotiations.* New York: Columbia University Press.

De Wulf, K., G. Odekerken-Schröder, and D. Iacobucci. 2001. "Investments in consumer relationships: A cross-country and cross-industry exploration." *Journal of Marketing* 65 (October):33–50.

Dibb, S., and M. Meadows. 2001. "The application of a relationship marketing perspective in retail banking." *The Service Industries Journal* 21 (1):169–94.

———. 2004. "Relationship marketing and CRM: A financial services case study." *Journal of Strategic Marketing* 12:111–25.

Elmer, G. 2004. *Profiling Machines*. Cambridge, Mass: MIT Press.

Fitchett, J A., and P. McDonagh. 2000. "A citizen's critique of relationship marketing in a risk society." *Journal of Strategic Marketing* 8:209–22.

Galbreath, J. 1998. "Relationship management environments." *CreditWorld* November-December:14–21.

Graham, S. 2005. "Software sorted geographies." *Progress in Human Geography* 29 (5):562–80.

Gummesson, C. 1999. *Total Relationship Marketing, Rethinking Marketing Management: From 4Ps to 30 Rs*. Oxford: Butterworth-Heinemann.

Hart, S., G. Hogg and M. Bannerjee. 2002. "An examination of primary stakeholders' opinions in CRM: Convergence and divergence?" *Journal of Customer Behaviour* 1:159–74.

Head, B. 2007. "Managing the legacy portfolio." *CIO* June:3–4.

Hewson, W., D. Hicks, A. Meekings, M. Stone and N. Woodcock. 2003. "CRM in the public sector in CMAT." *State Of The Nation III: A Global Study Of How Companies Manage Their Customers*. CMAT report.

Karakostas, B., D. Kardaras and E. Papathanassiou. 2005. "The state of CRM adoption by the financial services in the United Kingdom: An empirical investigation." *Information and Management* 42:853–63.

Knox, S., S. Maklan, A. Payne, J. Peppard and L. Ryals. 2003. *Customer Relationship Management: Perspectives from the Market Place*. London: Butterworth-Heinemann.

Kwakkelstein, T. 2002. "Customer over employee?" *Paper Presented at Emergence 2002*. http://www.emergence.nu (accessed March 2008).

Lyon, D. 1994. *The Electronic Eye: The Rise of Surveillance Society*. Cambridge: Polity.

——2001. *Surveillance Society: Monitoring Everyday Life*. Milton Keynes: Open University Press.

Murakami Wood, D., and K. Ball. 2008. "Brandscapes of control: Managing subjects and spaces in late capitalism." *Paper Presented at "InVisibilities", the 3rd Surveillance and Society Conference*, University of Sheffield April 2–3.

Nisnaken, W.A. 1971. *Bureaucracy and Representative Government*. New York: Aldine-Atherton.

Norris, C., and G. Armstrong. 1998. *The Maximum Surveillance Society: The Rise of CCTV*. London: Berg.

Parker, G. 1999. "The role of the consumer-citizen in environmental protest in the 1990s." *Space and Policy* 3(1):67–83

Peppers, D., and M. Rogers. 1993. *The One-to-One Future*. Piatkus: London.

——. 1997. Enterprise One-to-One. Tools for Competing in the Interactive Age. New York: Currency Doubleday.

——. 1999. The One-to-One Manager. New York: Currency Doubleday.

Perrien, J., and L. Ricard. 1995. "The meaning of a marketing relationship: A pilot study." *Industrial Marketing Management* 24:37–43.

Plakoyiannaki, E. 2005. "How do organisational members perceive CRM? Evidence from a U.K. service firm." *Journal of Marketing Management* 21:363–92.

Reichheld, F.F. 1996. *The Loyalty Effect*. Boston: Harvard Business School Press.

Reichheld, F.F., and W.E. Jr. Sasser. 1990. "Zero defections: Quality comes to services." *Harvard Business Review* 68 (September-October):105–10.

Reinartz, W.J., M. Kraft and W.D. Hoyer. 2004. "The customer relationship management process: Its measurement and impact on performance." *Journal of Marketing Research* 41 (August):293–305.

Reinartz, W.J., and V. Kumar. 2003. "The impact of customer relationship characteristics on profitability lifetime duration." *Journal of Marketing* 67 (January):77–99.

Ryals, L. and S. Knox. 2001. "Cross-functional issues in the implementation of relationship marketing through customer relationship management." *European Management Journal* 19 (5):534–42.

Sievewright, M. 2001. "Charting the future of financial services." *Credit Union Magazine* 67 (4):S4–S6.

Smith, G. J. D. 2007. "Exploring relations between watchers and watched in control systems: Strategies and tactics." Surveillance and Society 4(4):280–313.

Srivastava, R.K., T.A. Shrevani and L. Fahey.1999. "Marketing business processes, and shareholder value: An organizationally embedded view of marketing activities and the discipline of marketing." *Journal of Marketing* 63 (special issue):168–79.

Surveillance Studies Network. 2006. A Report on the Surveillance Society. Wilmslow: Information Commissioners Office.

Sussman, G., and L. Galizio. 2003. "The global reproduction of American politics." *Political Communication* 20 (3):309–28.

Swift, R.S. 2001. *Accelerating Customer Relationships: Using CRM and Relationship Technologies.* Upper Saddle River, New Jersey: Prentice Hall.

Thurston, C. 2000. "Financial services lead the way." *Global Finance* 14 (1):114–16.

Turow, J. 2006. *Niche Envy: Marketing Discrimination in the Digital Age.* Cambridge MA: MIT Press.

Verhoef, P.C. 2003. "Understanding the effect of customer relationship management efforts on customer retention and customer share development." *Journal of Marketing* 67 (October):30–45.

Vlcek, W. 2008. "A leviathan rejuvenated: Money laundering and the war on terror." *International Journal of Politics, Culture and Sociology* http://www.springerlink.com (accessed March 2008).

Walsh, K. 1991. "Citizens and consumers: Marketing and public sector management." *Public Money and Management* Summer: 9–15.

Yuan, S.T., and W.L. Chang. 2001. "Mixed-initiative synthesised learning approach for web-based CRM." *Expert Systems with Applications* 20:187–200.

Zeithaml, V.A., R.T. Rust and K.N. Lemon. 2001. "The customer pyramid: Creating and serving profitable customers." *California Management Review* 43 (4):118–42.

Zwick, D., and N. Dholakia. 2004. "Whose identity is it anyway? Consumer representation in the age of database marketing." *Journal of Macromarketing* 24 (31):31–43.

Chapter 7

The impact of communications data retention on fundamental rights and democracy – the case of the EU Data Retention Directive

Lilian Mitrou

Communications data retention as an answer to "pressing security needs"?

The images of the 9/11 terrorist attacks put "security" back on the political agenda with both a vengeance and a new accentuation. At the end of 2001 there was no doubt among the public or in political circles that 9/11 would trigger immediate legislative action. Legislative activism, expressed through regulations like the US Patriot Act or the European Union Data Retention Directive, was fuelled by the assumption that—despite the existence of information which might have thwarted the terrorists—the intelligence and law-enforcement agencies were unable to "connect the dots" to prevent the attacks (Taipale, 2004/2005). Added to this assumption was the widely shared belief that the existing legal framework contained considerable security deficiencies (Lepsius, 2004).

In the wake of a series of attacks in North America and Europe, security officials reintroduced proposals that had previously had "no chance to be accepted" (Hoffman-Riem, 2002: 498) or had been rejected on the grounds that they encroached too far upon civil rights and liberties (Levi and Wall, 2004). Threats were seen as arising from a qualitatively new and intangible terror network, which changed the geometry of freedom and security. Consequently, as Lepsius (2004) notes, "Whether a need for legislative regulation existed was never in doubt; the question of the 'if' had been answered by the evidence and needed no justification" (Lepsius, 2004:438). This perception reflects a disregard for fundamental civil rights and liberties, which characterizes many of the new, security-oriented, legislative initiatives.

The attacks in New York, Madrid, and London facilitated and accelerated the move towards policing focused on collecting intelligence (Institute for Prospective Technological Studies 2003). Access to communications content is a common way of gathering information for criminal investigations and security purposes. However, in the emerging "information society" more relationships and social interactions occur via electronic communications networks. It is not only the content of such information that is useful to the police and the security agencies; data on the use of communications systems are a valuable resource in preventing, investigating, detecting, and prosecuting threats and crimes. Communications data are used to trace and locate the source and route of information as well as to collect and secure evidence: "allowing investigators for example to establish links between suspected conspirators (itemized bill) or to ascertain the whereabouts of a given person at a given time, thereby confirming or disproving an alibi" (UK Home Office, 2002).

In Europe, the debate over the retention of communication data did not originate in recent terrorist attacks. Data-protection legislation now requires communication providers to erase traffic data, which includes information on source and recipient of the communication together with information on time, date, duration, location of devices, as soon as it is no longer needed for billing purposes. For several years, law-enforcement agencies in various European countries have urged governments to adopt retention requirements. As a compromise solution, the EU e-Privacy Directive (2002) provided that member states were allowed to adopt legislative measures to retain data for a limited period, if these are necessary to safeguard national security, defence, and public security, and prevent, investigate, detect and prosecute criminal offences, and so on. (Art. 15 § 1).

The call for harmonized data-retention legislation arose as a result of the Madrid train bombings in March 2004. Four years later, the permissive language of the e-Privacy Directive has been transformed into an obligation imposed on EU member states. Service and network providers situated in European Union member states are or will be legally mandated to indiscriminately retain all communication data of all subscribers. The Directive applies to electronic communication services offered via the internet, but it does not apply to the content of the communications. Data is to be retained for a period of six months to two years (depending on the member state) for the purpose of the potential investigation, detection, and prosecution of serious crime, and made available to the designated authorities, in the cases provided by domestic law. The "prevention" of crime was ultimately excluded from the scope of the Directive as a result of a privacy-enhancing approach adopted by the European Parliament and the critical voices of European data-protection commissioners who opposed the wide ambit inherent in a "preventive" approach. National legislators have to specify the procedures to be followed and the conditions to be fulfilled in order to gain access to retained data "in accordance with necessity and proportionality requirements" (Art. 4 of Data Retention Directive).

This regulatory development still raises significant concerns about the respect for privacy and other fundamental rights and freedoms. To date, European critics have focused on the disproportionality of the adopted measures, in particular their impingement on existing rights and liberties of the overwhelming majority of the population. This chapter, by focusing on the 2006 EU Data Retention Directive, addresses the question of data retention as a method of mass communications surveillance. It suggests that generalized and indiscriminate data retention reflects a shift from a constitutional state guarding against the threat of specific risks in concrete situations toward a security-oriented preventive, or even pre-emptive, state, which acts or is expected to act proactively.

Retention of communications data is discussed as a security measure, one which interferes with the right to privacy, freedom of communication, and freedom of expression. Privacy, in our approach, is not merely a residuum or a right "possessed" by individuals, but is a condition for making autonomous decisions, freely communicating with other persons, and participating in a democratic society, all of which are jeopardized by data-retention practices. There is a serious concern that data-retention policies may endanger open communication and affect democratic participation with further and considerable impacts on democracy.

Data retention and the changing range and nature of communications

Data-retention practices—understood as a "soft security measure"—mainly seek to exploit the interactivity of information communication technologies to identify risky individuals and the networks in which they operate (Levi and Wall, 2004). The convergence of communications and information technologies over the past few decades has led to more diverse technologies being used for personal communications. New, sophisticated technologies have also given governments and law-enforcement agencies an unprecedented ability to engage in powerful mass surveillance (Solove, 2004). The legal apparatus of data retention reflects new powers, investigative methods, and procedures, all supported by a new technological environment. The far-reaching impacts of communications surveillance on rights and liberties cannot be assessed without considering the technological mechanisms that enable the monitoring of systems as well as the deep changes in communicational exchanges that these mechanisms support or initiate.

In recent years the prevalence of the expression "telecommunications" has been steadily replaced by the term "(electronic) communications," which, in the wording of the relevant European Union regulatory framework, refers to the "conveyance of signals on electronic communications networks" (*Directive 2002/21/EC on a common regulatory framework for electronic communications networks and services*). The use of this expression makes it clear "that the form and the content of any communicative exchange is as central to [tele] communications as the technological system in place to enable it" (Green, 2006: 2). An exchange of signals or data between technological devices includes or generates mechanisms to monitor and store the information being exchanged. The digitalization of data and communication structures makes it possible to scrutinize and manipulate previously unimaginable amounts of information. Surveillance potential expands exponentially through data collection, storage, and mining as communication technologies become more interconnected and are used more extensively and intensively.

Different communications infrastructures aim to retain different forms of transactional data (Rotenberg et al., 2006). The relevant European statutes, which regulate the use of such transactions, cover traffic data either "in a technology neutral way," (i.e. the e-Privacy Directive, which addresses traditional circuit-switched telephony as well as packet-switched internet transmission) or in a functional way (i.e. the Data Retention Directive, which deals with any data necessary to identify the subscriber or user, as well as the source and the destination of a communication). Technological neutrality, in this sense, is regarded by policy-makers and legislators as necessary, if not unavoidable (World Summit on the Information Society, 2003). Technology-specific formulations that refer to the means of communication are undesirable in view of the "technological turbulence" at stake (Koops, 2006). Technology-neutral laws are also preferred by industry, which holds that legislation should not discriminate against certain technologies (Samuelson, 2000). ICT legislation should abstract away from concrete technologies in order to cope with technological changes and provide legal certainty. However the use of technology-neutral language ignores the specific challenges and risks of applying legal powers to different technological infrastructures (Escudero and Hosein, 2004).

Defenders of the new data-retention measures point out that the Data Retention Directive does not allow the content of communications to be monitored. In the landscape of electronic communications, however, the frontiers between communication data and content (the so called "envelope–content principle") no longer necessarily reflect a distinction between "sensitive" and "innocuous" information (Solove, 2004; Mitrou, 2008). Numerous network services cannot be easily categorized by distinguishing between data content and data traffic. The ambiguity of this separation is particularly acute in internet communication, as it is highly uncertain whether email, instant messaging, and other online activities analogous to "speaking" could be covered by this traditional distinction between content and envelope. In the case of an internet search that uses Google or AltaVista, for example, a result like "www.google.com/sites/web?q=aids+medical+treatment" reveals not only data necessary for the conveyance of an electronic communication but also elements of content, information which at least indicates the interests of the user (Coemans and Dumortier, 2003). The subject line of an email or the name of an attached file (for example "Communistmanifesto.doc" or "BinLaden.doc") could also arguably be viewed as data content. Technological changes such as the growing use of the Voice over Internet Protocol (VoIP), with which telephony signals are digitized and transmitted as "data packets" to their destination, are likely to have profound implications on an approach to communications that relies upon a distinction between content and external data. For example, VoIP telephony destroys the "old" distinction between "voice" and "data" (Shin, 2006) and creates the potential for telephone conversations to be routinely stored by the parties involved in the communications as well as being stored at the network level (Swire, 2004).

Apart from the difficulties of establishing clear distinctions between content and traffic data, it is disputable if—under changing technological circumstances—the surveillance of content is necessarily more of a privacy invasion than the retention of and access to traffic data. The informative value and the usability of traffic data is extremely high as they can be analyzed automatically, combined with other data, searched for specific patterns, and sorted according to various criteria (Breyer, 2005). It is worth mentioning that authorities are often, at least initially, only interested in obtaining traffic data (German Working Group against Data Retention, 2007). Without ignoring the particularities of monitored infrastructures and the data being retained, it is important to stress the unique feature of data retention as a method to gather information. Data-retention practices allow law-enforcement authorities to analyze the wealth of data at their disposal and develop models of what constitutes normal and "suspicious" communications networks, identifying individuals for further investigation (Crump, 2003).

When individuals communicate using such systems they often have a false sense of privacy and anonymity. There are an increasing number of situations in which users are either unaware that data is being collected about their behavior, that the communication systems used are accessed by authorities, or that users are unable to control such scrutiny. The exponential increase of internet use, in combination with the pervasive nature of online information-management systems, makes it extremely difficult for end-users to identify interference and abuse. The internet increases the quality, quantity, and accessibility of personal information relating to personal behavior, both in cyberspace and real space. It reduces the previous scope of zones-of-data anonymity and heightens uncertainty about which people or organizations are utilizing personal information, and the purposes and circumstances of such use (Schwartz 1999). However, it is exactly communication data retention which "dramatically re-architects the Internet from a medium that promotes relative obscurity to one of relative transparency" (Crump, 2003:192). By exploiting the specific features of information and communications technologies (ICT), data-retention practices make the past and the present evermore traceable, and in doing so jeopardize the privacy of individuals.

Data retention as interference with fundamental rights and freedoms: privacy, freedom of expression and freedom of movement

Privacy is commonly perceived as freedom from unwarranted and arbitrary interference from public authorities and/or private bodies into activities that society recognizes as belonging to the realm of individual autonomy (the private sphere) (EU Network of Independent Experts in Fundamental Rights 2003). However, it is not only a matter of preventing one's life choices from being conditioned by public and/or private influence. European theory and jurisprudence—including the jurisprudence of the European Court of Human Rights—do not restrict privacy considerations to conditions of "total secrecy" and/or "separateness." On the contrary, the European courts have provided expansive interpretations of the ECHR's reference to "private life." In its jurisprudence the European Court of Human Rights admitted that the scope of Art. 8 extends to the right of the individual "to establish and develop relationships with other human beings" (*Court of Human Rights, P.G. vs. United Kingdom, Niemitz vs. Germany*). The need for privacy emerges from within society itself.

The European approach towards privacy is largely grounded in the dignity of the person, understood as those individuals who operate in a self-determining fashion as members of a free society (German Federal Constitutional Court Census case, 1983). If a person can be "technologically invaded" then not only is their freedom diminished but so is their personal dignity (Marx, 2001). Within the concept of privacy, dignity refers to principles such as the protection of an individual's personality, non-commodification of the individual, non-interference with others' life choices, but also to the ability to act autonomously and freely (Rodota, 2004). Privacy therefore protects individuals against practices that erode individual freedom, their capacity for self-determination, and their autonomy to engage in relationships and foster social appearances and behavior.

Privacy and freedom of communication are strictly interrelated, at least in the European approach. The European Convention on Human Rights (ECHR), which is binding for both the member states and the European Union, guarantees everyone's "right to respect for his private and family life, his home and his correspondence" (Art. 8). The EU Charter of Fundamental Rights (2000/2007) adopts in Art. 7 the same wording with the exception of the term "correspondence," which is replaced by "communications," in order to "take account of developments in technology" (EU Charter, Art. 7 Explanatory Notes). Communicating with others and using communication services falls within the protected zone of (communicational) privacy (Covington and Burling, 2003). Governmental regulations that chill communication or inhibit the use of communications services amount to an interference with an individual's right to respect for their private life (Data Protection Working Party, 2005). As asserted by the European Court of Human Rights in the case *Malone vs. United Kingdom*, data related to the source, the destination, and in general to the conditions of communication are an "integral element of the communications made." The Court has recently accepted (*Copland vs. UK*) that information derived from the monitoring of internet use should be similarly protected under Art. 8 of the ECHR.

In this institutional context, data retention inevitably affects the right to privacy and confidential communications. The fact that data are retained by private parties (service and network providers) is not decisive in this regard. Instead, what is significant for classifying such practices as interference with personal privacy is that the authorities have the right, as specified by domestic law, to access the data at any time (Kosta and Valcke, 2006), whether or not the state subsequently uses the data against the individual (see the European Court of Human Rights case *Amann v Switzerland*).

Privacy also comprises one's ability to remain anonymous in certain contexts, such as the use of technology without revealing one's name (Mitrou, 2008). Anonymity, in the context of this discussion, should not only shield individuals while speaking or reading, but also when physically or electronically roaming about, interacting, and transacting through networks (Zarsky, 2004). As electronic communications leave "digital traces," communications surveillance also has a disturbing effect on the right to anonymity (Crump, 2003; Surveillance Studies Network, 2006). Data retention practices are therefore an important step in the "disappearance of disappearance," a defining feature of the information age characterized by progressively fewer opportunities to remain anonymous (Haggerty and Ericson, 2000).

Anonymity has to be assessed not only as a component of intimacy but also—and mainly—in relation to the right to freedom of expression. This fundamental freedom includes "the right to receive and impart information and ideas without interference by public authorities" (Art. 10 of the European Convention of Human Rights, First Amendment of the US Constitution). Part of the appeal of anonymity concerns how it helps individuals disseminate and consider information without bias. By making communicative activity traceable, data-retention practices discourage individuals from participating in public debate for fear of being identified and singled out for reprisal (USA Supreme Court *Talley v California*). When communications data are retained, citizens must constantly fear that this information might at some point lead to false incrimination, reprisals, or manipulation of their data. Individuals who fear that their communications might be used against them in the future by government or individuals will endeavor to behave as inconspicuously as possible or, in some cases, choose to abstain from communicating altogether (German Working Group against Data Retention, 2007).

Anonymous speech enriches public discussion and maximizes freedom of (anonymous) association (Crump, 2003). The danger in retaining all communication data pertains to how this might shape the public's willingness to voice critical and constructive ideas—forms of communications which are of paramount importance in democratic societies (Mitrou, 2008; Breyer, 2005; Kreimer, 2004). This is the so-called chilling effect, the concern that constitutionally protected forms of communication will be inhibited by the potential for individuals and authorities to engage in forms of post hoc surveillance of communication data (Taipale, 2004/05). The chilling effect could prove especially harmful in the case of organizations and individuals who are critical of the government (German Working Group against Data Retention, 2007).

If privacy and anonymity are prerequisites of making autonomous decisions and participating in social and political life, then "traditional" fundamental rights such as freedom of movement and freedom to travel are also imperiled. People use electronic means for more than accessing information or exchanging ideas. Information and communication technologies have produced radical changes in daily activities and "an unprecedented stretching of social relationships across time and space," (Lyon, 2002:27) in a way that makes it "more appropriate to think of technology as activity and environment than as a tool" (Lyon, 2002:31). People increasingly live their everyday lives in cyberspace. They run their errands and conduct their business online. They socialize with their friends in the virtual world and build online social networks. Movements and activities, which in the off-line world would take place without any traces, are now leaving a "footprint" in the form of traffic data. Our communicational actions and transactions, our "internet activity," is transmuted into identified or identifiable personal data (Schwartz, 1999). This technology-rich lifestyle routinely generates millions of pieces of data (Bignami 2007), which synthesize the puzzle of our daily online movements.

The "spatialized language" used in relation to the internet ("surf," "visit a website," "information superhighway," "cyberspace") reflects how informational networks have begun to transform traditional notions of "place" and "space." Participation in computer networks is described in quotidian terms drawn from every imaginable environmental situation, suggesting an entire virtual geography: (chat)rooms, lobbies, dungeons, cafes, pubs, offices, and e-classrooms. Social networks, like MySpace or Facebook, are expanding the boundaries of what societies see as a person's individual space (International Working Group on Data Protection in Telecommunications [IWGDPT] 2008).

In this sense, data retention also risks jeopardizing the historically fundamental right to "freedom of movement." It is worth mentioning that the NGO Digital Rights Ireland, in its action before the Irish High Court, argues that the tracking and storing of the movements of a person carrying a mobile phone infringes the right to travel, since data retention amounts to a system of state-mandated surveillance of the movements of the overwhelming majority of the population (McIntyre, 2008). As anchored in the Additional Protocol No 4 to the European Convention of Human Rights, freedom of movement concerns not only the right to move freely in physical space but also the right to move without being traced. Accordingly, both legal theorists and legislators need to rethink the fundamental rights and freedoms to fit a new context where many users not only use electronic systems to communicate, but increasingly "live" their life in cyberspace.

Data retention as the negation of proportionality

Both national constitutions and supranational texts like the European Convention on Human Rights allow restrictions on privacy and the freedom of communication in order to pursue legitimate public interests such as national security, public safety, prevention of crime and disorder, protection of health or morals, or protection of the rights and freedoms of others. Such provisions, if and to the extent that they are combined with counterbalancing legal or institutional guarantees, reflect the tension between the interests of the individual and those of the wider community. This is commonly expressed as the need to consider the interests of society, without infringing upon the intrinsic value of privacy in a democratic society.

The courts have held that the identification of communication partners is only appropriate in exceptional cases, for example if there is no other way for the government to achieve objectives that serve a compelling public interest. In democratic states, the police's powers to limit freedom have historically been focused on the person causing a disturbance or on those who represent a public danger. Criminal investigations are directed only against legitimate criminal suspects. Only in specified rare cases can the state bring measures against non-suspects (Denninger, 2004; Breyer, 2005). It is a fundamental precept that individual citizens who are not involved in crime, or who are not creating an immediate public danger, should be largely free from the exercise of state authority.

In light of such longstanding legal principles, the new data-retention framework represents a significant development in relation to personal security and freedom. That is, surveillance practices, which were once reserved for "suspect" or "deviant" individuals, have been extended to cover the majority of the population, making it increasingly possible to sort, categorize, and target innocent individuals (Surveillance Studies Network, 2006). Data-retention policies mandate the permanent, general recording of the communicational behavior of all subscribers/users, notwithstanding the fact that in the first instance they are not understood to be a source of danger, nor are their communications taking place in an unusually dangerous area (Breyer, 2005).

Laws that authorize the state to interfere in communications privacy must meet the standards of accessibility and foreseeability inherent in the rule of law (Court of Human Rights, *Malone v UK*, *Kruslin vs. France*). The indiscriminate collection of communications data therefore offends a core principle of the rule of law: that citizens should be made aware of all circumstances in which the state may engage in surveillance, so that they can regulate their behavior to avoid unwarranted intrusions (Covington and Burling, 2003).

Constitutional intervention in rights and liberties is also subject to the principle of proportionality, also known as the ban on undue intervention (Denninger, 2004). Proportionality, a key principle in European constitutional law, requires that any proposed measure be assessed as to its suitability for achieving its aims. According to the European Convention of Human Rights, communications surveillance is unacceptable unless a legal basis is provided: unless the measure is "necessary in a democratic society" and serves the legitimate interests of national security, public safety or the economic wellbeing of a country, the prevention of disorder or crime, protection of health or morals, or protection of the rights and freedoms of others. Even if "necessary is not synonymous with indispensible ... it implies a pressing social need" (European Court of Human Rights case *Handyside v UK*). The objective pursued must be weighed against the seriousness of the interference entailed in the measures. It is not only the practices of collecting and processing telecommunications data that have important social effects and regulatory implications, but the scale of the collection (Green, 2006). The seriousness and the impacts of the interference are to be judged by taking into account, *inter alia*, the competences granted to the security authorities, the number and nature of persons affected, and the intensity of the negative effects that will result (Mitrou, 2008; Breyer, 2005).

Restrictions on personal freedoms must be strictly minimized and legislators must try to achieve their aims in the least onerous way possible (European Court of Human Rights case *Hatton v UK*). The necessity and proportionality of any particular measure must be clearly demonstrated, recognizing that privacy is not only an individual right to control one's information but also a key element of any democratic constitutional order (Federal German Constitutional Court Census case, 1983).

The Data Retention Framework was adopted without demonstrating that "the (pre) existing legal framework does not offer the instruments that are needed to protect physical security" (European Data Protection Supervisor 2005; Erd, 2008). Nor was it demonstrated that this large-scale initiative, with its massive surveillance potential, was the only feasible option available to combat crime. Under the current dominant security ideology—which sometimes verges on a security obsession—the need for greater security is presented as a "self-evident fact," but "security" cannot be understood normatively nor does it allow for the usual constitutional balancing of process and principles (Lepsius, 2004; Denninger, 2004).

There are serious concerns about the proportionality of means and ends, and their connection to demonstrable security gains. Of the innumerable electronic communications taking place every minute, the probability that a random communication will need to be revisited and established as a legal fact by law-enforcement authorities is minuscule (German Working Group against Data Retention, 2007). According to research conducted by T-Online, a big German telecommunications provider, only 0.0004% of retained communications-traffic data are ever needed for law-enforcement purposes (Breyer, 2004). The routine retention of traffic and location data about all kinds of communications (mobile phones, SMSs, faxes, emails, chatrooms, and other use of the internet), for purposes that vary from national security to law enforcement, is extensive and completely out of proportion to the law-enforcement objectives ostensibly served (Mitrou, 2008; Covington and Burling, 2003).

In order to achieve an agreeable compromise the Data Protection Working Group, representing the data protection authorities of the EU member states, has advocated a data-preservation policy commonly referred to as the "fast-freeze, quick-thaw" model (Data Protection Working Party, 2005), adopted by the Council of Europe (Cybercrime Convention, 2001) and the United States (Covington and Burling, 2003). Within this model, data preservation occurs in relation to a specific investigation. Law-enforcement authorities can compel a service provider already in possession of data on a specific subscriber/user to conserve this information for a longer period before letting it disappear. This demonstrates the utility of internet traffic data as evidence of criminal wrong-doing, "whether data retention, by making it easier to link acts to actors, aims at the change of the communication context" (Crump, 2003).

Generalized data-retention practices conflict with the requirements for proportionality, fair use, and specificity in the European data-protection regulations. In that framework, personal data is not to be collected, processed, or transmitted for the sole purpose of providing a speculative future data resource (Simitis 2006). In light of the increased use of electronic communications in daily life, and the fact that the internet in particular provides an unprecedented ability to store and reveal information, the storage of such data amounts to an "extended logbook" of a person's behavior and life (Coemans and Dumortier, 2003). In a preliminary ruling, the German Federal Constitutional Court (March 2008) has emphasized that the retention of communication data constitutes a "serious interference into the freedom of communication that cannot be undone, as such an access (to communications data) enables far-reaching firm insights into the communicational behavior and the social contacts of individuals." The Court, pending review, has concluded that parts of the act are unconstitutional (Bundesverfassungsgericht, 2008).

The comprehensive storage of all communications data gives rise to an indefinite and ongoing interference with the privacy rights of all users, not just criminal suspects. Citizens are monitored purely for unsubstantiated, precautionary reasons. This effectively transforms surveillance from an exception (which can only be specifically and legally authorized in exceptional circumstances), to the rule (Data Protection Working Party, 2005). Ultimately, data retention shifts the focus of risk from suspect individuals to suspect subpopulations.

At the same time, data retention transforms the "burden of proof." The state no longer has to demonstrate individualized suspicion in order to target individuals and interfere with their rights. Every person who communicates with someone else becomes a potential suspect as both individuals are routinely involved in the state's monitoring efforts. In the event of being singled out for heightened scrutiny, individuals must defend themselves against the state's (potentially entirely mistaken) inferences and conclusions (Donohue, 2006).

Comprehensive data retention draws upon and nourishes the rapidly spreading motto that "those that are innocent have nothing to fear." Embracing such populist common sense could easily open a Pandora's box of universal surveillance where every person is treated as a potential criminal (Mitrou and Moulinos, 2003).

Data retention as a "risk to democracy"

Data retention is one manifestation of what Clark refers to as "dataveillance," the routine, systematic, and focused use of personal data systems to investigate or monitor the actions or communications of one or more persons (Clark, 1997). Such data are not gathered occasionally but via routinized discovery systems (de Hert, 2005; Surveillance Studies Network, 2006). As contemporary life increasingly depends upon information and communication, data retention practices record ever more of a citizen's behavior and social interaction (Mulligan, 2004; Breyer, 2004). In the process, it also "rigidifies one's past" (Solove, 2004). People who know they are under surveillance often shape and steer their behavior accordingly (Surveillance Studies Network, 2006). The US Department of Defense (2004) even acknowledges this fact, noting that "Awareness that government may analyze activity is likely to alter behavior," as "people act differently if they know their conduct could be observed." They might adapt their actions to the accepted social norms or decide to deviate from them; the latter behavior ultimately risks reprisal (Institute for Prospective Technology, 2003). Under pervasive surveillance, individuals are inclined to make choices that conform to mainstream expectations (Simitis, 1987; Solove, 2004). The "maximum security society" (Marx, 2001) relies exactly on such a refined technological framework to influence and even "program" people's daily lives.

Routine data retention encroaches on the everyday lives of most citizens and imperils the fundamental freedoms that people enjoy and cherish (Data Protection Working Party, 2006). Under extended (or even potential) surveillance, freedoms that form the underlying substance of constitutional democracies (freedom of speech, freedom of association or assembly) cannot be fully exercised. At the beginning of the twenty-first century, concerns about security have challenged the state's longstanding mandate to guarantee the constitutionally protected freedoms of its citizens. Such concerns may also serve as a new normative guiding principle, one that affects and weakens legal institutions and undermines "traditional" notions of freedom (Denninger, 2004).

The prevention and removal of risks has become a social and political imperative. New perceptions about risk mirror a critical change in our relation to freedom and security. The concept of the "risk society" implies a rational assessment of risks and the development of a proportionate response, but "it also masks a deeper felt need in the collective psyche" (Rowland, 2004:6).

Anxieties about risk have contributed to a culture of zero tolerance; restrictions on rights are tolerated, if not actively supported, by the majority, if they are presented as promising greater security (Crump, 2003).

The state's eagerness to keep its "security promise" under conditions where Western societies are facing new threats also reveals the state's readiness to suspend freedoms. The state's accentuation of its "protection duties" is its central justification for infringements on basic rights. By invoking such protective duties it is possible to place legally protected, collective security on the same level with individual civil liberties. In such situations collective duties override individual rights, particularly when collective duties claim to protect lives. Jurisprudence and theory in Europe emphasize that collective goods and interests may not, under any circumstances, outstrip individual rights: individual liberty has a higher status than collective security (Lepsius, 2006; Erd, 2008). Restrictions on individuals' rights are tolerated only in relation to the proportionality principle, which serves as a "limitation of limitations" of individual rights. The relatively recent "invention" of a "fundamental right to security" (Isensee, 1983: 22) has done nothing to resolve the problems of security. Instead, it is used as a justification of ever wider powers of state intervention (Denninger, 2002; Hustinx, 2006). The "right to security" is not conceived as a condition of freedom, but as an individual claim on the state that it must create conditions of safety. From a constitutional point of view, the individual's rights to freedom, to privacy, and/or to communicational secrecy could be more easily limited by invoking the "rights of other persons," i.e., in the context of this discussion, a right to be (or feel?) safe. The existence of a "fundamental right to security," in a general sense, however, is negated by the argument that constitutional texts and jurisprudence recognize only a much narrower right to physical integrity of the person and provide for a number of possible grounds for legitimate restrictions on other fundamental rights (Hustinx, 2006).

The decision to routinely retain communications data for law-enforcement purposes is historically unprecedented (Data Protection Working Party, 2006). Generalized and indiscriminate data retention reflects the shift from a constitutional state, guarding against the threat of specific risks in specific situations, to a security-oriented preventive or even preemptive state (Denninger, 2002). This dissociation of risk from individual acts, with its focus on risk prevention, has considerable and far-reaching impacts on fundamental rights and on democracy.

Communication-data retention reflects a transformation from the traditional constitutional model, where evidence of wrongdoing was collected on specified suspects, to a model of intelligence-gathering where information is gathered at random on all individuals (Levi and Wall, 2004; Denninger, 2002). In this latter model everyone is perceived "as exchangeable element(s) in a principally dangerous environment" (Lepsius, 2004:454). Here, Lepsius is referring to the "de-individualization of freedom," which concerns how "the weighing ratio has shifted away from the weighing of individual, subjective-legal positions to a weighing of objective-legal perspectives. Individual rights are replaced by collective interests" (Lepsius, 2004:455). The dominant emergent argument is that the individual, as a part of society, must accept greater interference in his or her fundamental rights, in order to secure societal freedom. Individual freedom is evaluated in light of broader social purposes (Lepsius, 2004).

Establishing affirmative duties for citizens leads, in principle, to disequilibrium in the process of balancing political rights and freedoms (Lepsius, 2004). The legitimization of the democratic state depends upon successfully balancing various public objectives and fundamental rights (i.e. freedom and security), under the terms and within the limits of core democratic values. Policy decisions, like the one made to routinely retain data, considerably alter the "balance" between freedom and security.

However, in calculating the costs associated with this development, we should not fixate on the dilemma of "security or freedom" or "how much freedom should we sacrifice to gain how much security?" The political impact of the state's power to obtain such a broad range of personal information should also be taken into consideration. The concentration of such power in the executive, and more specifically in law-enforcement authorities, transforms the balance of power among the different branches of the state (Donohue, 2006) and raises questions about the public's ability to control the state's data-collection and data-processing activities.

Moreover, systematic data retention is a paradigm for recently enhanced policies which aim to enable and promote increased data-sharing between the public and the private domain. The private sector now produces enormous pools of information. Corporations process unprecedented amounts of information about the everyday activities of each and every user. The new technological environment is characterized not only by the depth and the breadth of personal information available to and from private sources, but also by the capacity to analyze these data and draw from them patterns and conclusions (Dempsey and Flint, 2004). One of the inherent risks is that this information can also be placed at the disposal of the state (Solove, 2002; Kreimer, 2004). There is a growing trend in law enforcement of seeking to access data on airline passengers, telephone or internet use, and financial data (Hustinx, 2005).

Public and private enterprises are thoroughly intertwined. Privatization and diversification of traditionally state-controlled sectors (like telecommunications), combined with increasing interoperability and technological synergies, may foster forms of "function creep" (Rotenberg et al., 2006). Much of the surveillance activity, especially in the communications or banking sector, will be conducted and analyzed by private parties (Dempsey and Flint, 2004), enabling ubiquitous dataveillance. Financial institutes are required to monitor their customers for signs of suspicious transactions and European airlines are "allowed"—on the basis of an Agreement signed in July 2007 by the EU and the US—to transfer passenger information to American authorities.

The technique of folding private organizations into a government's surveillance network creates a system of "distributed surveillance," allowing the state to overcome practical limits on its resources (Steinhardt, 2005). The state's potential ability to access such vast amounts of data, initially collected by private entities for entirely different purposes, constitutes a threat to informational self-determination, which can chill not only political participation but also professional and personal activities.

Conclusion: data retention is here to stay?

The transmutation of communication and internet activity into data that is routinely retained by service and network providers may discourage communication. A recent survey (May 2008) conducted by the German research institute Forsa revealed that, once communications data retention became mandatory (January 1, 2008), one in two Germans (52 per cent) claimed that they would refrain from using phone or email for confidential contacts like drug counselors, psychotherapists, or marriage counselors. One in thirteen respondents (11 per cent) said they had abstained from using telephone, mobile phone, or email at least once this year because of concerns about data retention. This percentage extrapolates to a total of 6.5 million Germans (Arbeitskreis Vorratsdatenspeicherung, press release of June 3/6, 2008).

For individuals, data-retention policies may ultimately lead to personal inhibition and self-censorship (Solove, 2002). This makes it difficult for individuals to engage in the thinking aloud and deliberation with others on which democratic choice-making depends (Schwartz, 1999). The state's imperative to address new threats through pre-emptive measures and policies that affect an indefinite number of individuals, or even the whole population, ultimately "blows up the cornerstones of the rule of law" (Hoffman-Riem, 2002: 505).

The distinguishing feature of blanket, across-the-board, data retention is the absence of any plausible linkage between the intrusion on individual privacy rights and the law-enforcement objectives served. Indiscriminate data retention is diametrically opposed to a regime designed to minimally impair rights. The seriousness of interfering with the fundamental rights of privacy and freedom of communication is judged according to several criteria, including the conditions under which competences are granted to the designated security authorities, the number and nature of individuals affected, the intensity of potential negative effects (Breyer, 2005) and, last but not least, the provision of guarantees such as independent oversight mechanisms.

The Data Retention Directive leaves several important issues to the discretion of the member states, allowing them to regulate the retention of communication data in significantly different ways. The Directive allows for large variations in the retention period (six months to two years) as well as in the definition of "serious criminal offences," which may extend the scope of data-retention measures to trivial crimes, unrelated to attempts to combat public security. Member state governments tailor the Directive's provisions to suit their national interests. For instance, in Germany communication data should be stored for six months and made available for law enforcement in cases related to certain forms of crime. The British government intends to go further, with plans to introduce a draft communications bill in the autumn of 2009, requiring all telecommunications companies to hand over data to one central "super-database." Under the new law, it will be permissible for the authorities to access personal data for crime and public-order investigations or to prevent people from self-harmful actions.

Opposition to mandatory data retention has come from such diverse groups as data-protection officials, civil-liberties groups, and—last but not least— industry. The latter is concerned about the costs of complying with the new surveillance mandates (Steinhardt 2005), a powerful indication of the practical difficulties with data-retention requirements. At the European Union level, the European Parliament, the Group of the European Data Protection Commissions (Art. 29, Data Protection Working Group) and the European Data Protection Supervisors acted as institutional counterbalances to the Council and the governments of the member states. It is worth noting that the process of adopting the Data Retention Directive has proved to be substantially more transparent and open to public debate and participation than the corresponding, national-level process of transposing the Directive's imperatives into domestic legislation (McIntyre, 2008).

Against this background, the challenges to domestic data-retention laws in Germany, Ireland, and Hungary have, to varying degrees, provoked public discussion on the effects of pervasive data-retention policies on fundamental rights and (in the final analysis) on democratic society itself. McIntryre (2008) argues that these challenges offer an important opportunity to reflect on possible social consequences of pervasive surveillance.

The constitutional debate has been fruitful in Germany: the German Federal Constitutional Court has corrected the parliamentary one-side balancing of freedom and security by putting a limit on contemporary statutory approaches which claim to increase the level of security by decreasing the level of protection for fundamental rights and liberties (Erd, 2008; Lepsius, 2006). At the same time, concerned citizens are prepared to give up privacy for safety: 48 per cent of the people who participated in the Forsa survey still think that data retention is a necessary step for crime prevention. In a similar poll, for the Flash Eurobarometer Survey on Data Protection (conducted in January 2008 with 27,000 randomly selected participants from the 27 EU member states), a majority of respondents (72 per cent) agreed that it should be permissible to monitor telephone calls, if such monitoring served to combat terrorism.

Since 2003, the share of citizens who approve of monitoring telephone calls and internet use has increased by about 12 percentage points. However, as stressed in the survey, a considerable minority of EU citizens emphasized that restrictions on their privacy rights should have clearly defined limits:

25 per cent of the respondents agreed that communications monitoring should only be applied to suspects, under the supervision of a judge, or with equivalent safeguards. Independent oversight mechanisms are crucial to ensuring lawful access to communications data and records and to guaranteeing that the consequences for the individuals and their rights and freedoms are limited to the strict minimum necessary (Mitrou, 2008).

Despite the public's fears and perceptions, privacy, which is very closely associated with dignity, remains inalienable. Communications-data retention and surveillance beyond the bounds of clear and democratically defined limits threatens the process of deliberative democracy as well as the perpetrators of violence. Communication and information privacy is a key element of a democratic constitutional order; it enables individuals to develop their own identity and ideas in order to engage in public life (German Constitutional Court, Census Decision, 1983). Indeed, controlling a person's private life is one of the central repressive techniques used by totalitarian states (Solove, 2002). As contemporary societies are transformed into new forms of surveillance societies, privacy becomes more significant as a fundamental political value (Institute for Prospective Technology, 2003).

Once institutionalized, data-retention policies will be politically hard to dismantle. However, as long as dignity and freedom remain the basic parameters of the constitutional order in European states, respect for these values will be seen as an institutional condition for security measures and not as an encumbrance to providing effective security. Perceiving infringements to fundamental rights and freedoms as the inevitable collateral damage of security efforts risks "undermining or even destroying democracy on the ground to defend it" (European Court of Human Rights case *Klass v. Germany*, 1978).

References

Arbeitskreis, "Vorratsdatenspeicherung." 2008. Pressemitteilung vom 04.06.2008, available at http://www.vorratsdatenspeicherung.de.

Bignami, Francesca. 2007. "Protecting privacy against the police in the European Union: The data retention directive." *Duke Law School Working Paper Series – Paper 76*, available at http://1sr.nellco.org.

Breyer, P. 2004. "Bürgerrechte und TKG-Novelle – Datenschutzrechtliche Auswirkungen der Neufassung des Telekommunikationsgesetzes." *Recht der Datenverarbeitung Heft* 4:147–53.

———. 2005. "Telecommunications data retention and human rights: The compatibility of blanket traffic data retention with the ECHR." *European Law Journal* 11 (3):365–75.

Bundesverfassungsgericht-Pressestelle, "Pressemitteilung Nr. 37/2008 vom 19." März 2008 (Beschluss vom 11. März 2008–1 BvR 256/08), available at http://www.bundesverfassungsgericht.de.

Clark, Roger. 1997 [2006]. "Introduction to dataveillance and information privacy." Available at http://www.anu.edu.au.

Coemans, C. and J. Dumortier. 2003. "Enforcement issues—Mandatory retention of traffic data in the EU: Possible impact on privacy and on-line anonymity." In *Digital Anonymity and the Law*, edited by C. Nicoll, J.E.J. Prince and J.M., van Dellen, 161–83. The Hague: TMC Asser Press.

Covington and Burling, LLP. 2003. "Memorandum of laws concerning the legality of data retention with regard to the rights guaranteed by the European Convention on Human Rights." *Privacy International*. Available at http://www.privacyinternational. org. Crump, Catherine. 2003. "Data retention—Privacy, anonymity, and accountability online." *Stanford Law Review* 56:191–229.

Data Protection Working Party. 2005. Opinion 113/2005 on the proposal for a Directive on the retention of data processed in connection with the provision of public electronic communication services. Available at http://ec.europa.eu.

——. 2006. Opinion 3/2006 on the Directive on the retention of data generated or processed in connection with the provision of publicly available electronic communication services or of public communications networks and amending Directive 2002/58/EC. Available at http://ec.europa.eu.

de Hert, P. 2005. "Balancing security and liberty within the European Human Rights Framework. A critical reading of the Court's case law in the light of surveillance and criminal law enforcement strategies after 9/11." *Utrecht Law Review* 1:68–96.

Dempsey, J.X. and L.M. Flint. 2004. "Commercial data and national security." *George Washington Law Review* 72:1459–1502.

Denninger, Erhard. 2002. "Freiheit durch Sicherheit? Wie viel Schutz der inneren Sicherheit verlangt und verträgt das deutsche Grundgesetz?" *Kritische Justiz* 35 (4):467–75.

——. 2004. "Freedom versus security? Internal security in the area of tension between a constitutional state and a preventive state." *Goethe-Institut* – Online Redaktion Available at http://www.goethe.de.

Donohue, L.K. 2006. "Anglo-American privacy and surveillance." *Journal of Criminal Law and Criminology* 96:1059–1207.

Erd, Rainer. 2008. "Bundesverfassungsgericht versus Politik. Eine kommentierende Dokumentation der jüngsten Entscheidungen zu drei Sicherheitsgesetzen." *Kritische Justiz* 41(2):118–33.

Escudero-Pascual A. and I. Hosein. 2004. "Questioning lawful access to traffic data." *Communications of the ACM* 47:77–82.

EU Network of Independent Experts in Fundamental Rights – CRF-DF. 2003. *The Balance between Freedom and Security in the Response by the EU and its MS to the Terrorist Threat* (Comment) 1–52. Available at http://ec.europa.eu.

European Data Protection Supervisor. 2005. *Opinion on the Proposal for a Directive on the Retention of Data Processed in Connection with the Provision of Public Electronic Communication Services and Amending Directive 2002/58/EC*. Available at: http://www.edps.europa.eu.

Forsa (Gesellschaft fuer Sozialforschung und statistische Analysen mbH). 2008. Meinungsumfrage – Meinungen der Bürger zur Vorratsdatenspeicherung (Mai 2008) http://www.vorratsdatenspeicherung.de.

German Working Group Against Data Retention. 2007. Amicus Curiae brief that is to be presented to the European Court of Justice regarding the action started on July 6, 2006 – *Ireland vs. Council of the European Union*, European Parliament (Case C-301/06). Available at *http://www.edri.org*. Green, Nicola. 2006. "Communications."

In *Surveillance Studies Network, A Report on the Surveillance Society for the Information Commissioner-Appendices*, edited by D.M. Wood. September 2006.

Haggerty, Kevin D. and Richard V. Ericson. 2000. "The surveillant assemblage." *British Journal of Sociology* 51(4):605–22.

Hoffmann-Riem, W. 2002. "Freiheit und Sicherheit in Angesicht terroristischer Anschläge." *Zeitschrift für Rechtspolitik* 35:497–505.

Hustinx, Peter (European Data Protection Supervisor). 2005. *Data Protection and Citizens' Security: What Principles for the European Union?* Brussels: European Parliament, LIBE Committee, available at: http://www.edps.europa.eu.

——. 2006. *Human rights and public security: Chance for a compromise or continuity of safeguards?* in Conference on Public Security and Data Protection, Warsaw, 2006. Available at http://www.edps.europa.eu.

Institute For Prospective Technological Studies. 2003. *Security and Privacy for the Citizen in the Post-September 11 Digital Age: A Prospective Overview* – Report to the European Parliament Committee on Citizens' Freedoms and Rights, Justice and Home Affairs, European Communities. European Commission – Joint Research Center. Available at http://ec.europa.eu.

Isensee, Josef. 1983. Das Grundrecht auf Sicherheit – Zu den Schutzpflichten des Freiheitlichen Verfassungsstaates. Berlin/New York: Walter de Gruyter.

IWGDPT (International Working Group on Data Protection in Telecommunications). 2008. *Report and Guidance on Privacy in Social Network Services* (Rome Memorandum), Available at http://www.berlin-privacy-group.org.

Koops, Bert-Jaap. 2006. "Should ICT regulations be technology-neutral?" In *Starting Points for ICT Regulation. Deconstructing Prevalent Policy One-liners*, edited by B.-J. Koops, M. Lips, C. Prins, and M. Schellekens, 77–108. The Hague: T.M.C. Asser Press.

Kosta, E. and P. Valcke. 2006. "Retaining the data retention directive." *Computer Law & Security Report* 22:370–80.

Kreimer, S.F. 2004. "Watching the watchers: Surveillance, transparency and political freedom in the war on terror." *University of Pennsylvania Journal of Constitutional Law* 7:133–81.

Lepsius, Oliver. 2004. "Liberty, security and terrorism: The legal position in Germany, Part 2." *German Law Journal* 5(6). Available at http://www.germanlawjournal.com.

——. 2006. "Human dignity and the downing of aircraft: The German Federal Constitutional Court strikes down a prominent anti-terrorism provision in the New Air-Transport Security Act." *German Law Journal* 7(9). Available at http://www.germanlawjournal.com.

Levi, M. and D.S. Wall. 2004. "Technologies, security and privacy in the Post-9/11 European information society." *Journal of Law and Society* 31(2):194–220.

Lyon, David. 2002. "Cyberspace: Beyond information society." In *Living with Cyberspace: Technology and Society in the Twenty-First Century*, ed. John Armitage and Joanne Roberts, 21–33, New York: Athlone Press.

Marx, Gary. 2001. "Murky conceptual waters: The public and the private." *Ethics and Information technology* 3:157–69.

McIntyre, T.J. 2008. "Data retention in Ireland: Privacy, policy and proportionality." *Computer Law and Security Report* 24(4):326–34.

Mitrou, Lilian. 2008. "A Pandora's box for rights and liberties." In *Digital Privacy: Theory, Technologies and Practices*, edited by A. Acquisti, S. De Capitani di Vimercati, S. Gritzalis and C. Lambrinoudakis, 409–32. Auerbach Publications.

Mitrou, E. and K. Moulinos. 2003. "Privacy and data protection in electronic communications." In *Proceedings Int. Workshop Computer Network Security*, edited by V. Gorodetsky, L. Popyack, and V. Skormin, 432–36. Berlin-Heidelberg: Springer.

Mulligan, D.K. 2004. "Reasonable expectations in electronic communications: A critical perspective on the Electronic Communications Privacy Act." *George Washington Law Review* 72:1557–98.

Rodota, Stefano. 2004. "Privacy, freedom and dignity—Closing remarks." *26th International Conference on Privacy and Personal Data Protection*, Wroclaw, 16.09.2004. Available at http://26konferencja.giodo.gov.pl.

Rotenberg, M., Laurant, Galstee and Rodriguez-Pereda. 2006. *Privacy and Human Rights 2005 – An International Survey of Privacy Laws and Developments*. Electronic Privacy Information Center – Privacy International, available from http://www.privacyinternational.org.

Rowland, Diana. 2004. "Data retention and the war against terrorism – A considered and proportionate response?" *The Journal of Information, Law and Technology* 3. Available at http://www2.warwick.ac.uk.

Samuelson, Pamela. 2000. "Five challenges for regulating the global information society." In Regulating the Global Information Society, edited by C. Marsden, 316–32. London: Routledge.

Schwartz, P.M. 1999. "Privacy and democracy in cyberspace." *Vanderbilt Law Review* 5:1610–1701.

Shin, Dong Hee. 2006. "VoIP: A debate over information service or telephone application in US: A new perspective in convergence era." *Telematics and Informatics* 23:57–73.

Simitis, Spiros. 1987. "Reviewing privacy in an information society." *University of Pennsylvania Law Review* 135:707–32.

———. 2006. "Einleitung: Geschichte – Ziele—Prinzipien." In *Bundesdatenschutzgesetz – Kommentar*, edited by S. Simitis, 61–153. Baden-Baden: Nomos.

Solove, D.J. 2002. "Digital dossiers and the dissipation of Fourth Amendment privacy." *Southern California Law Review* 75:1084–1167.

———. 2004. "Reconstructing electronic surveillance law." *The George Washington Law Review* 72:1701–47.

Steinhardt, Barry. 2005. "How the American government is conscripting businesses and individuals in the construction of a surveillance society." *27th International Conference on Privacy and Personal Data Protection*. Available at http://www.privacyconference2005.org.

Surveillance Studies Network. 2006. *A Report on the Surveillance Society for the (UK) Information Commissioner*, ed.D.M. Wood, September 2006.

Swire, P.P. 2004. "Katz is dead. Long live Katz." *Michigan Law Review* 102:904–32.

Taipale K. A. 2004/05. "Technology, security and privacy: The fear of Frankenstein, the mythology of privacy and the lessons of King Ludd." *Yale Journal of Law and Technology* 7:123–220.

UK Home Office. 2002. *Justification for the Anti-Terrorism, Crime and Security Act*. Available at www.homeoffice.gov.uk.

U.S. Department of Defence – Technology and Privacy Advisory Committee. 2004. *Safeguarding Privacy in the Fight Against Terrorism*, (Report). Available at http://www.sainc.com.

World Summit on the Information Society. 2003. *Declaration of Principles*. Available at http://www.itu.int/wsis.

Zarsky, T.Z. 2004. "Thinking outside the box: Considering transparency, anonymity and pseudonimity as overall solutions to the problems of information privacy in the Internet Society." *University of Miami Law Review* 58:991–1041.

Legal Texts

Directive 2002/58/EC of the European Parliament and of the Council of July 12, 2002 concerning the processing of personal data and the protection of privacy in the electronic communications sector (Directive on privacy and electronic communications) OJ L 201, 31.7.2002, p. 37–47.

Directive 2006/24/EC of the European Parliament and of the Council of March 15, 2006 on the retention of data generated or processed in connection with the provision of publicly available electronic communications services or of public communications networks and amending Directive 2002/58/EC, OJ L 105, 13.4.2006, p. 54–63.

Directive 2002/21/EC of the European Parliament and of the Council of March 7, 2002 on a common regulatory framework for electronic communications networks and services (Framework Directive), OJ L 108, 24.4.2002, p. 33–50.

Convention on Cybercrime(Council of Europe), Budapest 23.XI. 2001. Available at http://conventions.coe.int.

Cases Cited

European Court of Human Rights

Klass and others v Germany, Judgment of September 7, 1973.
Handyside v United Kingdom, Judgment of December 7, 1976.
Malone v United Kingdom, Judgment of August 2, 1984.
Niemitz v Germany, Judgment of December 16, 1992.
Kruslin v France, Judgment of April 24, 1990.
Amann v Switzerland, Judgment of February 16, 2001.
P.G. and J.H. v United Kingdom, Judgment of September 25, 2001.
Hatton v United Kingdom, Judgment of July 8, 2003.
Copland v the United Kingdom, Judgment of April 3, 2007.

Deutsches Bundesverfassungsgericht (German Federal Constitutional Court)

Volkszählungsurteil (Census Case Judgment), Judgment of 15.12.1983.
Vorratsdatenspeicherung (Data Retention Case), Judgment of 11.03.2008. http://www.bundesverfassungsgericht.de.

Supreme Court (USA)

Talley v California, 362 US 60,65 (1960).

Chapter 8

"Full Spectrum Dominance" as European Union Security Policy

On the trail of the "NeoConOpticon"

Ben Hayes

This chapter identifies and explores a paradigm shift in the security strategy of the European Union (EU), characterized by the pursuit of the US military doctrine of "Full Spectrum Dominance," a euphemism for control over all elements of the "battlespace" using land, air, maritime, and space-based assets (Department of Defense, 2000). As military apparatuses have been given a "security" mandate, and "Homeland Security" policy has adopted a quasi-militarist posture, Full Spectrum Dominance has become a coherent political project geared toward imposing a ubiquitous and global surveillance system for the express purposes of maintaining and extending (Western) state power, authority, and control in the twenty-first century.

The EU has not *formally* adopted a strategy of Full Spectrum Dominance. Rather, EU policies on a whole host of formerly distinct "security" issues—including policing; counterterrorism; critical-infrastructure protection; border control; crisis management; external security; defence, maritime, and space policy—are converging around two interrelated objectives. The first is the widespread implementation of surveillance technologies and techniques to enhance security and law-enforcement capacity in these core "mission areas." The second is the drive for "interoperability," or the integration of surveillance tools with other government information and communications systems so that they may be used for multiple tasks across the spectrum of law enforcement and security. A culture of "joined-up surveillance" embedded in a culture of "joined-up government" is another way to describe this trend.

Characterizing these developments as constituting a "NeoConOpticon" accentuates concerns about the influence of transnational defence and security corporations in promoting the Full Spectrum Dominance agenda and the ideological orientation of this and other "Homeland Security" discourses. On one hand, the concept flags the close bond between corporate and political elites in the homeland-security sector (the "right to limitless profit-making" at the centre of "neoconservative" ideology [Klein 2007:322]). On the other, it refers to the inherently neoconservative appeal to the defence of the homeland and the eradication of threats to the Western way of life abroad, in which Full

Spectrum Dominance and related doctrines are embedded (Project for the New American Century, 2000; Department of Defence, 2000). The NeoConOpticon provides a fruitful line of enquiry for this analysis, but not a comprehensive theory of the contemporary security or surveillance policies of the EU.

This chapter argues that Full Spectrum Dominance in a European context relates to converging trends in the historical development of the EU: an increasingly sophisticated security apparatus; policy frameworks facilitating police surveillance and the collection and exchange of police information in the EU; the EU's external security, defence, and space policies; and the increasing influence of transnational defence and security corporations on the EU policy agenda. The second part of this chapter examines some of the policy programs, surveillance systems, and actors contributing to the development of Full Spectrum Dominance infrastructure for the EU. The final section considers some of the wider implications of this potentially omnipotent program of surveillance.

The EU security apparatus

With public support for the EU at an all-time low, following the rejection of the draft EU Constitution by voters in the Netherlands and France, and its successor the Lisbon Treaty by the Irish Referendum, security policy has moved steadily to the center of the EU's political agenda. Terrorist attacks in Europe, most notably in Madrid in 2004 and London in 2005, as well as 9/11, partly explain this reconfiguration of EU politics. The reality is a more complex apparatus; its sophistication was comparable to the internal security systems of the member states *prior* to the onset of the "war on terror" (Loader 2002). There were dozens of police and immigration control measures to "compensate" for the abolition of internal borders among the first five states party to the 1985 Schengen Agreement, under the 1990 "implementation convention," including the creation of a sprawling police and border-control information system containing information about persons to be refused entry, wanted and missing persons, persons to be placed under surveillance, and "high value" lost and stolen goods. The 1999 Amsterdam Treaty incorporated the Schengen framework into the EU legal order and over one million persons are registered, in various categories, in the "Schengen Information System." The SIS will soon be replaced by the "next generation" SIS II, which will include biometric data, more advanced policing and border-control functions, and ultimately will link hundreds of thousands of police and border guards across the 27 EU member states to tens of millions of records on persons and items of interest.

The contemporary EU security apparatus is also grounded in dozens of measures on EU border control, immigration, and asylum policy adopted in the 1990s. These increasingly restrictive regulations provide the foundation for heavily policed external borders and common EU policies to prevent the entry and residence of people fleeing poverty and persecution (Webber, 1995, 2004).

A number of member states began fingerprinting "irregular" migrants and applicants for asylum and a central EU database, EURODAC, went online in 2000. Laws criminalizing illegal entry and residence, together with those who "facilitate" such offences, combine with a detailed expulsion policy to produce ever greater surveillance inside what critics have dubbed "Fortress Europe."

While police cooperation and counterterrorism measures were inevitably prioritized in the wake of 9/11, the EU continues to reinforce its border controls as the "first line of defence." EUROPOL, the European Police Office, was developed during the 1990s and subsequently joined by a plethora of other EU security agencies: EUROJUST (the EU's judicial cooperation unit), FRONTEX (the EU "border management" agency), SITCEN (the EU's intelligence agency) and a host of civil and military agencies. In turn, these agencies are equipped with transnational databases and information systems. EUROPOL, for example, is mandated to collect and retain information on a potentially limitless cycle of criminals, suspects, associates, witnesses, and victims (Mathiesen 1999:20).

The development of the EU security apparatus consolidates political power within particular institutions and agencies instead of employing the usual "separation of powers" through the EU's "institutional triangle."[1] For the first ten years of EU justice and home-affairs cooperation, the Commission's "neutral arbitration" and the democratically elected European Parliament were all but excluded from policy deliberations, with "national sovereignty" justifying a member-state monopoly on decision-making. More substantive legislative proposals have been transferred to the normal "Community method" since 2004 but even now the European Parliament is merely "consulted" on EU police and criminal-law matters. More importantly, the member states in the EU Council retain their monopoly over the strategic direction of the EU policy agenda and all "operational matters." These "non-legislative" decisions are behind the development and implementation of many of the surveillance frameworks discussed in this chapter.

It is significant that EU security-policy decisions are made by an opaque and thinly accountable network of member-state and EU officials. An overwhelming majority of observers (and many participants) hold this system to favor two distinct interest groups. The first group represents the member states' interior ministries and law-enforcement agencies that dominate the decision-making structure. These policy-makers are inevitably "pro-security" in their orientation to migration, terrorism, organized crime, and other "threats," which in turn has had a detrimental effect on the protection of civil liberties and human rights (Loader, 2002; Curtin and Meijer, 2005; Bunyan, 2006; Bigo, 2006; Peers, 2007). The second group of beneficiaries are the governments of the largest EU states, who have a much greater say than the majority of small countries among the 27 member countries—it is telling that the "G6" (Group of Six largest EU member states) now meets independently to discuss the EU security agenda. The term "policy laundering" has been coined to explain how the governments of powerful countries use inter-governmental organizations to circumvent their national democratic processes, a problem particularly pronounced in the area of EU law on state surveillance (Hosein, 2004).

Surveillance states

This brief description of the EU security apparatus goes some way to explaining how, in the years since 9/11, the EU has surpassed the USA in facilitating the surveillance of its citizens. While the American Patriot Act achieved worldwide notoriety, the EU was quietly adopting legislation mandating the fingerprinting of all EU passport-, visa- and residence-permit holders, and the mandatory retention—*for general law enforcement purposes*—of all telecommunications data (our telephone, email, and internet "traffic" records [see Mitrou, in this volume]), all air-traveler data (on passengers into, out of, and across Europe), and all financial transactions. Conversely, in the USA fingerprinting was limited to foreign nationals and so-called "data-veillance," dependent upon an illegal domestic spying program and the dubious acquisition and use of personal data held by private companies and friendly governments (Webb, 2007).

According to the officials currently elaborating a new five-year plan for EU Justice and Home Affairs policy (the EU "Future Group"), this is just the beginning of a "digital tsunami" that will revolutionize law enforcement, providing a wealth of information for public-security authorities (Bunyan 2008). In November 2008, the lower house of the German Parliament approved legislation giving the police the power to conduct "remote searches" of personal computers (though this has recently been blocked by the Federal Council), essentially acknowledging that the security services are using "bugs," tracing technologies, or "spyware" that can be surreptitiously installed on a suspect's personal computer. This was quickly followed by a G6 call for "harmonized" legislation on "remote searches" and a new EU strategy on "cybercrime" including a series of operational measures such as "cyber patrols, joint investigation teams and remote searches" (European Commission, 2008b). The EU has also created a host of law-enforcement databases and communication systems. In addition to the SIS/SIS II, EURO-DAC, and EUROPOL databases described above, the EU is developing the Visa Information System (VIS, which will contain the fingerprints and application data from all visa applicants to the member states, even where visas are refused) and new automated data-comparison systems that will link the DNA and fingerprint databases of the member states (centralizing access, if not the data itself). SIS II and VIS are to be interlinked into a new "EU entry-exit system" based on fingerprint checks and automated searches for visa "over-stayers" and other "illegal aliens," fugitives, and suspicious persons "flagged" by the member states.

Even the EU's celebrated data-protection regime has proven largely power-less to rein in the EU's extensive surveillance program, with law-enforcement agencies almost exempted from the norms and standards that apply to other public data controllers (Hayes, 2005; Council of Europe, 2008).[2] Such laws are the antithesis of two strategic principles adopted by the EU: the principles of "availability" and "interoperability." Whereas the EU data-protection regime seeks to impose strict limits on the use and onward transfer of police data, the principle of availability means that *all* law-enforcement data held by any member state should *automatically* be accessible to all the others (European Commission, 2005b). This principle is now being implemented under the "Prum Convention," which will automate cross-border searches of member states' DNA and fingerprint databases, centralizing access and creating de facto EU databases. As noted above, interoperability refers to attempts to integrate these kind of databases and information systems with other surveillance tools and government agencies so that they may be used for multiple security tasks (European Commission, 2004b, 2006). This inevitably breaks down the "firewalls" around personal data that EU law is supposed to erect.

External defense and global policing

The European Security Strategy of 2003 (ESS) called upon the EU member states to rethink traditional concepts of self-defense. Arguing that new threats meant that "the first line of defense will often be abroad," the strategy favored a "strategic culture that fosters early, rapid and when necessary, robust [mili-tary] intervention" in "failed" and "rogue" states (EU Council, 2003). "Conflict prevention and threat prevention cannot start too early," it concluded. On January 1, 2007, with the support of Turkish forces, the EU reached its full operational capacity and "Headline Target" of 60,000 soldiers available for rapid-reaction operations. This includes 15 rotating EU battlegroups of at least 1,500 combat soldiers, two of which are ready for deployment at all times.

The battlegroups remain on standby, but since 2003 the EU has deployed peacekeepers and non-military (police and civilian) crisis-management person-nel in more than 20 operations in Africa, the Balkans, the Middle East, and Southeast Asia. The EU has also launched two ongoing "border management" missions in Moldova–Ukraine and Georgia–Southern Caucasus and, in response to the increasingly notorious piracy and armed robbery off the Somali coast, has just agreed to launch its first naval mission. EU military and non-military crisis-management operations are supported by a number of bodies including the EU Military Staff, the European Defence Agency, the EU Satellite Centre, and the EU Institute for Security Studies. The empowerment of this fledgling state apparatus is central to the emergence of the Full Spectrum Dominance scenarios described below.

NATO is also reaching for a global policing role. On the eve of its sixtieth birthday, five Generals have called for NATO to reinvent itself as an organization that can address the fallout from climate change, energy crises, food crises, uncontrolled migration, human trafficking, terrorism, and other contemporary "security threats" (NATO, 2007). There are also similarities among the USA, NATO, and EU maritime security and defense strategies. In 2005, inspired by the USA's "SeaPower21" strategy, the Chiefs of European Navies (CHENS) launched a 20-year "Vision for the Future Role of European Maritime Forces" to meet the demands of the European Security Strategy and NATO Maritime Dimension of Joint Operations (CHENS, 2005). The sub-sequent adoption of an EU maritime security policy and pursuit of an inte-grated border-surveillance system, considered below, represents a concerted attempt to impose *total surveillance* of the EU's maritime borders and the open seas beyond using land-, air-, and space-based assets in conjunction with EU agencies and police-information systems.

The EU's space-based assets include an increasingly sophisticated satellite surveillance, location, and tracking system called GMES (Global Monitoring for Environment and Security; recently renamed "Copernikus"). This will use the "Galileo" network conceived in the mid-1990s and lauded as the world's first *civilian* GPS system that would give the EU strategic independence from the US monopoly on global satellite surveillance. By 2004, Galileo had morphed into the EU's first "Public Private Partnership" (PPP) initiative, with defense giants Thales, European Aeronautic Defence and Space Company (EADS), and Finmeccanica among those selected to co-finance the deployment phase. By 2006, however, the consortium had collapsed, with corporate sour-ces publicly blaming the EU's "rigid governance" for the failure. Costs are now borne by the EU alone, with €3.4 billion of contracts for Galileo's deployment phase currently out to tender. As the EU's space program has developed, it has taken on an increasingly militaristic character (Slijper, 2008). The European Parliament recently dropped its long-standing (and increasingly untenable) political commitment not to develop military applications for Galileo. Parliament's report, authorizing the use of Galileo to assist EU Security and Defense Operations, also contains provisions favoring the development of satellite-based missile defense systems through NATO (European Parliament 2008).

The EU security research program

The EU Security Research Program (ESRP) is a seven year, €1.4 billion EU project predicated on the need to deliver new security-enhancing technologies to the Union's member states in order to protect EU citizens from a host of contemporary threats. The program also explicitly fosters the growth of a lucrative and globally competitive homeland-security industry in Europe. To this end, a number of prominent European corporations from the defense and IT sectors have enjoyed unprecedented involvement in developing the security "research" agenda. As the ostensibly public ESRP develops, more and more of its governance is outsourced to the very corporations that stand to benefit most from its implementation (Hayes, 2006, 2009).

This was really an extraordinary process. The "Group of Personalities" on security research (GoP) was convened in 2003. It met only twice but cemented the structure, objectives, and ideology of the future ESRP. The GoP included the European Commissioners for Research and Information Society, plus, as "observers," the Commissioners for External Relations and Trade, the High Representative for the EU's Foreign and Security Policy, together with representatives of NATO, the Western European Armaments Association, and the EU Military Committee. Also represented were eight multinational corporations—Europe's four largest arms companies (EADS, BAE Systems, Thales, and Finmeccanica), and some of Europe's largest IT companies (Ericsson, Indra, Siemens, and Diehl)—along with seven research institutions, including the controversial Rand Corporation. Among the "observers" were four members of the European parliament. While this added a democratic sheen to the process, one observer, Karl Von Wogau, was the European Parliament's keenest proponent of corporatist EU defense and security policies. Six members of the GoP later contributed to Von Wogau's book (2004), *The Path to European Defence*.

"Research for a Secure Europe," the final report of the Group of Personalities (GoP), was published in March 2004 (GoP, 2004). The argument it put forward can be summarized as follows. First, security, terrorism, proliferation of weapons of mass destruction, failed states, regional conflicts, organized crime, and illegal immigration are the main sources of anxiety for both citizens and policy-makers alike. Second, technology is vital for security: "Technology itself cannot guarantee security, but security without the support of technology is impossible. It provides us with information about threats, helps us to build effective protection against them and, if necessary, enables us to neutralize them" (2004:7). Third, there are "synergies" between the (military) defense and (civil) security sectors:

> ... technology is very often multi-purpose. Civil and defence applications increasingly draw from the same technological base and there is a growing cross-fertilisation between the two areas ... As a result, the technology base for defence, security and civil applications increasingly forms a continuum ... applications in one area can often be transformed.
>
> (2004:13)

Fourth, the ESRP should be developed to "bridge the gap between civil and traditional defense research, foster the transformation of technologies across the civil, security, and defense fields and improve the EU's industrial competitiveness" (2004:8).

The economic rationale for the ESRP was even more persuasive. The GoP (2004:21) argued that the US Department of Homeland Security (DHS) budget "includes a significant percentage devoted to equipment, and around $1 billion dedicated to research" (this is in addition to those activities funded by other defense and security agencies). The scale of US investment in Homeland Security research, said the GoP, meant that the US was "taking a lead" in developing "technologies and equipment which ... could meet a number of Europe's needs." This was most problematic because the US technology would "progressively impose normative and operational standards worldwide" and "US industry will enjoy a very strong competitive position. There is no reason why European security research should not be funded at a level similar to the US" (2004:21). A US annual per capita expenditure of "more than four dollars on security-related R&D for each citizen" would "mean that an overall EU security R&T budget of 1.8 billion for 450 million Europeans would be desirable" (2004:27). In its final analysis, the GoP recommended that the ESRP should receive a minimum of €1 billion per year in EU funds. After lengthy negotiations, just under €200 million per year was allocated to the security research component of the "FP7" program 2007–13, with the same amount again allotted to "space research." When additional EU research and technology budgets are taken into account, the total figure being spent on "security research" could be much closer to the GoP demands.[3]

The EU's Preparatory Action for Security Research (PASR) ran from 2004 to 2006, providing €65 million in EC funds to 39 projects (European Commission 2004a). In its first year the ratio of applications received to projects funded was 13:1 (with seven times as much money available in 2007 under "FP7" the program was still seven times oversubscribed). One of the most striking features of the PASR was the extent of the involvement of the defense industry. Of 39 security research projects, 23 (60 per cent) were led by companies that primarily service the defense sector. A third of the PASR projects (13) were led by Thales, EADS, Finmeccanica, SAGEM, and the Association of AeroSpace and Defence Industries of Europe (ASD, Europe's largest defense-industry lobby group). Together with BAE Systems, these enterprises participated in 26 (two thirds) of the 39 projects. Another evident feature of the PASR is its overwhelming concern with the *application of existing security technologies*, rather than research into security technology per se—geared more toward procurement than problematization, as it were.

In addition to the 39 projects funded under the PASR, the EU was also funding security-related research projects from its mainstream "framework research" program of 2002–6 (the €16.3 billion, "FP6" program). Bigo and Jeandesboz (2008:8) estimate that by the end of 2006, 170 projects relating directly or indirectly to the themes and priorities identified by the GoP and the European Commission had been funded under FP6.

Outsourcing policy, outsourcing governance

The European Security Research Advisory Board (ESRAB) was established by European Commission Decision on April 22, 2005, in accordance with recommendations of the GoP, "to advise on the content of the ESRP and its implementation, paying due attention to the proposals of the Group of Personalities" (European Commission 2005a). Like the GoP, ESRAB included "experts from various stakeholder groups: users, industry, and research organizations." There was no consultation with the European or national parliaments on who to appoint to ESRAB; nominations for the 50 positions on the board came instead from the then 25 EU ambassadors (the permanent representatives of the member states), the newly established European Defence Agency and other unspecified "stakeholder groups." ESRAB had a mandate to advise the Commission on any questions relating to the development of the ESRP and to make recommendations on the strategic missions and priority areas for security research, as well as implementation issues such as the exchange of classified information, IPR, the use of publicly owned research/ evaluation infrastructures, and a security-research communications strategy. There were two ESRAB working groups with 25 representatives on each. Group 1, the "Technology Group," dealt with "security research demand requirements" while Group 2, the "Enablers Group," addressed the "technology supply chain requirements." This structure clearly had less to do with research than with the needs of commerce and the objective of better integrating the supply chain (corporations) with the demand chain (governments).

The defense and security industries were again well represented, occupying 14 of 50 seats. Seven of the eight corporations on the GoP—EADS, BAE Systems, Thales, Finmeccanica, Ericsson, Siemens and Diehl—were there and the Board's two presidential terms went to Markus Hellenthal of EADS and Tim Robinson of Thales. The remainder of the ESRAB seats went to the member states (18 seats), academics and research institutes (14), the EU, which was represented by the European Defence Agency and EUROPOL, and two "civil liberty groups and think tanks." The European Commission made much of this last category, though while it apparently considered the Crisis Management Initiative set up by the Nobel Prize-winning ex-Finnish Prime Minister Martti Ahtisaari to be a "civil liberties" organization, with respect, this is not a core part of its mission. There were two contenders for the "think tanks"— the EU-funded Institute for Security Studies, which was part of the GoP, and the Italian Istituto Affari Internazionali (Institute of International Affairs)— both of which have very conservative agendas.

ESRAB's mandate expired with the publication of its final report in September 2006. Its replacement, the "European Security Research and Innovation Forum" (ESRIF) was announced at the Second European Conference on Security Research in March 2007. ESRIF was unveiled to the public six months later, somewhat cynically, on the anniversary of 9/11, in a Commission press release entitled "public–private dialogue on security research" (European Commission, 2007b). In all but name it was a simple continuation of the GoP-ESRAB governance of the ESRP with a broader remit: "ESRIF will go beyond FP7 security research; it will go towards meeting long term security research and technological development needs throughout the EU to be covered by national, EU and private investments." ESRIF's mandate includes the "identification of long term threats and challenges" and "linking predictions and expectations about future developments." The ESRIF "roadmap" on security research will be delivered late in 2009, taking a "mid and long term perspective (up to 20 years) ... not only addressing the European but also the national and sometimes regional level" (www.esrif.eu). At least seven member states have already established national-security research programs (the UK, France, Germany, Austria, the Netherlands, Sweden, and Finland) and an EU "network of national ESRP coordination points" is now being set up (the "SEREN" network).

The ESRIF "plenary" has 65 members (selected and appointed in the same opaque way as its predecessor ESRAB), while the forum as a whole contains 660 security-technology expert consultants. The plenary is chaired by Gijs de Vries (the former EU counterterrorism coordinator), with Giancarlo Grasso of Finmeccanica and Jürgen Stock (Deutsches Bundeskriminalamt) as deputies. Of the 65 plenary members, 30 represent the "supply side" of security research and 33 the "demand side," with five from "civil society" (several of the ESRIF plenary members represent more than one of these categories). Of the 50 organizations represented in ESRAB, 17 are also represented on the ESRIF plenary (including Thales, EADS, Finmeccanica, and Sagem). Several non-EU member-state representatives are also now represented, including the Counter Terrorism Bureau of the National Security Council of the State of Israel ("demand side").

The EU has again made much of the representation of European civil-society organizations in ESRIF, with Franco Frattini, former European Commissioner for Justice and Home Affairs, claiming:

> We need to listen to the technical experts to tell us what is technically feasible. Then we need to listen to experts on fundamental rights to see whether there are consequences of using these technologies that would put these rights in danger. It is only when we have considered all sides of the equation that we can find a balanced response.
>
> (European Commission, 2007a)

This time around, the "civil society" organizations are the German Federal Government Office for Population Protection and Disaster Relief (BBK); the European Institute for Risk, Security, and Communication Management (EURISC); the *European Corporate Security Association*; the Centre of Biomedical Engineering at the Bulgarian Academy of Sciences; and the Crisis Management Initiative. In addition to the 65-member plenary, ESRIF has 11 working groups comprising 660 security-research experts, of which two thirds are from the "supply side" (industry) and one third are from the demand side. Just nine of the 660 ESRIF consultants are from the much-vaunted "civil society side" and again, with respect, there are no recognized civil-liberties or fundamental-rights experts or organizations in sight.

While the EU treaties place a clear legal obligation on policy-makers to protect fundamental rights, the ESRP has taken a more fluid view of rights and liberties, viewing them as part of a broader "political challenge" to find a "socially acceptable" balance. In this "trade-off" scenario, civil liberties and human rights have effectively been reduced to "ethical concerns" that must be "balanced" with the needs of security, and, by implication, can be restricted when the case for security has been made. To the extent that many people hold this "baggage" to represent fundamental freedom developed over centuries and enshrined in the constitutional make-up of European democracy, this too is a paradigm shift. The ESRP is also promoting a "new" academic discipline of security economics dealing with risk analysis, public-finance analysis, the "economic costs" of insecurity, and research to combat terrorist financing. RAND Corporation and the University of Jerusalem are among those who develop "new analytical and conceptual insights" on security in the first ESRP-funded project in this topic (the SICMA project; see also the EUSECON project).

Full Spectrum Dominance: how "security research" is becoming security policy

"Meeting the challenge: the European Security Research Agenda," the final report of the European Security Research Advisory Board (ESRAB), was published in September 2006. It proposed a singular trajectory for EU security research, from border controls to counterterrorism and criminal investigations, for critical-infrastructure protection and crisis management, through to EU military operations. This is the model they propose: impose total surveillance (so-called situation awareness and assessment) using every viable surveillance technology on the market; introduce identity checks and authentication protocols based on biometric ID systems; deploy a range of detection technologies and techniques at all ID control points; use high-tech communications systems to ensure that law-enforcement agents have total information awareness; use profiling, data-mining and behavioral analysis to identify suspicious people; use risk assessment and modeling to predict (and mitigate) human behavior; ensure rapid "incident response;" then intervene to neutralize the threat, automatically where possible (ESRAB, 2006). Finally, ensure all systems are fully interoperable so that technological applications being used for one mission can easily be used for all the others (2006).

The ESRAB report was strongly influenced by two "high level" studies commissioned under the Preparatory Action for Security Research (above). The SENTRE project (Security Network for Technological Research in Europe), funded under the PASR (above), was led by the lobby group ASD (European Association of Aerospace and Defence Industries), with the support of 21 partner organizations, two thirds of which came from the defense sector. The ESSTRT project (European Security, Threats, Responses and Relevant Technologies), was led by Thales UK, with the support of the Institute for Strategic Studies and the Crisis Management Initiative. Contrary to the repeated European Commission claims that the ESRP is concerned with security technology and not security policy, ESSTRT's final report, "New Approaches to Counter-Terrorism," contained over 70 detailed recommendations—including 32 EU "policy actions"—many of which were incorporated wholesale into the ESRAB report. Among the other ESSTRT recommendations were that the European Commission "develop a communications strategy that fosters public awareness of threats and of the extent and limits of governments' ability to counter them." The communications strategy should stress "that it is a *long-term challenge*; that while it may be driven by external factors, considerable attention needs to be devoted to the capacity for *internal generation* of terrorist cells within EU member states" (emphasis in original). The advice continued with a call on the EU member states to adopt "minimum standards of law enforcement" that "allow necessary powers to security organisations" (ESSTRT 2006:6). As Lipschultz and Turcotte (2005:26) have observed: "Counter-terrorism is more than a response to acts of terrorism; it is an autonomous arena of supply that requires a demand to survive and succeed."

The "Stakeholders platform for supply Chain mapping, market Condition Analysis and Technologies Opportunities" (STACCATO) was a follow-up to the SENTRE project also led by the lobby group ASD. STACCATO produced an (unpublished) report entitled "How to Foster the European Security Market" and proposed "methods and solutions for the creation of a security market and a structured supply chain in Europe." STACCATO comprised four work packages: Stakeholder Platform (led by EADS), Market Condition Analysis (Finmeccanica), Integration of Priorities and Recommendations (Thales), and Analysis of Competencies of the Supply Chain (EU Joint Research Centre).

There were similar influences on the final ESRIF report, published in 2009. Working Group 1, on "Security of the citizens," had a mandate to "improve technologies" in the following areas:

> ... terrorism and organised crime, protection of soft targets (e.g. large scale events, crowds), urban security, civil protection, public health security (pandemics), cyber crime, on-line investigations, public–private trusted information exchange models, financial threats (e.g. currency manipulations, stock value manipulations) [and] non-proliferation of WMD and SALW [small arms and light weapons].
>
> (Berg, 2006:18)

The *rapporteur*, responsible for producing the findings of the working group, is Jean-Marc Suchier of *Sagem Défense Sécurité*, a company whose global mission is to provide "a cross-fertilization between solutions that belong to apparently different worlds: multibiometrics (fingerprint technologies) for making transportation more secure, optronics (usually military oriented) applied to homeland security, inertial navigation applied to unmanned air vehicles etc."

Identification of people and assets

The *rapporteur* for ESRIF Working Group 8 on the "identification of people and assets" is the European Biometrics Forum (EBF), a lobby group "whose overall vision is to establish the European Union as the World Leader in Biometrics Excellence by addressing barriers to adoption and fragmentation in the marketplace." The organization is also leading a PASR project on the "Testing and certification of biometric components and systems" (BioTesting Europe) in support of EU legislation on the fingerprinting of passport, visa, and residence permit-holders. This will produce a "roadmap" on "what needs to be tested," "which components should be certified (sensors/algorithms/sub-systems etc.)," "who is going to perform the tests," "what are the costs and who will pay/invest" (www.biotestingeuripe.eu). At least 20 other projects concerned with biometric identification systems have been funded by the EU to date, covering topics such as iris, voice, and facial recognition; infra-red vein imaging; entry and exit systems, including a "walk-by biometric identification system based on face recognition"; and a "virtual PIN" (personal identification number, as used in financial services) for e-commerce.

EU law has also placed obligations on the telecommunications, financial, and air-travel sectors to retain customer records for long periods for police purposes. Combining these and other datasets—such as consumer "lifestyle" databases built by specialized data-mining companies, or credit-reference agencies—creates a previously unimaginably detailed picture of peoples' lives and interests; their cultural, religious, and political affiliations; and their financial and medical health. Under the PASR, the EU funded projects on the identification of suspicious individuals through the analysis of communication, financial, and travel data (I-TRACS); on the cross-border exchange of differentiated sources of data, in order to "prevent, predict, and protect against potential terrorist activities" (HITS–ISAC); on "Human monitoring and authentication using biodynamic indicators and behavioral analysis" (HUMA-BIO); and on "interoperable" standards for data-exchange and profiling at the border (STABORSEC, see further below). The EU has already recommended that the member states use "terrorist profiling" systems as part of a program of measures to combat "radicalization and recruitment," despite objections from its own fundamental-rights experts and the European Parliament (EU Network of Experts on Fundamental Rights, 2003). As the Council of Europe Commissioner for Human Rights has explained, technologies that enable "profiling" and "data mining" may appear attractive, but they are just as likely to lead to actions against large numbers of innocent people on a scale that is unacceptable in a democratic society (Council of Europe, 2008:4). It is important to stress the inevitability in this—not everyone who bought product A will want product B—this is something that cannot be fixed by better design (2008).

From the battlefield to the border, from the border to the "barrio"

For ESRIF Working Group 3 on "border security" the challenge is integrated border management and maritime surveillance. The Group's *rapporteur* is the Italian defence giant Finmeccanica, which in 2007 published a "joint initiative" with Thales on "maritime management" to "promot[e] standards to foster the development of synergies between various civil and military maritime sectors" and "multi-user systems" (Thales, 2007: 5). This followed an earlier PASR project on the "surveillance of borders and harbors" (SOBCAH) led by Galileo Avionica (a Finmeccanica company) in conjunction with Thales Underwater Systems. The PASR also funded research projects on the "required specification standards" for interoperable EU border controls (STABORSEC 2007), led by Sagem, and "border surveillance using unmanned aerial vehicles" (BSUAV), led by Dassault Aviation, one of Europe's largest manufacturers of unmanned aerial vehicles.

At least a dozen projects on UAVs have been funded under the EU's framework research programs to date, including €5 million for a study on the "utilization of safe and low cost Unmanned Air Vehicles (UAVs) in the civilian commercial sphere" (CAPECON), led by Israel Aircraft Industries Ltd. (the state-owned, self-proclaimed "global leader in comprehensive UAV-based solutions—offering the widest range of combat-proven systems"); a €4.3 million "roadmap" for "innovative operational UAV integration" (INOUI, featuring Boeing Europe) and a project on the development of UAVs for the surveillance of urban environments (μDRONES, featuring Thales). The EU "Future Group" records that "with rare exceptions, drones (unpiloted, low-flying light aircraft that remain in view of their operators) are forbidden today in the European sky" (cited in Bunyan 2008:13). With "these technologies potentially very efficient for use in numerous security assignments" (2008), this may not be the case for long. Some member states, including the UK, are already piloting UAVs for public-order and domestic-surveillance purposes.

In 2008, the European Commission produced a Communication (EU position paper) on the creation of a European Border Surveillance System (European Commission, 2008a). The EUROSUR system will be implemented in three phases, by "interlinking and streamlining [of] existing national surveillance systems," developing "common tools and applications for border surveillance at EU level" and then creating "a common monitoring and information sharing environment for the EU maritime domain" (European Commission, 2008a: 5). In practice, all three phases are well underway. ESRP border surveillance projects funded under FP7 to date include OPERAMAR, led by Thales Underwater Systems in conjunction with Finmeccanica, which will examine the scope for "interoperability" of European and national surveillance assets (the "initial phase" of the two corporations' aforementioned joint initiative); and SECTRONIC, which concerns the "observation and protection of critical maritime infrastructures; passenger and goods transport, energy supply, and port infrastructures." Participants in the latter project—which will establish "control centres" equipped with "all accessible means of observation (offshore, onshore, air, space)" and "[be] able to protect the infrastructure by non-lethal means in the scenario of a security concerned situation"—include the NATO Undersea Research Centre.[4] Thales Airborne Systems is leading the WIMA2S project on "Wide Maritime Area Airborne Surveillance" (Dassault Aviation and Galileo Avionica are also participating); Thales Alenia Space is the *rapporteur* for ESRIF Working Group 7 on "situation awareness including the role of space." The €20 million TALOS project will "develop and field test a mobile, modular, scalable, autonomous and adaptive system for protecting European borders, [using] both aerial and ground unmanned vehicles, supervised by command and control centre ... first reaction patrols ... will undertake the proper measures *to stop the illegal action almost autonomously* with supervision of border guard officers."[5] (Emphasis added.)

Another "Autonomous Maritime Surveillance System" (AMASS) will use "autonomous, unmanned surveillance buoys with active and passive sensors" and "un-cooled thermal imagers" in coastal waters to detect and identify local threats to security.[6] A communications network between the national coordination centers for maritime surveillance and FRONTEX, the EU Border Management Agency, is being created. Saab has been awarded a European Defence Agency contract to produce a feasibility study on a Maritime Surveillance Network to fulfill the military's needs.

Despite the sea of acronyms, a somewhat alarming drive for "full spectrum dominance" is evident along the EU's external border (resplendent with autonomous threat neutralization), among just a handful of security-research projects funded under the first call for proposals under FP7. To date this has centered on what EU policy-makers now refer to as the EU's "southern maritime frontier," a border zone that stretches from the control rooms of Europe, across the open seas of the Mediterranean and Atlantic to the coastlines of the Middle East, North and West Africa. GLOBE, another FP7 project led by Telvent ("the IT company for a sustainable and secure world") will set out "the full scope of an integrated border management system, moving throughout the four main layers of border control (Country of origin, transit areas, regulated and unregulated border lines and internal territory)."[7]

Crisis management and critical-infrastructure protection

The extensively televised response of the United States' government to Hurricane Katrina appalled viewers around the world. The military were sent in to "secure" poor areas while people died in their homes and starved and froze in a sports arena. Was this just bad government by an overstretched administration—mainstream news organizations openly commented that they had seen better disaster relief in the Third World—or did it represent a deeper transformation, a new militarist era of "crisis management" in which the full force of the state may be deployed against the poorest sections of the domestic population? This question is beyond the scope of this paper, but those who have read *The Shock Doctrine* will have little trouble relating the failed-state response to the emergence of a powerful disaster-capitalism complex (Klein, 2007; Reifer, 2009).

Under the ESRP, crisis management and critical-infrastructure protection has already taken a distinctively militarist turn. This is not to say that this will inevitably lead to heavy-handed militarist deployments in domestic European crisis scenarios, though it certainly enhances this prospect. The *rapporteur* for ESRIF Working Group 4 on crisis management is Frequentis, Europe's self-proclaimed "number one" provider "of control centre solutions." It will report on Europe's preparedness to respond to natural catastrophes through internal and external "risk and crisis management." The *rapporteur* for ESRIF Working Group 2 on the "security of critical Infrastructure"—which has a mandate to improve the protection of critical infrastructure and utilities such as "energy infrastructures and supplies (including gas and water supply)," "food safety and security," health, "financial infrastructure," transport, the chemical industry, and space—is the defense giant EADS. EADS led earlier PASR projects on "mobile autonomous reactive information systems" for "urgency situations" (basically military command helicopters; MARIUS) and, with Thales, received funding for its "MANPAD" infrared aircraft missile-defense system for commercial aircraft (PALMA).

Finally, there are three "interoperable" ESRIF working groups which will provide "input to all the political mission areas." The Swedish Defence Research Institute FOI has been appointed *rapporteur* for ESRIF Working Group 7 on "foresight and scenarios," exploring computer modeling and prediction for crisis simulation; and the Dutch Defense Research Institute, TNO, is *rapporteur* on counter-CBRN [chemical, biological, radiological, and nuclear] proliferation strategy. RUSI, the UK's Royal United Services Institute, is *rapporteur* for Working Group 10 on "governance and coordination" of "security research strategy and implementation between the European Union and Member States and relevant institutions or organizations, such as ESA [the European Space Agency], EDA [the European Defence Agency], NATO" (Berg, 2006: 28)—Full Spectrum Dominance through full spectrum governance, perhaps? This uncertainty is critical: is anyone critically evaluating critical infrastructure protection and crisis management?

Disaster capitalism: a world of red zones and green zones

The pursuit of Full Spectrum Dominance may seem an absurd course of action for liberal democratic governments. But in a world that is systemically failing to address the *root causes* of most forms of global insecurity (or worse), it begins to make rather more sense. As the widely respected Oxford Research Group annual report on international security has warned:

> There is a great risk that the main effect of the financial crisis and consequent recession will be a sharpening of the wealth–poverty divisions worldwide ... If the response to the current financial crisis is primarily concerned with ensuring that the economic system works more effectively, this will benefit the world's elite communities but will do little or nothing for the majority, whose predicament will be worsened.
>
> (Rogers, 2008: 10)

In turn, an absence of adequate social-policy responses to protracted social, economic, and environmental problems could usher in counterproductive attempts to control social unrest with excessive force, leading to an escalation in violence in the South (Rogers, 2008). This is what Paul Rogers (2002:102) has called "liddism": "regaining and maintaining control, rather than addressing root causes ... keeping the lid on dissent and instability." Should the current economic crisis worsen significantly, EU member states with stark wealth disparities, growing inequalities and marginalized urban communities could face these dilemmas at home as well as abroad.

The costs of "liddism" are already abundantly clear, from the militarized borders of the EU and other rich countries, the stark inequalities between the gated communities and ghettoes of the world's global cities (where the latter keep the former at bay with their own localized versions of Full Spectrum Dominance) to the "disaster apartheid" of post-catastrophe and conflict zones. Reflecting on this last phenomenon, Naomi Klein records:

> At first I thought the Green Zone phenomenon was unique to the war in Iraq. Now, after years spent in other disaster zones, I realize that the Green Zone emerges everywhere that the disaster capitalism complex descends, with the same stark partitions between the included and the excluded, the protected and the damned.
>
> (Klein, 2007: 414)

In its haste to foster a globally competitive homeland-security industry, the EU is subsidizing the development of its own "disaster capitalism complex," which is in turn shaping high-level deliberations about security policy. At least to this observer, this too seems like an absurd course of action: a kind of arms race for technologies of control, a race in which all the weapons are pointing inwards. The rapid and apparently unopposed development of the EU's maritime surveillance system suggests that coherent political programs based on imposing ubiquitous, globalizing surveillance systems for the purposes of state control are certainly not as far-fetched as they may appear. It might be suggested that deploying such a system in a domestic context will meet far more public resistance, but this prospect is undermined by the relative invisibility of new surveillance technologies (both physically and politically).

The EU Security Research Program, the vehicle for the implementation of a Full Spectrum Dominance infrastructure in Europe, is largely off the radar of parliamentarians, civil society, and the public—and it is still very much in its infancy. The developments described above account for preparatory actions and just six months of the seven-year security-research component of FP7; the European Security Research and Innovation Forum is currently developing a 20-year vision. The merits of the "NeoConOpticon" as a conceptual framework is for others to discuss; at the very least, to disavow the now well-known phrase, it is starting to appear less a case of "sleepwalking into a surveillance society"—thousands of highly skilled people are hard at work designing this—and more a case of sleepwalking into the surveillance economy.

Notes

1 Under the so-called "Community method," the European Commission is responsible for developing and implementing policy and the EU Council (of member states) and the European Parliament are jointly responsible for deciding what these policies should be.

2 Just as the text of this chapter was being finalized, the European Court of Human Rights delivered a celebrated judgement in the case of *S. and Marper v The United Kingdom* (Applications nos. 30562/04 and), declaring that that the UK practice of keeping indefinitely the fingerprints and DNA of people not convicted of an offence is a violation of Article 8 of the European Convention on Human Rights on the right to privacy. This judgement has implications for the collection, storing, exchange, and use of biometric data by all parties to the Convention.

3 In addition to the €2.8 billion allotted to Security and Space, the Food, IT, Energy, Environment, and Transport components of FP7 are all likely to have a significant "security" research agenda. Finally, if the hype around "nano-technology"—which is to receive a staggering €3.5 billion under FP7 (more than Security and Space combined)—is translated into applied science, it has the potential to fundamentally affect military and security research by revolutionizing surveillance capabilities, biological and chemical warfare, and munitions and armaments (Langley, 2005:54–55). The EU has also established additional budget lines on border control and critical-infrastructure protection.

4 http://cordis.europa.eu.

5 Ibid.

6 Ibid.

7 Ibid.

References

Berg, F.R. 2008. *European Security Research and Innovation Forum*. Oslo: Kredittilsy-net [Norwegian Financial Services Authority]. Available at http://www.fsi.no.

Bigo, D. 2006. "Liberty, whose liberty?" In *Security Versus Freedom? A Challenge for Europe's Future*, edited by Thierry Balzacq and Sergio Carrera, 35–44. London: Ashgate.

Bigo, D. and J. Jeandesboz. 2008. *Review of Security Measures in the 6th Research Framework Programme and the Preparatory Action for Security Research*. Brussels: European Parliament.

Bunyan, T., ed. 2006. *The War on Freedom and Democracy: Essays on Civil Liberties in Europe*. London: Spokesman.

———. 2008. *The Shape of Things to Come: The EU Future Group*. London: Statewatch. Available at: http://www.statewatch.org.

CHENS (Chiefs of European Navies). 2005. *A Vision for the Future of EU Maritime Forces by the Chiefs' of European Navies*. Available at http://www.chens.eu.

Council of Europe. 2008. "Protecting the right to privacy in the fight against terrorism." *Issue Paper by Thomas Hammarberg, Council of Europe Commissioner for Human Rights* (CommDH/IssuePaper (2008) 3/04). Strasbourg: Council of Europe.

Curtin, D. and A. Meijer. 2005. "Five myths of European Union transparency: Delib-eration through the Looking Glass?" Paper presented at *Special Workshop on Deliberative Democracy and Its Discontents, IVR World Congress in Legal Philoso-phy*, Granada, May 2005.

Department of Defence. 2000. *Joint Vision: 2020*. Washington: USA Department of Defence.

ESRAB (European Security Research Advisory Board). 2006. *Meeting the Challenge: The European Security Research Agenda—A Report from the European Security Research Advisory Board*. Brussels: European Commission.

ESRIF [European Security Research and Innovation Forum]. 2009. *ESRIF final report*. Brussels: European Commission.

ESSTRT [European Security, Threats, Responses and Relevant Technologies]. 2006. *Final Report: New European Approaches to Counter Terrorism*. London: Thales Research and Technology, International Institute for Strategic Studies, Crisis Management Initiative (CMI) and Thales e-Security (TeS).

EU Council. 2003. *Thessaloniki European Council 19 and 20 June 2003: Presidency Conclusions*. October 1, 2003.

European Commission. 2004a. *Commission Decision 2004/213/EC of 3 February 2004 on the Implementation of the Preparatory Action on the Enhancement of the European Industrial Potential in the Field of Security Research*. Brussels: European Commission.

———. 2004b. *Towards Enhancing Access to Information by Law Enforcement Agencies*. COM (2004) 429 final, June 16, 2004.

———. 2005a. *Commission Decision 2005/516/EC of 22 April 2005 Establishing the European Security Research Advisory Board*. Brussels: European Commission.

———. 2005b. *Proposal for a Council Framework Decision on the Exchange of Infor-mation under the Principle of Availability*. COM (2005) 490 final, October 12, 2005. Brussels: European Commission.

———. 2006. *Interoperability for Pan-European eGovernment services*. COM (2006) 45 final, 13 February 2006. Brussels: European Commission.

——. 2007a. *New Challenges, New Opportunities.* Franco Frattini, European Commissioner Responsible for Justice, Freedom and Security. Speech to Security Research Conference, Berlin, March 26, 2007, press release dated 26 March 2007. Brussels: European Commission.

——. 2007b. *The European Security Research and Innovation Forum (ESRIF) – Public-Private Dialogue in Security Research.* Press release dated September 11, 2007. Brussels: European Commission.

——. 2008a. Communication from the Commission to the European Parliament, the Council, the European Economic and Social Committee and the Committee of the Regions – *Examining the creation of a European border surveillance system (EUROSUR)*, COM(2008) 68 final, February 13, 2008. Brussels: European Commission.

——. 2008b. *Fight against Cyber Crime: Cyber Patrols and Internet Investigation Teams to Reinforce the EU Strategy.* Press release dated September 11, 2007. Brussels: European Commission.

European Parliament. 2008. *Report on Space and Security.* Committee on Foreign Affairs, EP doc. A6–0250/2008, June 10, 2008.

EU Network of Experts on Fundamental Rights. 2003. *The Balance Between Freedom and Security in the Response by the European Union and its Member States to the Terrorist Threats.* Brussels: European Commission.

GoP (Group of Personalities). 2004. *Research for a Secure Europe: Report of the Group of Personalities in the Field of Security Research.* Brussels: European Commission.

Hayes, B. 2005. A failure to regulate: Data protection in the police sector in Europe in Open Society Institute (ed.) *Justice Initiatives: Ethnic Profiling by Police in Europe.* New York: Open Society Institute.

——. 2006. *Arming Big Brother: The EU's Security Research Programme.* Amsterdam: Tansnational Institute/Statewatch.

——. 2009. *Full Spectrum Dominance: The Corporate and Military Takeover of EU Security Policy.* Amsterdam: Tansnational Institute/Statewatch.

Hosein, G. 2004. "International relations theories and the regulation of international dataflows: Policy laundering and other international policy dynamics." Paper presented at the annual meeting of the *International Studies Association*, Le Centre Sheraton Hotel, Montreal, Quebec, Canada, March 17, 2004.

Klein, N. 2007. *The Shock Doctrine.* London: Penguin.

Langley, C. 2005. *Soldiers in the Laboratory: Military Involvement in Science and Technology – And Some Alternatives.* Folkstone, England: Scientists for Global Responsibility.

Lipschultz, R.D. and H. Turcotte. 2005. "Duct tape or plastic? The political economy of threats and the production of fear." In *Making Threats: Biofears and Environmental Anxieties*, ed. B. Hartman, B. Subramaniam, and C. Zerner, New York: Rowman and Littlefield.

Loader, I. 2002. "Policing, Securitization and Democratisation in Europe." *Criminal Justice* 2(2): 125–53.

Mathiesen, T. 1999. *On Globalisation of Control: Towards an Integrated Surveillance System in Europe.* London: Statewatch.

Mitrou, L. 2010. "The impact of communications data retention on fundamental rights and democracy – The case of the EU Data Retention Directive." In K. Haggerty and M. Samatas, eds., *Surveillance and Democracy.* London: Routledge.

NATO. 2007. *Towards a Grand Strategy for an Uncertain World: Renewing Transatlantic Partnership*. Lunteren: Noaber Foundation.

Peers, S. 2007. *EU Justice and Home Affairs Law*, 2nd Edition. Oxford: Oxford University Press.

Project for the New American Century. 2000. *Rebuilding America's Defenses: Strategy, Forces and Resources for a New Century*. Washington: Project for the New American Century.

Reifer, T. 2009. "Blown Away: U.S. Militarism, Hurricane Katrina and the Challenges of the 21st Century." In *Racing the Storm: Racial Implications and Lessons Learned from Huricane Katrina*. H. Potter, ed. Lanham, MD: Lexington Books.

Rogers, P. 2002. *Losing Control: Global Security in the Twenty-First Century*. London: Pluto.

———. 2008. *The Tipping Point? ORG International Security Report 2008*. Oxford: Oxford Research Group.

Slijper, F. 2008. *From Venus to Mars: The European Union's Steps Towards the Militarisation of Space*. Amsterdam: Transnational Institute.

STABORSEC (Standards for Border Security Enhancement). 2007. *Existing Specification Standards for Border Security*. (deliverable D4.1). Brussels: STABORSEC consortium.

Thales. 2007. *Thales Contribution to the Countation Process*. Unpublished paper dated 29 June 2007. Available at: http://www.statewatch.org.

Von Wogau, K., ed. 2004. *The Path to European Defence*. Brussels: Maklu-Uitgevers.

Webb, M. 2007. *Illusions of Security: Global Surveillance and Democracy in the Post-9/11 World*. San Francisco: City Lights.

Webber, F. 1995. *Crimes of Arrival: Refugees and Asylum-Seekers in the New Europe*. London: Statewatch.

———. 2004. "The war on migration." In *Beyond Criminology: Taking Harm Seriously*, edited by P. Hillyard, C. Pantazis, S. Tombs, and D. Gordon. pp. 133–55. London: Pluto.

Websites

ASD (AeroSpace and Defence Industries Association of Europe): http://www.asd-europe.org.

BAE Systems: http://www.baesystems.com.

Biotesting Europe: http://www.biotestingeurope.eu.

CORDIS (Community Research and Development Information Service): http://cordis.europa.eu.

Crisis Management Initiative: http://www.ahtisaari.fi.

Defense News: http://www.defensenews.com.

Diehl Group: http://www.diehl.com.

EADS: http://www.eads.net.

ESRIF (European Security Research and Innovation Forum): http://www.esrif.eu.

EU Institute for Strategic Studies: http://www.iss.europa.eu.

EU Joint Research Centre: http://www.jrc.ec.europa.eu.

EU Security research website: http://ec.europa.eu/enterprise/security/index_en.htm.

EURISC (European Institute for Risk, Security and Communication Management) http://www.eurisc.org.
European Biometrics Forum: http://www.eubiometricforum.com.
European Corporate Security Association: http://www.ecsa-eu.org.
European Space Agency: http://www.esa.int.
Finmeccanica: http://www.finmeccanica.com.
Frequentis: http://www.frequentis.com/internet.
GMES (Global Monitoring for Environmental Security): http://www.gmes.info.
Independent newspaper: http://www.independent.co.uk.
Institute for Security Studies: http://www.iss.co.za.
Instituto Affari Internazionali: http://www.iai.it.
Israel Aerospace Industries Ltd.: http://www.iai.co.il.
Rand Corporation: http://www.rand.org.
Sagem Défense Sécurité: http://www.sagem-ds.com.
Security and Defence Agenda: http://www.securitydefenceagenda.org.
Statewatch: http://www.statewatch.org.
Thales Group: http://www.thalesgroup.com.
Transnational Institute: http://www.tni.org.

Part III

Case studies in the dynamics of surveillance and democracy

Chapter 9

A trans-systemic surveillance

The legacy of communist surveillance in the digital age

Maria Los

Communist regimes have left their successors a poisonous surveillance legacy. The personal, political, and economic stakes in the struggles over communist surveillance records are so high that they dominate the aftermath of a regime's collapse. This is especially true for countries where due process protections for guardianship, access, and use of the secret archives were not swiftly established by new democratic laws. This includes the introduction of lustration laws, which are obligatory measures designed to identify former security-services functionaries, and their secret collaborators among those who seek or hold specified public offices.

In this paper, I ask how and to what extent current social/political power relations and practices in post-Communist democracies are affected by the former regime's surveillance records and mentalities. My query goes beyond "the policing of the past" (Cohen, 1995) and focuses on how the past may actually be policing the present, and possibly the future. What happens when secret information gathered by a totalitarian regime becomes available for use by its successor—a budding democratic state—and by other players in the murky waters of such so-called transitions? Does this body of information retain its surveillance potential under the changed political circumstances? If so, does this make the new surveillance culture of post-Communist countries significantly different from that currently evolving in well-established, neoliberal democracies? Are old habits of resistance useful in responding to these new challenges?

To address these questions, I point first to the main characteristics of the communist surveillance practices and habitual ways that people resisted or adapted to those measures. I also explore the sources and mechanisms of the lingering power of the Communist secret archives. Legal measures designed to deal with that legacy are briefly discussed and assessed for their compatibility with democracy. These laws are placed within the context of ongoing political struggles over the records of Communist surveillance practices, particularly in countries that delayed passing lustration laws.

Next, I briefly explain how the old fear of the state was replaced initially by a culture dominated by fear of crime, which eventually evolved into new forms of insecurity related to an unexpected bypassing of modernist processes and a direct move towards new, post-industrial forms of continuous surveillance. As post-Communist societies are faced with an uneasy combination of lingering police powers related to the old secret files and the new awareness of digital *dataveillance*, the suitability of old habits of resistance must be examined. To address this issue, I explore the main differences between the new and old surveillance practices, with a special focus on surveillance of the body and the self. By comparing contemporary biometric surveillance and the old form of monitoring practiced by Soviet states, I examine possible implications for the resisting self. The closing section of this paper briefly summarizes and discusses my findings.

Communist surveillance and lines of resistance

Soviet-style surveillance was essentially one-directional, centralized, and territorial; it was based on a scheme of immobilization, static visibility, state monopoly of surveillance technologies, and a rigid regimentation of life. It aimed to prevent the spread of contagious ideas and its surveillant logic was akin to that traditionally reserved for the control of epidemics (as depicted, for example, by Foucault, 1979:195–98). Its success was buttressed by strict controls over access to communication tools such as telephones, photocopiers, printing presses, and, naturally, computers.

Surveillance practices employed by Communist countries were part of a complex scheme of manufacturing fear. Fear was the principal premise of the control mechanism and was used by officials to break individuals, erode trust, and destroy social solidarity. The principle of fear was systematically applied as a tool of humiliation, while secret surveillance practices served both to promote and document this process. As I elaborate elsewhere, this led to the formation of the taboo mentality, whereby many areas of life were relegated to the forbidden land of topics automatically excluded from a conscious, rational reflection (Los, 2002, 2004). The key strategies for coping with the constant presence of fear included practices of invisibility and withdrawing into oneself, known generally as "internal immigration."

Under Communist regimes, any possible lines of flight or resistance were located inside a relatively static grid of continuous secret surveillance of state-owned workplaces, housing projects, leisure venues, and practically any other social space. This grid was underpinned by controls that immobilized population movement within and across state boundaries. The Soviet Bloc did not survive long enough for its surveillance/control measures to be tested by the inevitable invasion of borderless, interactive, postmodern, and post-panoptic technologies. Judging by the frantic efforts of Communist China, in collusion with international software producers, to curtail and subvert new communication technologies, such devices undoubtedly pose an enormous threat and challenge to the totalitarian system, while also providing it with new tools to track and control citizens (see Open Net Initiative, 2005).

Usually overlooked, however, is the fact that in the Communist era, resistance was very much imprinted in the body. Despite their early efforts to develop a comprehensive system of thought control, Communist rulers had to settle for an indirect system to detect independent thought by monitoring their subjects' overt behavior, oral and written expression, and, perhaps above all, their body language. Aware that their body might betray their thoughts, people developed refined regimes of bodily self-monitoring and self-control. While training their bodies to be inscrutable, they also treated them as a possible vehicle for resistance. Body language could either mask politically dangerous thoughts and attitudes or serve as an outlet to express them nonverbally, through various dignity-saving maneuvers. Thus, depending on the meaning they wanted to convey, bodies could nod, clap, look respectful or meek, and follow the rules of uniform appearance. Alternatively, they could refrain from clapping, look nonchalant, wear a sarcastic smile, and try to look distinct. Even more perversely, people developed an ability to signal with their posture and facial expression that their presence was a mere bodily façade; their inner souls were elsewhere, absent from the unbearable farce or torture. Confronted with this mass internal immigration, the authorities scaled down their utopian designs. When the withdrawal of souls from bodies advanced beyond a certain point, the system lost its bearing and the ideological façade started to crumble.

Communist secret archives and their lingering policing power

All Communist countries combined huge political police forces with a system of secret collaborators to enable totalitarian rule. Together they generated an enormous amount of secret personal data that was channeled into individual citizens' files as well as to other operational files and databanks. This information was routinely shared with their Soviet masters. Long after a regime's collapse, two categories of data remain especially potent and sensitive. They are:

1. Data pertaining to an individual's secret collaboration with the previous regime's civilian or military secret services.
2. Data pertaining to non-political, personal, embarrassing matters, recorded in the course of Communist surveillance.

Archival information might reveal or imply several types of secret collaboration, ranging from occasional contacts to a full, formalized, often paid, commitment in which a person provided information solicited by the authorities and performed secret tasks. Information about personal matters might concern sexual orientation, transgressions, addictions, health issues, private betrayals, or anything that the authorities thought potentially embarrassing for the individual if revealed publicly or communicated to specific people. This information was collected either as an integral part of a larger body of records, resulting from the comprehensive monitoring of an individual (or a group), or as a part of a profile of a secret collaborator or someone targeted for recruitment. A growing body of research based on secret-service archives in Poland clearly reveals that one major task of collaborators was to provide information about specific others to facilitate their secret recruitment (see various publications of the IPN—The Institute of National Remembrance, at www.ipn.gov.pl).

There were also special pools of detailed data about people believed to be particularly vulnerable to blackmail, such as the so-called pink archives containing files of people identified by the police as homosexuals. In Poland, much of this information was collected as part of Hyacinth, the secret operation, launched in the mid-1980s, when numerous suspected homosexuals were interrogated, fingerprinted, and pressured to enlist for secret collaboration (Stachowiak, 2007). Many victims of this operation—some of them now highly placed in public life—continue to conceal their sexual orientation and, therefore, live in fear that police information will be leaked, used for blackmail, or made accessible to researchers or journalists.

People were often targeted as candidates for secret collaboration because officials thought they possessed useful inside knowledge and access to groups or individuals of particular interest to the services. The information collected about such individuals concerned above all their relationships with others, which helped to assess the potential usefulness of prospective recruits. Officials also sought information about people's weaknesses, secrets, deviations, vices, and unlawful actions, as well as their particular needs, difficulties, and aspirations.

Any compromising information could be used in recruitment attempts to apply pressure or, in relatively rare cases, as a tool for full-blown blackmail. According to archival researchers, the services' priority in the post-Stalinist period was to secure a productive relationship with the informer and for this purpose it was more helpful to allude to any compromising information rather than explicitly engage in blackmail. As a result, blackmail was used as the main tool in successful recruitment only in approximately 1.5 per cent of cases in Romania (Stan, 2002a:55) and 2–3 per cent of recruitment cases in Poland (Rudzikowski, 2004:16; see also Korkuć, 2007:234).

Finally, information about someone's personal difficulties or aspirations was used to facilitate recruitment by enabling operatives to promise assistance in these areas and/or by helping to design strategies to psychologically manipulate the candidate. This comprehensive approach to recruiting informers resulted in an enormous amount of information both about those who agreed to collaborate and those who did not (Zając, 2006).

Formal measures to deal with the Communist surveillance legacy

Most Central/East European post-Communist countries have adopted some form of lustration law to regulate the status and access to Communist surveillance records and establish legal mechanisms to screen individuals who hold prominent public positions and candidates for such offices. Often, these laws require candidates and office-holders to obtain special certificates or submit personal statements concerning their possible collaboration with Communist secret services. Personal declarations are subsequently checked and made public to enable voters or decision-makers to make informed decisions. Under some laws, collaborators are given the option to quietly withdraw their candidacy or quit their post as an alternative to publicly disclosing their former roles. Several countries have also employed special *de-Communization* strategies that bar former secret-service functionaries and their collaborators and/or high Communist officials from occupying specified posts for a specified number of years.

An important aspect of lustration laws pertains to rules regulating the management of the old archives. Generally, the goal is to detach the archives from the new security agencies and establish separate, non-political, trusted bodies charged with cataloguing their content, supervising access, facilitating research, and helping implement lawful lustration.

Numerous public narratives and clashing political interests were involved in the campaigns to pass these pieces of legislation. Above all, they were motivated by the need to reduce the possibility that new, democratically appointed/elected politicians and other authority figures could still have unhealthy links to former secret-service networks or be blackmailed and manipulated by those with information about their secret past. The option for a person to quietly withdraw, incorporated into some lustration laws, was meant to combine protection of public offices and state security with respect for the privacy rights of ordinary citizens.

Czechoslovakia and Lithuania enacted their lustration laws in 1991, almost immediately after the regime collapse. Bulgaria, Hungary, and Albania did so in 1992, 1994, and 1995 respectively. Poland passed its first lustration law in 1997, followed by Romania, in 1999, ten years after the regime's collapse. The comparatively long period during which the former surveillance files in Poland and Romania were unregulated makes these countries particularly interesting for research. Slovakia could also be included in this category since it effectively abandoned its commitment to enforce the Czechoslovak lustration/de-Communization laws following the division of Czechoslovakia in 1993. It is generally recognized that the Czech Republic—with its timely combination of lustration, de-Communization, and the wholesale replacement of its security services—has largely prevented wild "file wars" and protracted political influence by the former police-state structures (see, for example, Williams, 1999).

Several publications have reviewed the constitutional and international human-rights challenges to lustration laws in various post-Communist countries and assessed whether they are compatible with national and international legal standards and practices (see, for example, Boed, 1999; David,

2003, 2004; Hatschikjan et al., 2005; Williams, 1999; Williams et al., 2003). The overall impression one gets from this research is that while there have been problems with some specific clauses, legal solutions, or the scope of some lustration laws, their underlying principles are compatible with international human-rights and labor conventions. Most democratic states have legal provisions designed to ensure that civil servants and other public officials meet specified criteria related to personal integrity and security. It seems legitimate to require that former registered Communist informers refrain from occupying high public offices for a specified period of time, or at least submit to a procedure that would publicly reveal their collaboration. The test of these laws lies in having clear criteria, transparent procedures, well-trained personnel, and due process in addressing the inevitable complexities of human behavior and historical context.

Insofar as they rely on the knowledge generated by the Communist secret services, lustration laws will always be vulnerable to accusations that they validate the previous regime's surveillance practices. Such laws are also often criticized on the grounds that they are technically unworkable because a large proportion of the contents of secret archives have been destroyed and the information contained in the files is generally unreliable. These claims have been answered by archival specialists, who have been in charge of or worked in those archives in the post-Communist period and publicized the archival research methods they use to address the inherent problems of working with the records of totalitarian regimes. They argue, for example, that because the same information and the same informants were, as a rule, recorded in many places and listed in many indexes, it is possible to reconstruct a large part of the missing records. Moreover, a good grasp of the logistics and functions of information-gathering by these services helps to evaluate the status and accuracy of the documents they produced (Bednarek and Perzyna, 2006; Gauck, 1992, 1996; Grocki, 1992; Kieres, 2005; Korkuć, 2007; Kurtyka, 2006; Musial, 2006; Rudzikowski, 2004; Stan, 2002a; Szustrowa, 1992; Zając, 2006).

The struggle over the legacy of Communist surveillance

A number of publications have examined public discourses surrounding lustration laws in several countries (see, for example, Barańska, 2007; Boed, 1999; David, 2003, 2004; Los, 1995; Los and Zybertowicz, 2000; Sojak, 1998a, 1998b; Sojak and Wicenty, 2005; Stan, 2002a, 2002b, 2004, 2006; Williams et al., 2003). In Poland, where attempts to pass such laws were unsuccessful until a weak version of lustration was finally enacted in 1997, myths about extraordinary dangers related to lustration have been very prominent in the media and other public venues. This helped to widen and transform the policing powers of previous surveillance practices by creating often-unjustified public fears, including anxieties amongst former opposition activists who had ambiguous or inconclusive encounters with the Communist secret forces. Although such individuals would likely not be covered by any legal definition of secret colla-boration, the lack of legal lustration procedures, and the scaremongering dis-courses surrounding proposals to introduce such laws, might have discouraged many qualified people from entering public life. Conversely, former colla-borators have often been skillfully promoted by former security networks and catapulted to influential positions, or they have sought such positions in the hope of erasing or controlling their secret files.

It is worth noting that although secret informers constituted a vital compo-nent of the totalitarian system of control, only a tiny minority of citizens were involved in such a role. For example, in the late 1980s—when the level of collaboration was at its highest in both Romania and Poland—the number of active registered collaborators was less than one percent of the total popula-tion of Romania and only around one third of one percent of the Polish population. Similarly, the number of registered collaborators in East Germany amounted to just over one percent of the population (Gauck, 1996; Rudzikowski, 2004; Stan, 2002a).

Despite the small numbers of people who were successfully recruited as informers, their representation among the post-Communist elites is dis-proportionately high, especially in those countries which delayed or subverted legal lustration. The secret file's long shadow, artificially elongated by those who continue to use it to their advantage, represents one of the most painful and least understood formative phenomena of post-Communist societies. Moreover, in countries such as Poland and Romania, where the communist secret archives were left for many years under the management of the new state security agencies—which still employed a large proportion of former Communist operatives—Communist surveillance files were blatantly exploited to manipulate political and economic arenas.

Interestingly, public-opinion surveys in Poland have shown an over-whelming public support for lustration throughout the post-1989 period (Ośrodek Badania Opinii Publicznej (Centre for Public Opinion Research, OBOP) 1996, 1999, 2005; Centrum Badania Opinii Publicznej (Public Opinion Research Centre, CBOS) 2005a, 2007; PENTOR, 2007). Generally, the higher the level of education a person has, the greater their support for lustration (OBOP, 2005). All these studies—conducted by reputable polling organizations on random, representative samples of adult Poles—show that the high profile anti-lustration rhetoric is not shared by the majority of the population and that Communist secret archives have not lost their troubling relevance in the changing surveillance culture. Similarly, Romanian surveys have also shown an overwhelming support for the lustration laws (BBC TV, 2006).

The strong public support for lustration and de-Communization notwith-standing, the media and Left-to-liberal elites have promoted a view that equates lustration with a witch hunt. This rhetoric ignores the reality of the presence of undisclosed former secret-services operatives and agents in the post-1989 power structures and the harm that such individuals may produce.

This "culture of denial" (Cohen, 1993) is evident in the persistent assertions that lustration laws deal with an invented problem.

Lustration delayed: a subversive role of former secret services

Based on his comparative research on the Czech Republic, Slovakia, and Poland, Roman David (2003) concludes that lustration laws help consolidate democracy. He notes that the periods when there was no lustration law in those countries were associated with a higher prevalence of "blackmail, subversive and criminal activities, mutual accusations, political scandals and the abuse of power" (David, 2003: 427).

Among the Central European post-Communist countries, Romania, Poland, and Slovakia seem to have suffered a disproportional number of spectacular political scandals, corruption cases, and organized economic scams that are either traceable to or are alleged to be linked with the wide-ranging infiltration of high echelons of public life by former secret-services members and collaborators.

The longer legally authorized lustration is delayed, the greater scope there is for wild, unregulated lustration ploys and scare tactics that give those with access to secret files unprecedented power to make and break careers and personal lives. Functionaries of former and current secret services—and in these countries there is a significant overlap between the two—engage in and profit from high-profile file wars, fueled by political, business, and criminal interests. Secret surveillance files are routinely turned into a weapon in political struggles, seriously undermining democratic processes and freedoms. Unregulated, secretly manipulated, "wild lustrations," involving strategically orchestrated leaks of compromising information to the media and black markets have turned the old secret police files into a potent blackmail tool (Baleanu, 1995a, 1995b; BBC TV, 2006; Cenckiewicz and Gontarczyk, 2008; Los and Zybertowicz, 2000; Lovatt, 2000b; "Romanian Daily ... ", 2002; Stan, 2002b).

Evidence from several post-Communist countries suggests that functionaries leaving the Communist secret services treated stolen or photocopied files and other types of secret information as an insurance policy. Their personal information treasure chests contained enough dirt to let them prosper and dominate the processes of political and economic transition (Arel, 2001; Cenckiewicz and Gontarczyk, 2008; Darden, 2001; Los and Zybertowicz, 2000; Zybertowicz, 2004a). A lucrative private security sector, founded by the Communist secret-services veterans, amassed as much past and current compromising data as possible to secure their continuing influence (Knight, 1999; Los, 2003; Los, and Zybertowicz, 2000; Nikolov, 1997; Wicenty, 2008). In the process, the new surveillance systems were contaminated by the old ones, transplanting the old surveillance culture into the new post-Communist environment.

Drawing on her research on Romania, Lavinia Stan (2002a, 2002b, 2004) paints a picture of a country run by networks of functionaries and informers of the former political-police *Securitate*, who have dominated the new security service (SRI) as well as political parties and the private sector. She comments:

> Given the Securitate's considerable hold over Romanian post-communist political and economic life, it is not surprising that few politicians have dared to call for file access and even fewer for lustration.
>
> (Stan, 2004: 353)

> Parliament has conveniently sided with the SRI in the name of an illusionary national interest better served by keeping secret the activity of the Securitate and names of *securists*.
>
> (Ibid:354)

The ominous power of the networks of the former secret services is well illustrated by a comment made in 2000 by the then President of Romania, Emil Constantinescu: "I feel more terrorized by Ceauşescu's Securitate today than I did before 1989" (quoted in Lovatt, 2000a:6).

One of the few Polish social scientists doing systematic research in this area is sociologist Andrzej Zybertowicz. He has been able to trace the key role that past/current networks of secret-services operatives and their agents play and have played within the justice system, defense and security sectors, and politics, as well as in many major economic scams and takeovers of key state assets (Los and Zybertowicz, 1997, 2000; Zybertowicz, 2002, 2003, 2004a, 2004b, 2008; see also Macierewicz, 2007). He and his colleagues have uncovered a unique mechanism used to shield large-scale criminal scams. Criminal activities are conducted under the cover of legitimate security-services operations, skillfully fused with official political and economic activities. When there is a threat of investigation into the suspected illegal dealings, arguments about the protection of state secrets and security are invoked and often upheld, thereby precluding any investigation of illegitimate activities (Zybertowicz, 2002:244; Sojak and Zybertowicz, 2005). This helps sustain a façade of democracy while precluding any real transparency in public life (Los, 2003).

In a 2004 poll of a representative sample of Polish business people, based on a questionnaire authored by a team headed by Zybertowicz, almost 68 per cent of respondents claimed that there were some economic sectors in which it was impossible to conduct business by legitimate means. These sectors were mostly located at the junction of business and security services and included the energy industry, military and police contracts, and trade with states that used to be part of the Soviet Union (Spławski, 2008). The same research indicates that former "functionaries of secret services and communist *nomenklatura* elites are the key group for whom violence represents a work tool, a resource in the business game" (Spławski, 2008:74, translation from Polish-ML; see also Wicenty, 2008).

The scale of the problems created by the lack of proper lustration and supervision over the old regime's archives is demonstrated by the numerous scandals surrounding real or supposed Communist files, which were directly instrumental in toppling governments, the fall of prime ministers, dismissals of ministers and other high-ranking politicians, incrimination of presidents, and, on a more general level, manipulation of state agendas and election campaigns. Built on a thick web of secret knowledge and mutual blackmail, these complicated games contributed to the anarchization of the state that made it difficult to institutionalize any form of accountability.

The tight lid that the rulers of the Soviet Bloc kept on emerging digital technologies was blown off after the collapse of Communism. Yet, since access to communications know-how and equipment was nearly monopolized by secret services, it is not surprising that their operatives moved quickly to dominate the process of expanding such technological markets in transitional societies. Former secret-service operatives and collaborators had enormous opportunities to solidify and consolidate their networks in the burgeoning field of computerization of government departments, utilities and social-insurance agencies, telecommunications industry, and internet service provision. They also played a major role in the private security/surveillance sector, databanks and data brokerages, the financial sector, and media markets. Gaining influence over these sectors not only helped establish former security operatives and associates as top business players, but also provided them with privileged access to population data and a strategic place within the newly emerging post-Communist, supranational, almost postmodern, surveillant assemblage(s) (Los and Zybertowicz, 2000:159–64; Los, 2002; see Haggerty and Ericson, 2000).

New surveillance and the old culture of fear

The post-Communist countries' new surveillance landscape, with its omnipresent cameras, unobtrusive identity checks, and aggressively marketed electronic security systems, contributes to the continuation of a culture of suspicion and division. The opacity of the new surveillance harkens back to the secrecy and murkiness of the old Communist practices. The feeling of being constantly spied upon brings—even if subconsciously—grim memories. The lack of human contact with communal agents of control reinforces old fears of the omnipresence of secret eyes and ears in an environment where there is no room for meaningful exchange or clarification. The question asked by John McGrath seems applicable here:

> If video cameras provide chief inspectors with dozens of extra pairs of eyes, what happens to the policing voice? ... The interpellating voice of the policeman ... carries the promise that if we are in a position to

answer politely—"Who me, officer? I live here," we will not be arbitrarily crushed by the state's power. Yet with the policing camera we are offered no such opportunity to respond ... [This] reintroduces the possibility of arbitrary power displays by the state, of an irrational totalitarianism.

(McGrath, 2004:31–32)

The impression conveyed by McGrath, who is referring to the British context, is particularly evocative for former subjects of totalitarian states. As I have shown elsewhere (Los, 2002), in the early transition period, the pervasive fear of the Communist state was quickly replaced by a fear of crime. This happened as the secret police / *nomenklatura* networks sought to privatize, and thereby preserve the old police-state structures. A vast private-security industry absorbed a large proportion of the personnel, technical resources, and power / knowledge of the police state, effectively privatizing law and order. The industry positioned itself as the primary provider of both risk definitions and risk-management technologies. By weakening the state and contributing to the rise of an anarchic regulatory framework, they helped to incite an intense fear of crime, thereby creating an escalating demand for the products and services of the new security industry (Los, 2002).

A well-coordinated effort to perpetuate the "fearing subject" (Lee, 2001) was related to the reconfiguration of sites and practices of control, including the promotion of selective self-control and vigilance. With time, the fading urgency and intensity of fear of crime (as evidenced by various public-opinion surveys—CBOS 2005b; Kojder 2008) has made room for the public to vocalize concerns about ubiquitous surveillance systems, but they are still mitigated by the ever-present concern about a return of terrifying forms of crime.

A surveillance culture in transition: the perils of skipping modernity

The historical convergence of the collapse of Communism and the advent of an information age that rewards skills in surreptitious information-gathering and processing, has inadvertently elevated former Communist secret operatives to positions of authority within rapidly changing knowledge hierarchies. This process paralleled post-Cold War developments in the West, where much of that era's sophisticated surveillance technologies, personnel, and know-how were suddenly released into the service of globalizing commerce, with its voracious appetite for information and customer tracking (see Ball et al. 2010 in this volume).

Unlike the hostile Cold War surveillance culture, the new Western art of surveillance evolved in part along seductive lines that enticed citizens with rewards and promises of safety and convenience. This soft surveillance net has, however, been complemented and reinforced by efforts to shore up demoralized (counter)intelligence services and push for more intrusive, security-oriented, surveillance technologies now legitimized by wars on international crime and terror. Their different logic and rationale notwithstanding, these two types of surveillance have increasingly blended together. Ayse Coyhan (2008) makes a similar point, and sees three types of logic included in this fusion process. They are: "First, a logic of security that corresponds to the identification of risks and dangers and to the interception of risky people. Second, a logic of management of flows of people, goods, and transportation. And third, a logic of ambient intelligence (AmI), which integrates microprocessors into individuals' daily routines to make life more comfortable. In other words, these new technologies move easily between the governmental, security, and domestic spheres" (Coyhan, 2008: 108; see also Haggerty and Ericson, 2000 and Lyon, 2003).

The ability of individuals to move freely, in both real and virtual spaces, remains an important aspect of governance in prosperous late-liberal societies, although this is increasingly restrained by security concerns. For the Communist authorities, however, the very idea of moving freely was antithetical to their guiding doctrine. Their apparatus of surveillance was based on principles of infiltration, invigilation, and social incapacitation.

Unlike the Western *modern* paradigm that required disciplined and productive *subjects,* Communism promoted mechanisms to purge individuals of their subjectivity to ensure their mechanical uniformity and obedience within the dense net of state surveillance/control. With both the failure of Communism and a gradual passing of modernist market conditions, these quite differently positioned societies now face a rapidly evolving reality of *postmodernity* and its uncanny surveillance culture. This culture is characterized by an irresistible tendency to turn the individual subject into information—to separate humans from themselves, render them divisible, easily reduced or multiplied, repeatedly decoded and recoded by virtual means of monitoring, simulation, and profiling (Bogard, 2006:106; Deluze, 1997; Lianos, 2001, 2003). It also splits and rearranges the individual in ways that render obsolete any unified concept of the self. As William Bogard observes: "the individual subject is a relic of a productive system that demanded functional unities ... Today, the global system of capital and control demands fluid, flexible and heterogeneous subjects" (2006:106). A de-territorialized, virtual control uproots the individual and eliminates the ideal of personal integrity (Los 2006).

Citizens of post-Communist societies are thus pushed to bypass the stage in the development of the democratic modern state where individual subjects navigate within the frame of an autonomous and ostensibly rationally organized *real* world. Instead, information-starved survivors of Communism are inscribed with new identity markers that allow them to share in vast virtual information markets and, at least in principle, outgrow their fear of *the file.* Yet, their much anticipated experience of the market has exposed them, with little warning or preparation, to aggressive strategies to marketize human subjects, converting them—and often encouraging them to convert themselves—into digital traces ready to be bought, sold, stolen, or played with. Finally, their hope for privacy, something they long associated with freedom, is turning before their eyes into a phenomenon that must be managed through myriad defensive strategies and forms of constant vigilance that ultimately surpass realistic human capacities (Whitson and Haggerty, 2008).

Their newly gained sense of sovereignty over their bodies has also proven to be illusionary. New forms of surveillance refocus on the body in a highly instrumental and objectifying manner. Bodies are treated as both the carrier of identifying personal information and a moving object to be perpetually scanned in search of any automatically detectable deviations from the norm. This, to the extent that it prevents anonymity and promotes uniformity, is reminiscent of Communist surveillance. The survivors of Communism are therefore faced with a situation where the modernist framework for personal growth and privacy protection, which invokes the treasured right to self-definition and anonymity, is rapidly eroded by the external assignment and certification of new forms of documentary identity by surveillance systems, which structure access to diverse spaces and opportunities. Toshimaru Ogura's (2006:293) prediction that "anonymity will be criminalized" and that we will lose control of our identity (or identities) seems accurate—as new surveillance-based forms of governance make it simply impossible for individuals to go about their lives anonymously and/or identify themselves on their own terms and in their own words (although cyberspace may give an illusion to the contrary). This creates a gulf between the expectations of citizens in East / Central European societies, who long for "old fashioned" forms of modernity, but experience postmodern forms of digitized capitalism.

The initial expectation shared by many survivors of the Communist surveillance regimes was that any new patterns of governance coming from the West would be well tested and essentially benign. The whole frame of reference for people living under Communist regimes was linked with a modern vision of liberal democracy, citizens' rights, sovereignty, free markets, steady economic growth, openness, rationality, a system of governmental checks and balances, an independent mass media, and division between private and public spheres.

Yet daily experience of new forms of surveillance, combined with the well-ingrained habit of conspiratorial thinking, soon created fears that powerful mafias were busy building new information empires on the basis of the old repressive system, now legitimized by global security and marketing strategies. Politicians and commentators who acknowledge and address these concerns are routinely discredited by political campaigns that portray them as paranoid, a label that effectively pathologizes any attempts at resistance (see Harper, 2008, on narratives about paranoia in debates on surveillance).

Dilemmas of resistance

In this new political era, the re-emergence of bodily forms of surveillance which draw upon new technological instrumentation may prompt the return of familiar strategies to salvage the soul by playing the body against the surveillance regime. However, the new mechanisms designed to turn bodies into information do not need any reference to individual subjectivity to remain effective. The controlling power of biometrics is particularly notable because it is not diminished by efforts to conceal the self. Any search for resistance strategies must therefore address the body/self information linkages in a new way.

With the shifting focus of surveillance and the explosion in biometric technologies, bodily boundaries are constantly renegotiated. In the process, the concept of bodily integrity and its link to consciousness is problematized (van der Ploeg, 2003). Kirstie Ball (2006) recently explored these new political dilemmas of resisting bodily surveillance. In her view, the current tendency to treat the body as an authenticator of identity and a source of fixed truth can be challenged by recognizing that the body is more than simply an observable (social) object. Since our consciousness is embodied and people need to be aware of their bodies to fully experience themselves, any meaningful resistance to bodily surveillance has to engage our ability to manipulate the inherently volatile flow of information from our bodies, thus destabilizing the fixed assumptions and codes (Ball, 2006). This may, however, entail new strategies of self-manipulation, repression, and deception that in themselves prove detrimental to one's sense of freedom and integrity.

The power of biometrics lies, as Coyhan (2008) points out, in its ability to produce and assign identities based on digitized body measurements. "By collecting and storing the biological features of an individual ... that make him / her unique, biometrics fixes the uniqueness of the person in databases" (113). This process of immobilizing identity through biometric reification of the body/person pre-empts many potential resistance strategies related to both postmodern and post-Communist identity politics. The postmodern ethos of heterogeneity, fluidity, and the negotiability of identity(ies) is undermined by the requirement to constantly authenticate oneself according to digitally petrified criteria. Biometrics is also immune to the old resistance habits employed by the survivors of Communism, which were founded on the separation of body and soul and expressed in the practice of maintaining a "poker face" or going on "internal immigration." Not only are these new scanning practices more technologically sophisticated than Communist methods of body monitoring, they also serve a surveillance system that has the unique ability to shape people's choices without engaging their selves. As I have argued elsewhere, we are witnessing the emergence of a new, surveillance-directed persona engendered by a major transformation in social control, one where the self is left out of an internalized control mechanism and replaced by the visualization of highly volatile and fragmented electronic doubles (Los, 2006, 2007; see Haggerty and Ericson, 2000, on the concept of the data double).

As elaborated by Lianos (2001), the new control is geared to produce subjects who are no longer conditioned by their conscience and internalized values but who respond to pragmatic codes of finely structured accessibility. This is an extra-moral type of control that works through the formalized configuration of contexts of action, interaction, and observation. As Lianos (2001) points out, actions that are contrary to the preprogrammed options of the structural grid become an absurdity even before they have a chance to be articulated as defiance. It is not smart to drive against the traffic, and no one would see doing so as a meaningful protest. So, people train their bodies to flow with the traffic, consigning an ever-increasing number of rules to the incontestable, procedural realm.

Withdrawing into oneself entails minimizing one's engagement with the organized world. However, the new grid of control demands a recognizable, active, and efficient user. Failure to meet these criteria is unlikely to be validated as a meaningful protest and is bound to result in an escalating spiral of exclusion threatening vital existential interests of the individual. This seemingly resistance-proof control logic is enabled by the recent revolution in information/surveillance technologies and cannot be understood apart from them. Therefore, to be consequential, attempts to resist manipulation and preserve individuality must involve an active intellectual resistance to these technologies and not just an imaginary flight into the private self. Given the complexity of the technologies involved, however, the means of resistance (or the means of designing lines of resistance) are available only to a small stratum of highly knowledgeable, technologically savvy individuals. Yet their specialized skills give them a stake in preserving and refining the system. They are thus often the most zealous practitioners of new, polyvalent, technology-based power that binds and profiles individuals for a multitude of purposes.

The general public is not equipped to manipulate or even recognize the hidden workings of this system. People are repeatedly told to take care of their personal data, use precautions against the theft of their identity, and eliminate traces of their existence, while simultaneously being obliged to provide ever more data, preserve all kinds of personal records, and constantly legitimize themselves through individual codes, voice-recognition recordings, and other identifying information (Whitson and Haggerty, 2008). Caught in this contradictory logic, they cannot talk back to the system, because there is no one to talk to. Any attempts to do so are identified as a sign of incompetence and lead to either rejection or more thorough inspection that further expands the stock of documentary personal data (or electronic doubles). This system of desocialized control renders human/social forms of negotiation/resistance empty, while internal immigration is interpreted as ineptitude. Under such conditions, rage, insanity, or desolation may displace any search for rational responses.

The specific circumstances of post-Communist countries lend an additional dimension to this process because of how they contribute to a trans-systemic surveillance flow. This happens when both the surveillance records of a totalitarian regime and the creators of those records are surreptitiously incorporated into the many private and public surveillance systems of an emerging democratic state and its wider global environment. Several East/Central European countries have a long tradition of intelligentsia-led opposition to oppressive regimes. Yet, in post-Communist societies, the new knowledge stratum—a class of specialists who guide and implement new control mechanisms—is dominated by former secret-services operatives, a group highly unlikely to pursue or enable technologies of resistance. Mechanisms to digitize and dehumanize subjects thus reinforce the relations of domination inherited from the former regime, while their application in ostensibly non-political areas, such as commerce and leisure, tends to defuse their political connotations.

Conclusion

In this time of confusing systemic change in East / Central Europe, the image of *the file* remains vivid (for comparison, see Samatas, 2004; 2005 on the role of filing in dictatorial Greece). First, the old Communist file has retained its policing powers—and this is especially true for those societies that delayed or mismanaged lustration and the legal regulation of access to the Communist secret archives. Second, the new surveillance, with its technologically innovative, rapidly expanding systems of identification, registration, tracking, and monitoring, raises new fears of centralized banks of hidden data. While this is still not a major political issue, the media are devoting more attention to the topic, while new privacy laws—introduced as a condition of joining the European Union—alert people to the potential dangers and abuses of their routinely collected personal data. Third, the leading role played by former secret-services networks in new surveillance strategies, technologies, and data management undermines the processes of democratization and contributes to the suspicion that the old file-centered political mechanism has simply metamorphosed into a new form of multi-purpose, digitally enhanced, shadowy, data-based surveillance.

These processes are facilitated by a massive anti-crime hysteria led by the private security industry, which itself emerged as a result of the privatization of secret services. Fear of crime, a hallmark of the post-totalitarian transitions, made possible the rapid expansion and legitimization of new control systems and ensured that the emerging surveillance culture grew out of the old foundations. The digital age offers spectacular career opportunities for those with skills related to new technologies, investing them with both inside knowledge and huge stakes in new control systems. In post-Communist countries this has inexorably bolstered the position of former secret services by giving them a prominent place in emerging knowledge hierarchies and data empires.

The European survivors of Communism yearned to embrace modernity, which was the essential frame of reference for their resistance and dreams. Freed from oppression, they took over public spaces that used to intimidate them; celebrated new unthreatening opportunities for visibility and free movement; packed new shopping centers and embraced the freedom of the internet. They felt released from the menacing eyes and ears of the system. Yet modernity was already passing them by. The Western world was venturing into the novel realm of postmodernity, with its omnipresent, de-territorializing, digital surveillance. This contributed to the growing sense of an evolutionary displacement. Time did not wait for them and the anticipated transition to an idealized modern state was no longer an option.

The new surveillance culture fuses two very different control paradigms, merging a seductive market-based *menu culture* with a belligerent *securitization culture* of the state / private security apparatus. In post-Communist societies, this process is additionally infused with the persistent legacy of the *totalitarian surveillance culture*. The enduring policing potential of the secret file is but one aspect of this legacy.

It remains to be seen whether the fear of the Communist file will eventually mutate from the notion of its trans-systemic, lingering, posthumous ability to police the present to the image of a revitalized new/old virtual file acting as a magnet for the wide-ranging, dispersed data produced by the new surveillance. Certainly, a timely and well-conceived legal regulation of the Communist surveillance legacy—like the one implemented in the Czech Republic—may play some role in preventing old data from being indiscriminately fused with new data in a monstrous megafile. The emerging global-surveillance trends may, however, supersede the differences in political biographies of new and old democracies, as new information and governance technologies promise an unprecedented expansion of capacity to build data linkages and a virtual totalization of surveillance. The remarkable surveillance capacity of new technologies and their unique focus on creating a parallel world of data doubles renders traditional, pre-digital resistance modes inoperative. The emerging focus on biometrics, with its ability to assign fixed identities, undermines both postmodern and (post) Communist resistance strategies.

In Communist societies, the need for resistance exclusively referred to a state that was essentially unmodern—undemocratic, closed, repressive, irrational, backward, based on a command economy and ruled by pervasive surveillance, secrecy, and fear. People resisted or adapted to the state's surveillance measures by protecting a private sphere, building informal systems of communication (covering both social logistics and linguistic codes), and practicing prudence, inscrutability, and self-control. There was little awareness of other modes of surveillance and resistance either with respect to the modern state or to the futuristic global/virtual sphere of postmodern surveillance.

The main mode of resistance to Communism, the so-called internal immigration, was widely perceived as a form of defense against state indoctrination and penetration. The body was used as a mask and a barrier against the colonization of the soul by the state. Yet the new surveillant mechanisms are meant to bypass subjectivity, thereby rendering irrelevant an interiorized, disembodied resistance. This approach to resistance is also challenged by the seductive postmodern ethos of self-creation and versatile, imaginative body / identity fusion. Yet the postmodern resistance culture itself is rendered defenseless when confronted by the omnipresence of the new technologies for automatic, biometric identification and profiling. With these two major resistance strategies clearly failing to address the daunting dilemmas presented by new surveillance technologies, the focus should be on developing strategies to prevent/undo the ongoing amalgamation of different logics of surveillance as well as to destabilize the mechanisms of external identity-fixing and the marginalization of the self.

As my research shows, it is vital that any inquiry into the formation of a new culture of surveillance in post-Communist countries pays attention to the surveillance legacy they inherited from the previous regime. This legacy encompasses a whole host of phenomena, such as the structure and lingering influence of the old secret surveillance mechanisms, the posthumous role of the Communist power/knowledge complex (including the content and control over its secret archives), the nature and extent of the reorganization of secret services and their role in the transition to democracy, the processes of conversion of the former police-state structures into a powerful private security sector, and a covert promotion of former secret agents to positions of power and influence. As I have discussed in this article, all these factors have shaped the unique environment in which the new, global surveillance trends are adopted and adapted.

References

Arel, Dominique. 2001. "Kuchmagate and the demise of Ukraine's geopolitical bluff." *East European Constitutional Review* 10(2/3):54–59.

Ball, Kirstie. 2006. "Organization, surveillance and the body: Towards a politics of resistance." In *Theorizing Surveillance. The Panopticon and Beyond*, ed. D. Lyon, 296–317. Cullompton, UK: Willan.

Ball, Kirstie, Elizabeth Daniel, Sally Dibb and Maureen Meadows. 2010. "Democracy, Surveillance and 'knowing what's good for you': The private sector origins of profiling and the birth of 'citizen relationship management' ", in Kevin D. Haggerty and Minas Samatas eds., *Surveillance and Democracy*. London: Routledge.

Baleanu, V. G.1995a. "The enemy within: The Romanian Intelligence Service in transition." *Federation of American Scientists*, http://www.fas.org.

——1995b. "A clear and present danger to democracy: The new Romanian Security Services are still watching." *Federation of American Scientists*, http://www.fas.org.

Barańska, Maria. 2007. "Zasada państwa prawnego w dyskursie publicznym na temat lustracji." *Studia Socjologiczne* 2:83–116.

BBC TV. 2006. "Secret police row grips Romania." *BBC TV* August 17, 2006. http://news.bbc.co.uk.

Bednarek, Jerzy and Paweł Perzyna, eds. 2006. *Z kręgu 'teczek.' Z badań nad zasobami i funkcjami archiwum IPN*. Łódź: IPN and Wyd. Adam Marszałek.

Boed, Roman. 1999. "An evaluation of the legality and efficacy of lustration as a tool of transitional justice." *Columbia Journal of Transnational Law* 37 (2):357–402.

Bogard, William. 2006. "Surveillance assemblages and lines of flight." In *Theorizing Surveillance. The Panopticon and Beyond*, ed. D. Lyon, 97–122. Cullompton, UK: Willan.

CBOS (Centrum Badania Opinii Społecznej). 2005a. Research report. *Vetting and Decommunization*, http://www.cbos.pl.

——2005b. Research report. *Reduced Fear of Crime*, http://www.cbos.pl.

——2007. Research report. *O lustracji i sposobie ujawniania materiałów zgromadzonych w IPN*, http://www.cbos.pl.

Cenckiewicz, Sławomir and Piotr Gontarczyk. 2008. *SB a Lech Wałęsa. Przyczynek do biografii*. Gdańsk-Warszawa-Kraków: IPN.

Cohen, Stanley. 1993. "Human Rights and crimes of the state: The culture of denial." *Australian and New Zealand Journal of Criminology* 26 (July):97–115.

——1995. "State crimes of previous regimes: Knowledge, accountability, and the policing of the past." *Law and Social Inquiry* 20 (1):7–50.

Coyhan, Ayse. 2008. "Technologization of security: Management of uncertainty and risk in the Age of Biometrics." *Surveillance and Society* 5 (2):102–23.

Darden, Keith A. 2001. "Blackmail as a tool of state domination: Ukraine under Kuchma." *East European Constitutional Review* 10 ():67–71.

David, Roman. 2003. "Lustration laws in action: The motives and evaluation of Lustration Policy in the Czech Republic and Poland (1989–2001)." *Law and Social Inquiry* 28 (2):387–439.

——2004. "Transitional injustice? Criteria for conformity of Lustration to the right of political expression." *Europe-Asia Studies* 56 (6):789–812.

Deluze, Gilles. 1997. "Postscript on the societies of control." In *Rethinking Architecture: A Reader in Cultural Theory*, edited by N. Leach, 309–12. London: Routledge.

Foucault, Michel. 1979. *Discipline and Punish. The Birth of the Prison*. New York: Vintage Books.

Gauck, Joachim. 1992. "Interview with J. Gauck." In *Konfidenci są wśród nas*, edited by M. Grocki, 114–18. Warszawa: Editons Spotkania.

——1996. "Interview with J. Gauck." *German Life*, February/March, http://www.germanlife.com.

Grocki, Michał. 1992. *Konfidenci są wśród nas*. Warszawa: Editions Spotkania.

Haggerty, Kevin D. and Richard V. Ericson. 2000. "The surveillant assemblage." *British Journal of Sociology* 51 (4):605–22.

Harper, David. 2008. "The politics of paranoia: Paranoid positioning and conspiratorial narratives in the surveillance society." *Surveillance and Society* 5 (1):1–32, http://www.surveillance-and-society.org.

Hatschikjan, Magarditsch, Dušan Reljić, and Nenead Šebek, eds. 2005. *Disclosing Hidden History: Lustration in the Western Balkans. A Project Documentation*. Thessaloniki: Center for Democracy and Reconciliation in South Eastern Europe.

Kieres, Leon. 2005. "Interview with L. Kieres" ("Trzysta tysięcy nazwisk"). *Polityka* No 4, 29 January:19–22.

Knight, Amy. 1999. "The security services and the decline of democracy in Russia: 1996–99." *The Donald W. Treadgold Papers in Russian, East European and Central Asian Studies* No.23 (October). Seattle, WA: University of Washington.

Kojder, Andrzej. 2008. *Kontakty z prawem, ocena instytucji prawnych i poczucie bezpieczeństwa Polaków. Komunikat z badań.* Warszawa: Centrum Badania Opinii Społecznej.

Korkuć, Maciej. 2007. "SB wobec Kościoła Katolickiego – sprawa ks. Mirosława Drozdka." In *Kościół Katolicki w czasach komunistycznej dyktatury. Między bohaterstwem a agenturą.* Studia i Materiały, Tom 1. Instytut Pamięci Narodowej, 231–59. Kraków: WAM.

Kurtyka, Janusz. 2006. "Interview with J. Kurtyka (Nie jestem politykiem)." *Biuletyn Instytutu Pamięci Narodowej* 1–2: 5–20.

Lee, Murray. 2001. "The genesis of 'fear of crime.'" *Theoretical Sociology* 5 (4):467–85.

Lianos, Michalis. 2001. *Le Nouveau Côntrole Social: Toile Institutionelle, Normativité et lien Social.* Paris: L'Harmattan.

——2003. "Social control after Foucault." *Surveillance and Society* 1 (3):412–30.

Los, Maria. 1995. "Lustration and truth claims: Unfinished revolutions in Central Europe." *Law and Social Inquiry* 20 (1):117–61.

——. 2002. "Post-communist fear of crime and the commercialization of security." *Theoretical Criminology* 6 (2):165–88.

——. 2003. "Crime in transition: The post-communist state, markets and crime." *Crime, Law and Social Change* 40:145–69.

——. 2004. "The technologies of total domination." *Surveillance and Society* 2 (1):15–38.

——. 2006. "Looking into the future: Globalization and the totalitarian potential." In *Theorizing Surveillance. The Panopticon and Beyond*, ed. D. Lyon, 69–94. Cullompton, UK: Willan.

——. 2007. "Pytania o przyszłość i widmo totalitaryzmu." *Studia Socjologiczne* (Warsaw) 2:117–44.

Los, Maria and Andrzej Zybertowicz. 1997. "Covert action. The missing link in explanation of the rise and demise of the Soviet bloc." *Periphery* 3 (1/2):16–20.

——. 2000. *Privatizing the Police-State: The Case of Poland.* Houndmills, UK: Palgrave Macmillan.

Lovatt, Catherine. 2000a. "Dirty election campaigning." *Central Europe Review* 2 (9), 6 March, http://www.ce-review.org.

——. 2000b. "Securitate schaffle." *Central Europe Review* 2 (15), April 17, 2000, http://www.ce-review.org.

Lyon, David. 2003. *Surveillance after September 11.* Cambridge: Polity Press.

Macierewicz, Antoni. 2007. *Raport o działaniach żołnierzy i pracowników WSI.* Warsaw, 374 p., http://www.raportwsi.ipn.pl.

McGrath, John E. 2004. *Loving Big Brother: Performance, Privacy and Surveillance Space.* London: Routledge.

Musiał, Filip, ed. 2006. *Wokół teczek bezpieki – zagadnienia metodologiczno-źródłoznawcze.* Kraków: IPN.

Nikolov, J. 1997. "Organized crime in Bulgaria." *East European Constitutional Review* 6 (4):85–90.

OBOP (Ośrodek Badania Opinii Publicznej). 1996. Research report Opinia publiczna o lustracji," http://www.tns.global.pl.

——. 1999. Research report Polacy o lustracji i dekomunizacji," http://www. tns-global.pl.

——. 2005. Research report Lustracja w lustrze TNS OBOP," http://www.tns-global.pl.

Ogura, Toshimaru. 2006. "Electronic government and surveillance-oriented society." In *Theorizing Surveillance. The Panopticon and Beyond*, ed. D. Lyon, 270–95. Cullompton, UK: Willan.

Open Net Initiative. 2005. *Internet Filtering in China in 2004–2005: A Country Study*. http://www.opennetinitiative.net.

PENTOR (Research International Pentor). 2007. Kto powinien poddać się lustracji, http://www.pentor.pl.

Romanian Daily Published List of Securitate Agents Working in Intelligence. Federation of American Scientists, http://www.fas.org.

Rudzikowski, Tadeusz. 2004. *Instrukcje pracy operacyjnej aparatu bezpieczeństwa (1945–1989)*. Warszawa: IPN.

Samatas, Minas. 2004. *Surveillance in Greece. From Anticommunist to Consumer Surveillance*. New York: Pella Publishing Co.

——. 2005. "Studying surveillance in Greece: Methodological and other problems related to an authoritarian surveillance culture." *Surveillance and Society* 3:181–97, http://www.surveillance-and-society.org.

Sojak, Radosław. 1998a. Porządki wykluczeń: Ekskluzja społeczna w świetle socjologii wiedzy na przykładzie dyskusji wokół lustracji. Master's thesis. The Nicholas Copernicus University, Toruń, Poland.

——1998b. "Demaskowani i wykluczeni. Dyskurs anty-lustracyjny w Polsce w świetle socjologii wiedzy." *Teraźniejszość. Człowiek. Edukacja* 2:29–59.

Sojak, Radosław and Daniel Wicenty. 2005. *Zagubiona Rzeczywistość. O społecznym konstruowaniu niewiedzy*. Warszawa: Oficyna Naukowa.

Sojak, Radosław and Andrzej Zybertowicz. 2005. "Czy Polskę stać na dalsze odsuwanie wiedzy o zakulisowych obszarach transformacji ustrojowej?" *Rzeczpospolita*, February 22, 2005.

Spławski, Marcin. 2008. "Przemoc w polskiej polityce i gospodarce w świetle badań ogólnopolskich i badań przedsiębiorców." In *Transformacja podszyta przemocą: O nieformalnych mechanizmach przemian instytucjonalnych*, ed. R. Sojak and A. Zybertowicz, 27–82. Toruń: Wydawnictwo Naukowe Uniwersytetu Mikołaja Kopernika.

Stachowiak, Jakub. 2007. "Różowe archiwum." *Polityka*, 4 (2626), 27 October:28–30.

Stan, Lavinia. 2002a. "Moral cleansing Romanian style." *Problems of Post-Communism* 49 (4):52–62.

——. 2002b. "Access to securitate files: The trials and tribulations of Romanian law." *East European Politics and Societies* 16 (1):145–81.

——. 2004. "Spies, files and lies: Explaining the failure of access to securitate files." *Communist and Post-Communist Studies* 37:341–59.

——. 2006. "Lustration in Romania: The story of a failure." *Studia Politica* 3 (1).

Szustrowa, Petruszka. 1992. "Kontrowersyjna lustracja." In *Konfidenci są wśród nas*, ed. M. Grocki, 108–14. Warszawa: Editons Spotkania.

Van der Ploeg, Irma. 2003. "Biometrics and the body as information: normative issues of the socio-technical coding of the body." In *Surveillance as Social Sorting: Privacy, Risk and Digital Discrimination*, ed. D. Lyon, 57–73. London and New York: Routledge.

Whitson, Jennifer and Kevin D. Haggerty. 2008. "Identity theft and the care of the virtual self." *Economy and Society* 37(4):571–93.

Wicenty, Daniel. 2008. "Przemoc jako kapitał w życiu gospodarczym." In *Transformacja podszyta przemocą: O nieformalnych mechanizmach przemian instytucjonalnych*, ed. R. Sojak and A. Zybertowicz, 165–86. Toruń: Wydawnictwo Naukowe Uniwersytetu Mikołaja Kopernika.

Williams, Kieran. 1999. "A scorecard for Czech lustration." *Central Europe Review* 1 (19), 1 November, http://www.ce-review.org.

Williams, Kieran, Aleks Szczerbiak, and Brigid Fowler. 2003. "Explaining lustration in Eastern Europe: A post-communist politics approach." *Sussex European Institute Working Paper* No 62. Falmer, Brighton, UK, 30 p.

Zając, Ewa. 2006. "Ślad pozostaje w aktach. Wybrane zagadnienia dotyczące funkcjonowania ewidencji operacyjnej w latach 1962–89." *Biuletyn Instytutu Pamięci Narodowej*, no 1–2:21–36.

Zybertowicz, Andrzej. 2002. "Odwrócone spojrzenie: czy służby specjalne znajdują się na marginesie transformacji ustrojowej?" *Colloquia Communia. (Idee i ludzie demokracji)* 2 (73), July–December: 233–49.

——. 2003. "Paradoksy wiedzy i ukryci aktorzy." *Ius et Lex* 1: 269–82.

——. 2004a. "Nieformalne grupy interesu w procesach prywatyzacji." Próba analizy modelowej. Unpublished research report, 37p.

——. 2004b. "Interview with A. Zybertowicz, by Piotr Bączek." *Głos*, no. 52/53.

——. 2008. "Przemoc układu – na przykładzie sieci biznesowej Zygmunta Solorza." In *Transformacja podszyta przemocą: O nieformalnych mechanizmach przemian instytucjonalnych*, ed. R.Sojak and A. Zybertowicz, 187–266. Toruń: Wydawnictwo Naukowe Uniwersytetu Mikołaja Kopernika.

Chapter 10

Balancing public safety and security demands with civil liberties in a new constitutional democracy

The case of post-1994 South Africa and the growth of residential security and surveillance measures

Anthony Minnaar

In 1994, South Africa gained full democracy after many years of apartheid rule, under which political oppression was the norm. In keeping itself in power, the government of the day trampled on civil liberties, *inter alia* by routinely using covert surveillance to collect information about political dissidents. However, after 1994 South Africa instituted a strong constitutional democracy, incorporated a liberal and wide-ranging Bill of Rights into the new Constitution of 1996 and, for the first time in its history, established a Constitutional Court. State institutions were set up to protect the rights of its citizens, such as the South African Human Rights Commission; The Public Protector; The Commission for the Promotion and Protection of the Rights of Cultural, Religious, and Linguistic Communities; and The Commission for Gender Equality.

In the ensuing years crime has emerged as one of the major challenges for South African citizens and state institutions. In the context of extremely high levels of crime, in particular of violent crime, the public has made numerous and vociferous calls for the state to be tougher on criminals. Since the late 1990s, the exponential growth of security measures—gated neighborhoods, road closures, "security villages," and armed-response private security companies with the attendant use of both open-street public and private CCTV surveillance (as one component of integrated security systems)—has largely been premised on an almost paranoid fear of crime and extreme feelings of insecurity. Crucially, when it comes to the implementation of both public and private CCTV surveillance in an integrated security system, there has been an almost total absence of any public debate regarding issues of public consultation (no public authority established these measures, nor consulted with civil-society stakeholders on whether such systems should be installed using public monies), invasion of privacy, evidentiary use of surveillance information, and other humanrights and civil-liberties issues. The implications of the ever-expanding CCTV surveillance footprint covering large areas of central business districts in the major metropolitan urban areas of South Africa are simply not being debated, largely because such systems are seen as expedient and necessary measures to assist in the fight against crime.

Fear of crime combined with a desire to improve feelings of safety and security have led to more access-control systems being implemented based on road closures (many making use of private CCTV surveillance systems as part of integrated security measures linked to a central control room). These are most apparent in the more affluent suburbs, in so-called gated neighborhoods and the private-security villages/estates that have sprung up all over the country. Some commentators have, however, questioned the legal underpinnings of both the principle of gated or secure private areas and the installation of such surveillance systems. This includes questions about the possible abuses of these measures, including restriction of free movement, the covert "screening" of who is allowed entry, demanding identification information, stopping and searching vehicular traffic, and the use of information gathered by such means for other purposes.

Other ancillary issues regarding accountability and oversight of such "private" systems of security have also been raised. However, some proponents point to the need to balance security (*inter alia* surveillance) needs with certain restrictions on human rights, precisely in order to fulfill the constitutionally enshrined right of the state and police to "protect and secure its citizens."

This paper explores some of these issues within the context of South African constitutional democracy, with reference to constitutionally enshrined principles of the right to privacy, information, free movement, personal safety and, more specifically, the South African Human Rights Commission public hearings on the issue of "road closures and boom gates." It addresses one of the most high profile issues in South Africa, and how new constitutional governmental frameworks sensitive to individual rights have played themselves out in trying to address the complex issues raised by these developments.

Political context

In April 1994, South Africa held its first full democratic elections. The victory by the African National Congress replaced the previous apartheid white minority regime, which in its last few years in power had become repressive in its fight for survival against the liberation movements and in its efforts to oppress all political dissent and protest—largely in the black townships. In its place, a black majority government was installed in South Africa for the first time.

However, the transformation to a full democracy was not easy and involved lengthy negotiations for a peaceful handover of power. The main thrust of the formal negotiations—the Convention for a Democratic South Africa (CODESA) during the period 1991–93, which negotiated the end of apartheid—involved establishing a strong constitutional democracy that protected but also limited a wide range of rights.

The "Interim" Constitution (Act 200 of 1993) was an important outcome of the CODESA negotiations, as it laid the foundation for the final Constitution (Act No. 108 of 1996). One of its most important provisions established the first ever Constitutional Court for South Africa, with the final say over all matters "relating to the interpretation, protection and enforcement of the provisions of this Constitution" (and its 1996 successor) (Constitution Act 1993: s 98[2]).

One other relevant institution within the context of this paper, set up by the 1993 Interim Constitution, was the South African Human Rights Commission (SAHRC), which was to "promote respect for human rights and a culture of human rights; promote the protection, development and attainment of human rights; and monitor and assess the observance of human rights in the Republic" (Constitution Act 1996: s 184[a–c]).

One aim of the 1996 Constitution Act was to "improve the quality of life of all citizens" (Constitution Act 1996: Preamble). Furthermore, it formalized a Bill of Rights (again the first time that any rights were specifically enshrined). This Bill of Rights was mooted as the "cornerstone of democracy in South Africa," establishing as it does the rights of all in South Africa while simultaneously affirming the "democratic values of human dignity, equality and freedom" (Constitution Act 1996: Chapter 2: Bill of Rights).

The following rights, as mentioned in the Bill of Rights, are specifically relevant to the discussion that follows: the "freedom and security of the person" (s 12); the right to privacy, which includes the right not to have your person, home, or property searched; your possessions seized; or your privacy of communications infringed (Constitution Act 1996: s 14[a–d]).

Most democracies commonly accept these privacy rights, but they are doubly important in the context of the new democratic South Africa, where such rights were ignored, trampled, and suppressed wholesale during the apartheid era. This was particularly true in the mid-1980s and early 1990s with the successive imposition of States of Emergency and the workings of the repressive apartheid political system, which were formalized into law in the years after the all-white National Party ascended to power in 1948. These issues are acutely important when examining the imposition of access control and surveillance security measures in private residential neighborhoods.

A final right relevant to this discussion is the "right of freedom of movement and residence" which gave everyone the right to "enter, to remain in and to reside anywhere" in South Africa (s 21[1–3]). While this might seem an "insignificant" right in Western democratic countries, within the context of historically restrictive Pass Laws and restrictions on where black persons could live (most were forced to reside in specific demarcated black areas and tribal homelands under the political policy of segregation), this was an extremely significant development in South Africa. The apartheid Pass Laws required every black male (and later female) person over the age of 18 to carry a "Pass Book" (Identity Document book) if they wanted to come into the "whites only" demarcated urban areas for work and remain there. If they were granted residential rights, which were usually linked to a permanent job, they were forced to live in special demarcated township areas ("Locations") that were solely for blacks. Without residential rights, they could be arrested for transgressing the Pass Laws—frequent Pass Law raids by police occurred in the black townships—and deported back to their tribal homeland areas. Frequent transgressors were imprisoned and their fingerprints placed on one of the largest fingerprint systems in the world. Hence any restrictions on movement, demands for ID (reminiscent of police Pass Law raids), and residential exclusivity were particularly sensitive issues for the black South African population.

The new South African police services were also responsible for constitutional obligations and responsibilities, namely "to prevent, combat and investigate crime, to maintain public order, to protect and secure the inhabitants of the Republic and their property, and to uphold and enforce the law" (Constitution Act 1996: s 205[3]). Particularly significant here was the use of the terms "protect and secure," which were taken very literally by many citizens, and used to justify individuals contracting and implementing "paid-for" private-security measures because of the perceived inability of the state's police agencies to provide effective "safety, security and protection" for individuals and their homes.

Policing and the growth of the private security industry

In subsequent policy documents the new South African Police Service (SAPS) was charged with transforming itself to become more democratic and human-rights oriented. As early as the end of 1994, and building on the Interim Constitution, a Green Paper on Safety and Security was issued as a policy guide for policing in the "new democratic" South Africa. This outlined principles such as community policing (see Minnaar, 2008a, 2009b), democratic control and accountability, and introduced a new demilitarized style of policing whereby civilian values would inform every aspect of the new policing services. This latter was important as a reaction to the previous way of policing (pre-1994) in South Africa, but it did little to reduce the continuing high levels of crime—some of which were close to the highest in the world.

In South Africa, fear of crime and high levels of insecurity and concerns about personal safety have been fuelled by the very real high rates of reported crime. For instance, there were 25,965 murders in 1994–1995 (a rate of 67 per 100,000 of the population). Other violent crimes show an equally high rate. There were 18,795 attempted murders in 2007–2008; 118,312 robberies with aggravating circumstances in 2007–2008 (a rate of 247 per 100,000); 36,190 rapes in 2007–2008 (a rate of 7 per 100,000); and researchers estimate a 40 per cent under-reporting of rape in South Africa.

While the police are charged with addressing these dramatic crime problems, any mention of policing in the new democracy must first be contextualized by briefly referring to the policing surveillance legacies of the old South African Police (SAP) (Force), especially the covert surveillance and repressive tactics employed by the SAP's Security Branch. This policing unit was responsible for placing any and all political dissidents and activists under covert surveillance. During the late 1980s in particular this involved the widespread use of illegal wire- and telephone tapping, opening of mail, conducting 24/7 surveillance of residences, placing individuals under "house arrest," i.e. restricting daily movement, and the iniquitous "detention-without-trial" arrests of citizens on the Security Branch lists of "persons endangering state security." Some of the Security Branch tactics involved clandestine assaults, beatings, and the "disappearance" or "removal from society" (covert state-sanctioned murder) of political opponents (see Minnaar, Liebenberg and Schutte, 1998). Moreover, it did not take much—attending a protest rally or writing a critical newspaper article—to be listed in the Security Branch's surveillance files. Such activities in the post-1994 newly democratic South Africa, or anything that smacked of similar tactics, were anathema to many activists and politically aware citizens. Some of the opposition to gated neighborhoods was colored by this previous experience of covert surveillance.

Since 1994, South Africa has also seen a significant growth in the size of the private security industry. By the end of March 2007, approximately 900,000 persons were registered with the Private Security Industry Authority (PSIRA) (see Minnaar and Ngoveni, 2004; Minnaar, 2005). At the same time, the numbers of the South African Police Service (SAPS) stood at approximately 128,000. Private policing services also infiltrated the terrain of the traditional public police by responding to alarms, patrolling, and even investigating crimes. Much of this growth was related to public perceptions of the police's poor service delivery and their virtual absence in many suburban areas (Minnaar, 2005). Those who could afford it hired armed-response companies to protect their homes and businesses and installed sophisticated surveillance and alarm systems. "Security villages/estates" proliferated and there was an increase in "gated neighborhoods"—which involved installing boom gates ("booming off" access control via road closures) and CCTV surveillance systems to control access to suburban communities.

Those communities that cannot afford to pay for private security have tried to institute more self-policing activities including street committee patrols, e-block, or neighborhood watch systems. These typically involve volunteers patrolling residential areas, or attempting to be the "eyes and ears" of the police, as in "e-block watches" where private citizens organize themselves in "blocks" and report any suspicious activities either to each other or directly to the local police. There has also been regular and frequent recourse to anti-crime vigilante actions (mob justice) by communities tired of the depredations of criminals and perceptions that such criminals act with impunity (See Minnaar 2002).

More affluent communities contracted private security companies to install, manage, and respond to increasingly sophisticated integrated security barriers, alarms, and detection and surveillance systems. These were usually linked to a security-company control room via information technology or as part of the houses' integrated surveillance security systems. Private residences continuously upgraded and "hardened" their security measures, which could entail installing perimeter lights and electric fencing; infra-red beams (movement activated) in gardens, cameras mounted on building corners etc. Many also opted for armed-response services.

A number of public surveys have graphically demonstrated that the public exhibits high levels of insecurity and fears for their personal safety and rank high crime levels as their number one concern. Ordinary citizens face a high probability that they will be victimized at least once every three years. This was also due in part to the changing modus operandi of crime in South Africa. For instance, in the early 1990s when new motor vehicles came equipped with improved security and anti-theft features, thieves took to hijacking vehicles (Minnaar and Zinn, 2000).

In the early 2000s, the same occurred with house burglaries as burglars turned to engaging in house robberies in order to circumvent security measures at private residences (Zinn, 2008). House robbery involves perpetrators overpowering, detaining, and robbing residents inside their home, most often resorting to threats, intimidation, and violence (sometimes murder and rape). Over the last few years the number of such incidents has increased dramatically. In 2002–2003 (the first year that this "new" crime subcode appeared on the SAPS crime statistics) there were 9,063 house robberies and by 2007–2008 there were 14,481 such incidents. At the same time, the number of residential burglaries (as opposed to the separate crime category of burglaries at business premises) stabilized at around 240,000 per annum. This is an extremely high (by international standards) rate of 497 per 100,000.

Controlling access to residential neighborhoods

Partly as a response to these crime concerns, groups sought to control access to their communities. According to Landman (2002:6), in South Africa the "fear of crime is generally considered to be the biggest reason for the establishment of gated communities in urban areas." It was assumed that crime would be deterred by controlling all movement into neighborhoods and installing public street CCTV systems.

As noted, many of the more affluent neighborhoods resorted to controlling access to their particular neighborhoods by establishing Neighborhood Watches, conducting their own night-time patrols or erecting boom gates and other road closures. These areas were termed "gated neighborhoods" to distinguish them from areas merely patrolled by a local Neighborhood Watch, and from the "security villages or estates," the difference being that the latter are private property for collective use. This enabled property owners to legally set up stringent security measures by building security barricades/walls entirely around their properties and controlling access (usually having a security gate or controlled access point with a security guard) to the cluster of enclosed residences. Such security estates are typically private developments with private streets/roads inside walled-off areas where management and upkeep is carried out by a private body (Landman, 2002:5, 8).

In comparison, residents of gated neighborhoods often got together in a residents'association, to which they paid a monthly levy. These associations would then contract with a private security company, erect a makeshift boom gate across an entry street, and (illegally) stop all motorists and pedestrians entering in an effort to control movement in and out of their "gated" neighborhood. The roads in these areas remain "public property" and local councils are responsible for providing community services and the upkeep of such roads / streets.

Road closures and gated neighborhoods

A piece of local (provincial) legislation (the Gauteng Local Rationalisation of Government Affairs Act 10 of 1998) regulated security access restrictions in Gauteng Province and provided the foundation for local neighborhood enclosures in urban areas with the "Restriction of Access to Public Places for Safety and Security Purposes." Chapter 7 of the Act governs security access restrictions, and municipal council procedures must comply with its provisions. Consequently, the Act allows for *authorized* access restrictions to public areas by private persons or bodies. However, such closures are only allowed *as a security measure* and can only be approved if it is demonstrated that they are in the interest of residents' safety and security. Enclosure applications can be approved *only as a last resort to curb crime in a specific area*. The policy states that security restrictions are supported only as a short-term solution to combating crime and proposes long-term solutions, such as encouraging the public to take reasonable measures to protect themselves, and discouraging crime in various other ways.

Residents invoked the specific terminology about safety and security (see below) when applying for wholesale closures for "personal safety and protection from the depredations of violent criminals." However, many applications were motivated by other factors, including quieter suburbs, less traffic, and over 20 per cent higher property prices once an enclosure was in place. Furthermore, insurance companies typically offered residents of particular types of enclosures a reduction of between 25 and 30 per cent on their premiums (SAHRC, 2005:24).

To support this legislation the Metropolitan Council of Johannesburg developed a "Security Access Restrictions Policy" which more clearly defines security access restrictions as:

> ... any means that discourages access to any other person and may include measures such as traffic calming measures, guards and guardhouses. A restriction of access does not necessarily mean the erection of gates, fences or booms. Restriction of access shall mean restriction is limited to access control, no denial of access and no discriminating actions nor infringements on the rights of individuals.
>
> (SAHRC, 2005: 8)

In slight contrast to the Johannesburg and Pretoria municipalities, the Thekwini Metropolitan Council (Greater Durban Municipality in the KwaZulu-Natal Province) operates in terms of Section 209 of the Local Authorities Ordinance 25 of 1974. This allows the local authority to act in the best interests of the public, provided that its actions do not result in the "deprivation or substantial deprivation of the public of the enjoyment of its right in, or to, any public street or public place." eThekwini used less restrictive measures to address crime and drew up a management plan in relation to its Safer City strategy that prohibits erecting any device which partially or fully obstructs a public roadway. Applications for security measures were only considered for residential access roads. In such cases a guard can monitor access, but not stop or search any person or vehicle, nor collect names and/or vehicle registration numbers. Additional traffic-calming measures, whether temporary or permanent, are not permitted. Furthermore, in eThekwini municipality service providers and essential services may not be restricted from entering such areas and guardhouses must be erected in accordance with national building regulations. The municipality designed a set of forms to assist the council in making informed decisions about such applications, which, if approved, are only valid for six months at a time (SAHRC, 2005:25).

So, if the residents of Gauteng Province wanted to install road closures or access-control barricades they first had to obtain approval from at least 80 per cent of the area residents. Since some of these enclosure schemes involved erecting barricades and walls and contracting with a private security company, they also had to obtain contractual agreements from residents to pay monthly levies. To get residents to "buy-in" to an enclosure plan the initiator (often an outside consultant) had to call a public meeting, get 80 per cent agreement, draw up an implementation plan, and then submit this application to the local municipal council.

One practical obstacle that was often encountered was the fact that some residents had already contracted for security services from different security companies. Getting residents to agree to one service provider, which meant canceling their individual contracts, was a major stumbling block that often stood in the way of any successful application.

Most road-closure approvals depend upon the nature and route layout (traffic volumes) of the roads and streets in the area concerned. As the policy does not allow for major through-routes to be closed, it is usually the neighborhoods designed on a "closed road network system" (i.e. fewer traffic intersections and fewer roads to close) which are likely to be approved (Landman, 2002:9).

Security is an integral factor, not only in motivating applications (motivations usually cite "local crime patterns and high incidence"), but also in getting the "buy-in" of residents (a safer and more secure area to live in). An ancillary selling point of such closure plans is that property values are increased in a secured area. Overall, the concept of "total security" has become a lifestyle marketing strategy to gain acceptance for implementing strict security measures, something that is particularly apparent with private security villages (see Landman, 2002:14–17). The "total security" package features such "standard" security measures as guardhouses, entrance gates or booms, fences, walls, 24-hour patrolling guards, intercom systems, CCTV surveillance cameras, and individual residences' security systems (alarms, cameras, lights, and so on) linked to a contracted security company's central control room, often with an armed rapid-response team on 24/7 standby.

The property developers of private security villages (often linked to a golf estate) had little problem incorporating security measures as standard urban planning and development features. However, it often took many months and even years for a residents' association with 80 per cent or more resident support to obtain official approval for road closures, boom gates, and other security measures designed to gate off their neighborhood. The whole process is fraught with a number of legal hurdles. In the case of enclosed neighborhoods, for example, in order for residents to submit a formal application for the right to control access to their neighborhood they must also form a legal body, generally taking the form of a Section 21 company (a legally established "not-for-profit" company). In addition, some residents have increasingly resisted neighborhood closure plans, as have government agencies such as public transport, emergency and hospital services, and community service providers (electricity, water, refuse removal, and so on). Domestic and garden workers who must come from outside an enclosed neighborhood to work for local residents have also opposed closures. The difficulties and delays in obtaining approval prompted many residents to undertake their own arbitrary and illegal closures (Landman, 2002:24).

Gatings and road closures increased dramatically after 2000, especially in the Gauteng Province cities of Johannesburg and Pretoria (Tshwane). A number of civil-rights organizations, including the South African Human

Rights Commission, became concerned that these developments might limit rights guaranteed in the South African Bill of Rights. A number of metropolitan councils, particularly Johannesburg and the City of Tshwane (Pretoria), where the highest number of such closures were occurring, in 2004 placed a moratorium on any new road closures and neighborhood gatings until the legislation (municipal bylaws) could be reviewed.

Security measures at enclosed areas as an abuse of rights

Implementing and operating security measures led to a number of abuses not only in enclosed areas but also in neighborhoods with Neighborhood Watches, where security companies were contracted to patrol and provide armed response. Some patrolling guards randomly stopped and questioned pedestrians or those standing on street corners perceived to be "loitering" purely on the basis of suspect appearances or some perceived suspicious behavior, or because they were suspected of being undocumented immigrants. These persons were asked to produce identification documentation and questioned about why they were in the area. Guards who manned boom gates and other access-control structures might insist that anyone entering the area sign in, divulge personal identification information (such as full name, ID number, telephone number, and in some cases even a home address), and provide reasons for entering the area or the name and address of the person(s) they were visiting. Guards at a number of security villages used surveillance cameras to record the registration numbers of vehicles entering and exiting. Patrolling guards would also arrest undocumented immigrants, persons who were carrying the "tools of the trade" for burglaries and even those who could not prove that they owned goods in their possession. As my own interviews and discussions with guards attest, such arrests could involve illegal detention, with some guards even locking up individuals in a storeroom/office for several hours before handing them over to the nearest police station, and then only at the end of a twelve-hour shift.

Hearings of the South African Human Rights Commission

As closures proliferated (particularly in Gauteng Province) the public lodged a number of complaints with the South African Human Rights Commission concerning the erection of boom gates, road closures, and the security measures and practices at some enclosures (SAHRC, 2005:3). These complaints prompted the SAHRC to hold public hearings on this issue. The SAHRC first called for written submissions from the public and interested parties. After receiving such submissions a number of key players were identified and invited to make oral submissions to a SAHRC panel in September 2004 (SAHRC, 2005:8).

Allegations of rights abuse lodged with SAHRC: arguments and counter-arguments

Among the arguments advanced to support booms and road closures was that they had reduced crime while not prejudicing road users or other members of the community (SAHRC, 2005:4). That said, no statistically reliable evidence was presented to the SAHRC that substantiated the contention that these measures permanently reduced high levels of crime, nor that they fundamentally enhanced safety and security in enclosed areas. Much of the evidence for crime reduction was anecdotal and could not be substantiated with the SAPS crime statistics, which are usually based on provincial and national figures and cannot be broken down into smaller geographical units. While precinct-level crime statistics are available to each police station for analytical (e.g. GIS Spatial Analysis and Crime Mapping) and operational needs it would be a mammoth task to produce numbers for individual streets or enclosed neighborhoods, let alone making that data available to private citizens.

While in most cases crime reduction appears immediately following the implementation of these measures, crime slowly returns. This is attributable to several factors: criminals learn more about the effectiveness and procedures of the new security measures; guards become more lackadaisical in performing their security screening and surveillance duties; and residents become less observant of the required procedures. The end result is that several months after the start of operations crime often returns to the previously high levels.[1] Others have argued that this initial crime reduction results from crime displacement, whereby criminals target other nearby areas that might not have the same level of security measures. As a consequence, any reductions in crime levels experienced in a particular enclosed area would not be reflected in a precinct's overall crime statistics since the crime is still occurring in that precinct.

At the SAHRC hearings, and in the written submissions, those in favor of security access restrictions argued that the state was constitutionally obligated to protect individuals from all forms of violence. While the state's law-enforcement capacities were considered inadequate and the police particularly ineffective in relation to this obligation, they argued, private citizens were well within their rights, and, in fact, felt compelled by the realities of violent crime and lack of personal safety in their neighborhoods, to provide their own protection by whatever means they considered appropriate. If this meant contracting with private security companies who might abrogate rights and freedoms in providing such protection, it was further argued that this should be seen in the context of the "wider good" of ensuring the "public safety and security" of ordinary citizens. It was also suggested that such restrictions should be viewed as short-term and temporary measures to be employed until the crime situation had been sufficiently "stabilized." Some also maintained that such measures advanced the constitutional aim to "improve the quality of life of all citizens" (Constitution of South Africa 1996: Preamble) which, it was felt, was palpably not being fulfilled by the state (SAHRC, 2005:11–12).

Coincidentally, opponents of the measures also used the "right to freedom and security of the person" to argue against security access restrictions. They pointed to incidents where individuals had allegedly been handcuffed to gates by security guards, or where residents opposing the closures had been threatened and intimidated because they refused to either support or comply with the restrictions imposed at road closures/boom gates (SAHRC, 2005:12). In one area, mini explosives were thrown onto the property of an opponent of closure, while other opponents had been publicly threatened with a shotgun (SAHRC, 2005:12).

Both sides of the debate also used the "right to privacy" to justify or oppose road closures (SAHRC, 2005:19). It is evident that a person's right to privacy is infringed by arbitrary searches at security access points, and demands for personal information by security guards. Privacy, however, is not an absolute right and can be constitutionally limited. To satisfy the limitation clause in the Constitution, the action infringing a human right must be done in terms of a law of general application (SAHRC, 2005:19). However, in South Africa the legislation (see Code of Conduct for Security Service Providers, 2003 and The Private Security Industry Regulation Act [56 of 2001]) governing the private-security industry does not give security officers the power or authority to conduct searches and seizures (Minnaar, 2005; 2007).

In one case it was reported (Own Correspondent 2002) that certain residents were being forced to sign a log each time they entered or exited their enclosed residential suburb if they did not agree to, approve of, or support (by paying a levy or monthly service subscription) the neighborhood closure. In contrast, the paid-up residents were given vehicle stickers showing they had done so, and consequently were allowed unhindered, unfettered, and undocumented access. This palpably discriminatory measure was justified by this residents association's chairperson by claiming that there had been an "80 per cent" drop in the crime rate for the enclosed area, and furthermore that property values in the area had increased dramatically, making the suburb more sought-after by homeowners.

Several submissions supporting the closures argued that personal details such as name, identity number, and vehicle registration number should not be considered private information. Furthermore, they stressed that the information requested at security access points was not obtained in an intrusive manner and was not used for ulterior purposes. The counter-arguments suggested that being required to disclose such information to strangers (the security guards at the boom gates) was indeed an infringement on people's right to privacy and also intimated that such information could be used for ill gain (e.g. providing information to criminal syndicates) (SAHRC, 2005:19).

Another document referred to in the SAHRC submissions and hearings in support of the access-control restrictions was the Bill of Rights Handbook (interpretation of the Bill of Rights in the South African Constitution) statement that: "violence against an individual is a grave invasion of personal security." The Constitution (s 12[1][c]) requires the state to protect individuals, both by refraining from such invasions itself and by restraining or discouraging private individuals from such invasions (De Waal et al., 2001). Accordingly, it was claimed that road closures/boom gates deterred criminals and therefore enforced the rights of residents within enclosures to be "free from violence." Furthermore, as s 152(1)(d) of the Constitution requires local authorities to promote "a safe and healthy environment," proponents argued that approving enclosures should also be seen as fulfilling this Constitutional obligation. There were, however, heated disputes over whether closures do in fact reduce crime (SAHRC, 2005:12).

The majority of submissions that opposed enclosures were based on the claim that such access restrictions "infringed on an individual's right to freedom of movement on a public road" (SAHRC, 2005:14). This right is particularly relevant in South Africa due to the country's history of apartheid, which rigidly controlled the movement of people purely on the basis of their race. The use of security access restrictions in enclosed communities and security villages sparked similar fears. As the SAHRC graphically stated:

> ... the fear of forced segregation arises if communities are permitted to box themselves off from the rest of society and have the power to determine who can be granted or denied access to public places.
>
> (SAHRC, 2005:15)

In addition, it was suggested that guards at these enclosure points wield tremendous powers in deciding whom to let in and on what basis.

Many of the submissions alleged that racial discrimination was occurring at security access points; the security guards at these booms would routinely stop black and not white people in order to enquire about their movements (SAHRC, 2005:17). Such practices, whether real or perceived, were, in the context of South Africa's racial-discriminatory past, extremely sensitive and politically charged. The SAHRC was adamant that such racial bias had no place in the "new democratic" South Africa, irrespective of whether such bias was intentional or merely procedural (i.e. that the majority of residents— and their visitors—in affluent enclosed areas were white, while their domestic workers and gardeners and other manual-service workers were largely black).

Another argument against security access restrictions was that they can compromise the freedom and security of the person and violate the right to access health services (see Constitution Act 1996: ss 24, 27), since they could prevent emergency vehicles from reaching persons in need if their quickest route to the emergency was unnecessarily delayed by road closures or gates. Such delays are a potential health risk since, as submitted by the Johannesburg

Emergency Services, it is time-consuming for emergency personnel to search for alternative entrances and exits (SAHRC, 2005:12).

The constitutional provisions for "freedom of trade, occupation and profession" (Constitution Act 1996: s 22) were raised to a lesser extent in submissions to SAHRC. Here it was alleged that the right to choose a trade, occupation, or profession could be infringed when persons are denied access to seek employment at residences in enclosed suburbs, or even when hawkers are not allowed to enter and sell their goods. In addition, plumbers, electricians, house painters, and so on could not solicit work from residents if they could not go directly to a resident to perform these services (i.e. if they were routinely refused entry to market their services). Such access restriction could also negatively affect small businesses operating from private residences located within enclosures because they would not be easily accessible to customers outside of the enclosed area. It was also feared that if these business owners did not support the security initiatives, customers might view them in a negative light and avoid their businesses (SAHRC, 2005:20).

SAHRC findings and recommendations

The SAHRC had to consider all evidence/information presented to it and judge whether boom gates and closures impinged upon the rights of others. This included considering whether such measures were so unduly restrictive that they could not be constitutionally justified or sanctioned (SAHRC, 2005:4).

The SAHRC made a number of findings and recommendations. One of these was that security access-restriction points should not be implemented if they denied or hindered access to public spaces, including roads, nor should they require anyone to furnish private information (for example, destination, purpose of visit, or identity document). Moreover, they should not allow arbitrary searches of persons or vehicles, or the detention (arrest) of anyone, or deny any entry (other than serving as a security measure delaying open entry or acting to deter the movement of criminals). If any of these enclosed neighborhoods operated in such a manner this would be a violation of the rights of those affected (SAHRC, 2005:4).

Furthermore, the SAHRC did "not generally support the use of boom gates and gated communities" (SAHRC, 2005:5), largely because of how these affect urban mobility, restrict freedom of movement and the ability of the public to freely engage in business, social activity, and recreation. They also expressed the fear that these measures created "no-go closed areas" and "enclaves of privilege." In addition, the SAHRC felt that these measures "cause social division, dysfunctional cities and lead to the further polarization of our society." Moreover, the purported benefits they bring by way of enhanced safety and security "are in doubt and the subject of considerable debate" (SAHRC, 2005:5–6).

According to the SAHRC, there was "little recourse [to the law] for those whose rights had been violated" (SAHRC, 2005:5). This was notwithstanding the fact that approvals for such closures were accompanied by relatively strict conditions of implementation. For instance, a residents association and their contracted security providers had to commit to providing "free and unhindered access." But it was evident that numerous communities flouted these conditions, or even illegally implemented gating and road closures and their accompanying security measures. One factor that contributed to this situation was the lack of official capacity to monitor the myriad of closures that occurred in Gauteng Province from 2000 onwards. This, in turn, was due to practical difficulties and manpower shortages at the local-government level. As a consequence, most breaches and/or instances of noncompliance were never sanctioned. This is a glaring shortcoming of the regulatory policy for road closures since there are no monitoring or enforcement provisions for noncompliance within the Gauteng Local Rationalisation of Government Affairs Act 10 of 1998. Moreover, there are no prescribed penalties for noncompliance, which leads to a situation where people can argue that noncompliance to the statutory terms is not unlawful. To further compound these difficulties complainants had to report such breaches so that local authorities, the police (if a suspected criminal breach had occurred), or SAHRC (violation or abuse of a constitutional right) could investigate and impose legal sanctions. This happened very rarely, if at all, until a few public complaints began to be submitted to the SAHRC in 2002–2003.

To the question of whether "road closures and boom gates are effective in preventing crime?" the SAHRC could not conclusively demonstrate the effect road closures and boom gates had on crime rates. The SAPS do not keep crime statistics for specific enclosures and the official SAPS crime statistics do not (and are unable) to directly address the question of whether road closures are effective.

Some concluding remarks

The SAHRC hearings punctuated a public debate that made people think far more carefully about the practical use and implementation of security measures for access control in enclosed and gated neighborhoods—particularly as these pertain to crime reduction and public safety. Moreover, the process also emphasized that in a constitutional democracy with a strong human-rights base one can only act in public spaces within a framework that strictly respects everyone's rights and freedoms.

The "road closure/boom gate" debate also increased the public awareness and profile of the SAHRC as an independent-rights "watchdog" that would follow up and investigate any alleged rights violation complaint they received.

This issue also initiated a vigorous public debate that for the first time linked rights, freedoms, and public safety with the perceived private-security restrictions. An ancillary debate also sprang up regarding the stricter regulation, oversight, and monitoring of the conduct of security officers (Minnaar, 2007) as the number of complaints against security abuses and service-delivery problems against registered private security companies began to rise (PSIRA, 2007).

It appears that the violations that occurred in residential areas and at security villages in Gauteng were a function of operational implementation and not because the security measures were prohibited. In other words, these rights violations occurred outside of the policy guidelines, or resulted from the failure of residents associations to live up to their commitments as outlined in the policy. The negligible monitoring by local authorities of the implementation and operation of security access control further contributed to these violations.

What came through clearly in the SAHRC hearings and submissions was that access-control security measures were mostly implemented with a view to enhancing public safety and residents' feelings of safety. Sometimes this involved overzealous security guards who were unaware of the legislative underpinnings or policy guidelines for operating such security access-control measures.

One important development in this process that deserves ongoing scrutiny is the increased use of CCTV in enclosures. When enclosures and gating were being implemented the only CCTV surveillance measures in place in enclosed (gated) neighborhoods and security villages were those at access boom gates, guardhouses, gated street entrances, and the walled entrances to security villages. While CCTV surveillance systems are officially implemented in public open streets in several central business districts in South Africa (Minnaar 2007), currently in the Gauteng Province there are only two CCTV surveillance systems using multiple linked cameras in residential neighborhoods. Such systems have a camera footprint that covers not only a boom gate or entrance access-control point but also covers public streets and other public spaces. These two systems, one in the Sandton suburb in Johannesburg and the other in the Erasmuskloof suburb of Pretoria, have been approved, but unlike the official public open-street CCTV systems in central business districts (CBDs) they are being funded by residents associations, and routed through a private-security control room. Rights activists have only just begun to address the concerns raised by such systems, including who would be employed to do the monitoring; how video images would be stored; their potential use as evidence; whether crime information will be routinely handed over to or routed through law-enforcement agencies; the possible exploitation of private information databases, and so on. All these aspects of such crime prevention/reduction security surveillance measures need more investigation and further debate.

Note

1 This statement is based on the perceptions of residents living in such areas about how they experience the perceived initial reduction and then slow rise of crime in the first few months of gating or closure. The author has gleaned this information

from residents' reports in a number of forums, *inter alia* residents committees, local Community Police Forum (CPF) meetings, news media, and discussions with residents and security managers in an ancillary Department of Security Risk Management research project on security measures in gated neighborhoods.

References

Bremner, L. 2000. Crime and the emerging landscape of post-apartheid Johannesburg. In *Blanc Architecture, Apartheid and After*, edited by H. Judin and I. Vladislavic. Rotterdam: Nai Publishers.

De Waal, J., I. Currie, and G. Erasmus. 2001. *The Bill of Rights Handbook*, 4th Edition. Lansdowne: Juta & Co. Ltd.

Hook, D. and M. Vrdoljak. 2000. "From power to power: Strydom Square and the security park." Paper presented at the Urban Futures Conference, July 10–14, 2000. Johannesburg.

——. 2001. "Gated communities, heterotopia and a 'rights' of privilege: A 'heterotopology' of the South African security-park." Paper presented to the University of the Witwatersrand (WITS) Housing Seminar, May 17, 2001. Johannesburg.

Landman, K. 2000. *An Overview of Enclosed Neighborhoods in South Africa*. Pretoria: Council for Scientific and Industrial Research (CSIR) Publication, BOU/I 187.

——. 2002. *Gated Communities in Brazil and South Africa: Comparative Perspectives*. Pretoria: Council for Scientific and Industrial Research (CSIR).

Lipman, A. and H. Harris. 1999. "Fortress Johannesburg." *Environment and Planning B: Planning and Design* 26: 727–40.

Minnaar, A. 2005. "Private-public partnerships: Private security, crime prevention and policing in South Africa." *Acta Criminologica: Southern African Journal of Criminology* 18(1): 85–114.

——. 2007. "Oversight and monitoring of non-state/private policing: The private security practitioners in South Africa." In *Private Security in Africa: Manifestation, Challenges and Regulation*, edited by S. Gumedze, 127–49. ISS Monograph No. 139. Brooklyn: Institute for Security Studies.

——. 2008a. "Community policing in a high crime transitional state: The case of South Africa since democratisation in 1994." In *Community Policing: International patterns and comparative perspectives*, ed. D. Wisler and I.D. Onwudiwe (19–57). Boca Raton: CRC Press/Taylor & Francis.

——. 2008b. "Transforming policing in a high crime transitional democracy: The South African experience." In *Current Problems of the Penal Law and Criminology*, ed. E. Plywaczewski, (377–404). Bialystak: Temida 2.

Minnaar, A., I. Liebenberg, and C. Schutte, eds. 1994. *The Hidden Hand: Covert Operations in South Africa* 2nd Edition (revised and updated 1998). Pretoria: Human Sciences Research Council/Institute for a Democratic Alternative for South Africa (IDASA)/Friedrich-Naumann Stiftung.

Minnaar, A. and P. Ngoveni. 2004. "The relationship between the South African Police Service and the private security industry: Any role for outsourcing in the prevention of crime?" *Acta Criminologica: Southern African Journal of Criminology* 17(1): 42–65.

Minnaar, A. and R. Zinn. 2000. "Vehicle hijacking in South Africa: An examination of victimisation patterns and an evaluation of current prevention/interventionist strategies with specific reference to Gauteng Province, South Africa." Paper presented to the Xth International Symposium on Victimology: *Beyond Boundaries: Research and Action for the Third Millennium*. Montreal, Canada. August 6–11, 2000.

——. 2002, "The 'new' Vigilantism in post-April 1994 South Africa: Searching for explanations," in Informal Criminal Justice Ed. D. Feenan. Advances in Criminology series, Aldershot: Dartmouth/Ashgate Publishing.

Own Correspondent. 2002. "Boom policy infuriates residents." *The Star*, November 16, 2002.

The Private Security Industry Regulatory Authority (PSIRA). 2007. *Annual Report 2006/2007*. Pretoria: PSIRA. Available at www.sira-sa.co.za. Accessed July 27, 2007.

South Africa. 1993. *Constitution of the Republic of South Africa Act No 200 of 1993*. Pretoria: Government Printer.

——. 1996. *Constitution of the Republic of South Africa Act No 108 of 1996*. Pretoria: Government Printer.

South African Human Rights Commission (SAHRC). 2005. *Road Closures/Boom Gates Report*. Johannesburg: SAHRC. Available at www.sahrc.gov.za. Accessed October 2, 2008.

Zinn. R. 2008. *Incarcerated Perpetrators of House Robbery as a Source of Crime Intelligence*. Unpublished DLitt et Phil dissertation. Pretoria: University of South Africa.

Chapter 11

The Greek Olympic phone tapping scandal

A defenceless state and a weak democracy

Minas Samatas

Despite technological advances in blocking interceptions, there is still little privacy afforded to cellular telephone or internet communications (Alexandropoulou, 2008; Garfinkel, 2000; Ogura, 2006). In an age of wireless mobile communications, it is common to hear of both legal and illegal telephone tapping (Edwards, 2004). Although electronic interception by individual hackers is a crime, it no longer makes headlines. In the aftermath of the 9/11 attacks, authorities have used heightened security concerns to further legitimate state-initiated communication interceptions (Beck, 2002; Schulhofer, 2002; Sidel, 2004). Individual hackers, corporate rivals, and government agencies use interception technologies to monitor communications for assorted purposes.

Phone tappings only become scandalous when they unlawfully target the power elite and those who supposedly protect telecommunications privacy and security; that is, when they target the traditional state watchers and eavesdroppers. If such monitoring is discovered it is usually not disclosed publicly to avoid embarrassment. Nonetheless, in recent years the public has learned about several telecommunication scandals, including the Telecom Italia spying incident, the phone tapping of the British Royals, the Hungarian, Brazilian, and Portuguese political hacking scandals, and so on.[1]

This chapter analyzes the Greek phone-tapping scandal. At first glance just another in a procession of comparable incidents, it relates to the Athens 2004 Olympic Games, and the targeting of the Greek prime minister, his government, and top military and security officials. Commentators call it "the most spectacular cell-system penetration ever" (Cherry and Goldstein, 2007), "the most audacious cell-network break-in ever," and "the most bizarre and embarrassing scandal ever to engulf a major cell phone service provider" (Prevelakis and Spinellis, 2007: 1–2). The perpetrators of this crime and their motives had not been identified by the conclusion of investigations in January 2008. The dominant theory is that these cell-phone taps were orchestrated by the US secret services in light of concerns about Olympic security and mistrust of the Greek government. If so, the case touches not only on communications privacy and human rights, but also on sensitive areas of national security and sovereignty.

I emphasize three main aspects of this event. First, the phone tappings are Greece's "Olympics-gate," given their connection with security for the Athens 2004 Summer Olympic Games. Second, officials at Vodafone and in the Greek government blatantly covered up this scandal. Third, Greek state and democratic institutions appear defenseless against such high-tech crimes.

This case was a political scandal that unmasked the weakness and defenselessness of the Greek state and its systems of democratic oversight and accountability. For the first time the Greek state, traditionally the main agent in tapping the telephones of Greek citizens and political opponents, has admitted that it was a prolonged victim of such monitoring. The state failed to protect its leaders and citizens from eavesdropping and, more importantly, to take necessary measures to avoid comparable disasters. This failure also reflects the tremendous democratic deficit of the Greek political system, in which the executive can cover up scandals without offering public explanations or fearing meaningful sanction. The actual telephone tapping is far less scandalous than the demonstration of the inefficiency of the Greek state, the blatant cover-up, and the failure to guard against such actions in the future.

Official accounts and cover-ups

Since the specifics of this scandal are not well known to an international audience, this section details the chronology of events. On February 2, 2006, the Greek government announced that during the Athens 2004 Olympics, and for nearly a year afterwards, unknown individuals had tapped the telephones of Prime Minister Kostas Karamanlis, as well as those of the ministers of foreign affairs, defense, public order, justice, and many other top government, military, and security officials. In a remarkable press conference, the government spokesman, backed by the ministers of justice and public order, revealed that the phone tapping started before the Athens 2004 Olympic Games and probably continued until it was discovered on March 7, 2005. Officials did not identify the perpetrators of this unlawful surveillance: "It was an unknown individual, or individuals, who used high technology" (Smith, 2006a).

Spy software allowed calls to and from the tapped numbers to be monitored and recorded by other cell phones. This monitoring was detected by Vodafone Greece after customers complained about problems with their service. Public Order Minister George Voulgarakis gave credit to Vodafone Greece CEO George Koronias for informing the government, and noted that "Had it not been for the check [by Vodafone] it is very conceivable the wiretaps would have continued beyond [March 2005] when they were discovered" (Smith 2006a). During the press conference, several indecipherable diagrams, containing intersecting lines and diminishing circles, were used to try to explain the specifics of the surveillance operation. The most interesting revelation, however, was that the focal point of the tapping program was the area around the US Embassy in central Athens, raising suspicions that US intelligence services were involved. The Greek government subsequently denied that it has evidence of such involvement, and the US Embassy and State Department have refused to comment.

The Greek press revealed more details about this extraordinary security breach. The technology used was spy software installed in the central system of Vodafone, which is Greece's second-largest mobile telephony provider. The list of illegally tapped telephone numbers rose to over 100, including most officials in Greece's foreign ministry, top security officers, journalists, and foreign embassy workers. Topping the first announced list of 46 names were: Kostas Karamanlis (Prime Minister), Petros Molyviatis (foreign minister), Spilios Spiliotopoulos (defence minister), George Voulgarakis (public order minister), Anastasios Papaligouras (justice minister), Yiannis Valinakis (deputy foreign minister), Stavros Dimas (EU Environment Commissioner), Dora Bakoyannis (then mayor of Athens) and former defense minister and PASOK MP Yiannos Papantoniou. On February 7, 2006, Public Order Minister Voulgarakis publicized the names of 10 more people, including those of most senior police officers. Other numbers that were tapped included one used by the former chief of the Greek National Intelligence Agency (EYP), three left-wing activists, a journalist, a few foreign citizens, Athens-based Arab businessmen, and a Greek-American employee at the US Embassy in Athens (*Athens News*, February 10, 2006:A03). Even the prime minister's wife had her telephone tapped. The day after the news conference, an urgent judicial investigation was initiated to discover the culprits.

Officials now believe that the tappings commenced in the run-up to the 2004 Olympic Games and continued until March 2005. The security breach was kept under wraps until February 2, 2006, when the Athens daily *Ta Nea* first broke the story. Security officials launched a secret investigation in the period between discovery and announcement, but this apparently bore little fruit.

On February 9, 2006, Vodafone Greece's CEO, Koronias, told the Greek Communications Privacy Protection Authority (ADAE), an independent watchdog responsible for protecting the security of information and communication networks, that someone working for Vodafone, or the Swedish telecom firm Ericsson, must have activated the spy software. He also said the system was deactivated by Vodafone Greece immediately after it was discovered because of fears about national security. Koronias blamed the breach on Ericsson, who provide Vodafone's central software system, and hinted that " 'the perpetrators of the phone-tapping belong to the secret service of a major power.' In ambiguous terms, he let it be known that 'if he was made a scapegoat, he will have much more to say' " (*Athens News* February 10, 2006:A03).

In fact, the spy software was discovered on March 7, 2005, by Ericsson technicians. Vodafone deactivated the program the next day and then informed the government. The spy software was eventually found on four of Vodafone's Ericsson telephone exchanges, allowing calls to and from around 100 numbers to be diverted to 14 pay-as-you-go mobile phones, from which conversations could then be recorded. The Ericsson technicians who examined the spy software were amazed by its sophistication, according to Bill Zikou, Ericsson's then managing director of the Greek subsidiary.[2] He suggested that whoever was behind the tapping had "excellent knowledge of technical matters and a big budget" (eKathimerini, March 16, 2006). This effectively excludes individual hackers from the pool of potential suspects.

Two days after the spy software was discovered, and one day before Vodafone CEO Koronias informed the government, a Vodafone software engineer, Kostas Tsalikidis, was found dead. Tsalikidis, who was in charge of network planning, allegedly committed suicide by hanging himself. There was considerable suspicion that his death was linked to the scandal and speculation that he either committed suicide because he was involved, or was murdered because he had discovered, or was about to discover, the perpetrators. In June 2006, after a four-month investigation, Supreme Court prosecutor Dimitris Linos concluded that Tsalikidis' death was directly linked to the scandal: "If there had not been the phone tapping, there would not have been a suicide," but that no third party was involved in his final act (Cherry and Goldstein 2007). Tsalikidis's family appealed this report on the grounds that it was inconsistent and contradictory. The appeals court prosecutor Miltiadis Andriotelis rejected the family's appeal, concluding that he "found nothing wrong with Diotis's investigation and that Tsalikidis decided to commit suicide because he was under great stress as he had been in charge of software that was hacked into and used to spy on some 100 mobile phones" (Smith, 2006b).

On February 13, 2006, a few days after the government's announcement, Prime Minister Karamanlis met with representatives of ADAE, the National Telecommunications Commission (EETT), and a group of law professors. These individuals were asked to examine Greece's telecommunications system. Eventually, this academic team, under Professor Dimitris Tsatsos, recommended to the prime minister that: (a) legislation be adjusted to give industry watchdogs clearer and larger roles, and (b) there be stiffer penalties for firms or individuals who breach privacy laws. The team also said it was vital that law-makers keep up with technological advances and suggested a national-level public dialogue about communications freedom and security. Following that meeting, Karamanlis publicly announced his government's intention to tighten up the operating framework for telecommunications companies. In an attempt to stem criticism that the government had done little since the phone taps were discovered, Karamanlis outlined broad measures designed to protect phone privacy. He also pledged that his government would get to the bottom of the phone tapping and hold those responsible accountable: "whoever they may be ... The era of cover-ups has passed, never to return ... We will adopt stricter penalties, both for those involved in such crimes and for those who make use of data gathered from this type of criminal activity" (Kathimerini, February 14, 2006).

Approximately five weeks later, on April 6, 2006, both George Koronias, the CEO of Vodafone in Greece, and Bill Zikou, the managing director of Ericsson Hellas, appeared before a parliamentary committee investigating how the phone tapping occurred and who was responsible. They disagreed on whether Vodafone knew that the software to legally tap phones (which was hijacked by the eavesdroppers) was included in the package supplied by Ericsson. Zikou said that in January 2003 Ericsson began delivering software which enabled the legal tapping of mobile phones. This contradicted Koronias's claim the previous week that Vodafone had no such software. The program was apparently unlocked just before the 2004 Olympics, allowing the eavesdroppers to listen in on their targets. The Ericsson chief left MPs in no doubt that he held Vodafone responsible for the breach of security: "Once we deliver something to a customer, it is their responsibility to protect it," said Zikou (*eKathimerini*, March 16, 2006). When MPs asked Zikou who might have been involved in the tapping, he said it certainly was not Ericsson staff, but he could not rule out the involvement of Vodafone employees, internet hackers, or the possibility of an inside job.

On the same day, Yiannis Angelou, the director of the prime minister's political office, and the first government official to meet with Vodafone's CEO on March 10, 2005, told the parliamentary committee that Premier Karamanlis had some twenty cell phones, two of which were on the list of numbers that were illegally tapped.

In December 2006, ADAE fined the Greek branch of Vodafone €76 million for the illegal wiretapping of 106 cell phones and a "number of infringements attributed to the company." The fine was calculated at €500,000 for each phone that was illegally monitored, as well as a €15 million penalty for impeding the investigation. The watchdog accused Vodafone of failing to adequately protect its network and of failing to inform subscribers that their phones were being tapped. ADAE officials also claimed that by removing the bugging devices after they had been discovered, Vodafone made it impossible to trace the perpetrators. The firm paid the fine but appealed the decision. Vodafone Greece has also been fined €19.1 million by EETT, the national telecommunications regulator, for breaching privacy rules. Notwithstanding these penalties, Vodafone's exact role in the affair was never clarified.

Finally, on January 17, 2008, almost two years after the initial announcement by the Greek government, judicial authorities shelved the investigation into the wire-tapping, claiming they could not trace the culprits. This, despite the fact that at least 500 witnesses were questioned.

Revelations by the Greek Communications Privacy Protection Authority (ADAE)

The Greek government and judiciary also excluded the Greek independent Authority for Communications Privacy Protection (ADAE) from the phone-tapping investigation until the scandal was made public. Asked why ADAE was not informed immediately and asked to help, the government's spokesman pointed out that at the time the agency was new and not in a position to carry out regular inspections. It was only in January 2005, a month before the wiretaps were discovered, that ADAE acquired a rudimentary staff of ten specialists. Moreover, he noted, the government is not legally obliged to inform ADAE of such matters.

Nevertheless, ADAE took just a few weeks to prepare a report that reached a surprising initial conclusion. Published on March 18, 2006, this report revealed that additional phone numbers beyond those listed in the initial announcement were also tapped, a fact that broadened the geographic area of the monitoring. Hence, the ADAE report raised questions about why this information was not immediately released and who had withheld it.

ADAE also offered damning testimony to the parliamentary committee on February 21, 2006, of how state authorities and Vodafone had handled the tapping. The wiretaps, ADAE argued, required the help of someone who had technical knowledge of Vodafone Greece. Verification of this claim was precluded because the phone company had destroyed relevant records. Moreover, ADAE's head, Andreas Lambrinopoulos, warned Greek ministries and state agencies that Greece still lacked effective measures to protect telecom security, which could lead to future national security breaches (*Athens News*, February 24, 2006:A07). Professor Iakovos Venieris, ADAE's expert on these matters, confirmed that the software used to illegally monitor the mobile phones was part of Vodafone's system to allow authorities to conduct legal phone taps. Although Vodafone said it discovered the spy software on March 7, 2005, Venieris argued that, with the help of Ericsson, which was responsible for the operating software, Vodafone began installing upgrades to stop eavesdroppers at the end of January 2005, that is, before the announced discovery of the tappings. This surprised MPs, who had been led to believe that Vodafone discovered the spy software in March 2005 and shut it down immediately. Venieris told the deputies that it was not clear when the phone tapping began and refused to comment on when the spy software was deactivated.

ADAE's president, Lambrinopoulos, prompted further consternation when he refused to answer a question about whether the spyware had been installed at Vodafone or by someone hacking into the system from outside. This was an important silence given the claim of computer scientists Prevelakis and Spinellis that extraordinarily knowledgeable hackers "either penetrated the network from outside or subverted it from within, aided by an agent or mole ... In either case, the software at the heart of the phone system was reprogrammed with a finesse and sophistication rarely seen before or since ... " (2007:3). The members of the parliamentary committee were also surprised to hear the head of ADAE state that Ericsson did not upgrade the software at seven of Vodafone's centers, including those where the spy software had been activated (*Kathimerini*, February 24, 2006). The report and testimony from ADAE raised questions about how the investigation might have progressed had there not been a year-long delay in informing ADAE about the discovery of the phone-tapping software.

Besides ADAE, computer scientists Prevelakis and Spinellis also underlined that Vodafone has yet to explain why it wiped out vital evidence after they discovered the eavesdropping:

> ... key material has been lost or was never collected. For instance, in July 2005, while the investigation was taking place, Vodafone upgraded two of the three servers used for accessing the exchange management system. This upgrade wiped out the access logs and, contrary to company policy, no backups were retained. Some time later a six-month retention period for visitor sign-in books lapsed, and Vodafone destroyed the books corresponding to the period where the rogue software was modified ... Most crucially, Vodafone's deactivation of the rogue software on 7 March 2005 almost certainly alerted the conspirators, giving them a chance to switch off the shadow phones. As a result ... the perpetrators not only received a warning that their scheme had been discovered but also had sufficient time to disappear ... Physical logbooks of visitors were lost and data logs were destroyed.
>
> (Prevelakis & Spinellis, 2007:8)

In brief, Vodafone ignored the telecommunications industry's best practices which "require that the operator's policies include procedures for responding to an infiltration, such as a virus attack: retain all data, isolate the part of the system that's been broken into as much as possible, coordinate activities with law enforcement" (Ibid:8).

The "Olaf" tapping program: legal phone tappings boomerang back on the Greek government

Prior to the Olympic Games, the Greek government, which has traditionally controlled phone tappings in Greece, tried to organize a phone-tapping network to coordinate the monitoring capacities of private mobile-phone providers. While this initiative failed, it also ultimately boomeranged on the Greek government.

The newspaper *Sunday's Kathimerini* (February 5, 2006) reported that before the Athens Olympics in 2004 a specialist team, known as "OLAF," was assembled under the auspices of the Greek National Intelligence Agency (EYP). The team was to monitor phone calls in the run-up to and during the Games. The Public Order Ministry denied that this surveillance team existed, and said that "OLAF" was working under the auspices of the European Anti-Fraud Office to tackle financial crime. However, his statement was contradicted by documents obtained by *Kathimerini* (February 6, 2006) indicating that the "OLAF" team was mainly involved in phone tapping.

These efforts began shortly before the Athens Olympics, when the government established a team to tap phones. OLAF was set up under then Prime Minister Kostas Simitis, within the framework of EYP, and was to report directly to the EYP director. Yet a series of Greek press reports in the dailies *Ta Nea, Ethnos,* and *Eleftherotypia* (February 2–8, 2006) indicate that while a lawful operation was set up to tap specific conventional phones in the months before and during the Athens 2004 Olympic Games, there were no legal grounds to tap mobile phones in Greece as late as five months after the Games ended. Although Olympic security would certainly fall under the government's purview, in fact the mobile companies failed to agree on the legal framework for tapping during the Olympics. Ultimately, the companies flatly refused to conduct surveillance in the absence of iron-clad legal indemnification. This refusal may have prompted certain individuals or groups to install the illegal surveillance software on Vodafone's servers.

The Athens daily *Eleftherotypia* of March 26, 2006 insisted that the government knew that EYP and American intelligence agents jointly conducted telephone surveillance related to the Athens Olympics using the Vodafone network and equipment stationed on the EYP premises. The report stated that: (a) the Americans dismantled the EYP equipment after the Games, but continued their bugging through the stealth software they installed at several Vodafone hubs, and (b) EYP also continued an independent bugging operation after the Games using surveillance equipment contained in mobile suitcases. On March 27, then Public Order Minister Voulgarakis vehemently denied these reports, and accused the Panhellenic Socialist Movement (PASOK) administration of conducting illegal phone tapping in the past. Referring to security lapses in the period before the Athens 2004 Games, he told the state television network: "I did not open my mouth, because I realized that by speaking out the Olympics might not have been conducted in Greece and our relations with foreign countries would be torpedoed" (*Athens News,* March 31, 2006:A3).

In addition to the Greek press reports, a former US diplomat, John Brady Kiesling, who had recently served at the US Embassy in Athens, published an article in the US weekly *The Nation* on March 20, 2006, which points to the US Embassy in Athens as the likely source of the comprehensive phone-tapping operation. The article, entitled "An Olympian Scandal" (www. thenation.com) suggests that exaggerated Olympic security concerns motivated the eavesdropping.

The intercepted calls were forwarded from four cellular antennas. Their coverage circles overlapped atop the US Embassy. The list of victims was also damning. Anyone might eavesdrop on a defense minister, but only one organization still cares about the electrician whose brother-in-law was implicated in the 1975 murder of CIA station chief Richard Welch by the terrorist group called 17 November.

Kiesling claimed that the officials of the American Science Applications International Corporation (SAIC) company, builders of the high-tech C4I security system that was failing operability tests in advance of the Olympics (Samatas, 2007; 2008), were afraid that the Greek government would take them to court for breach of contract. He argued that "by bugging more Greek Olympic security officials than local radicals, the eavesdroppers fuelled speculation that they were less concerned for the safety of athletes and spectators than for the fortunes of SAIC" (op cit). Kiesling's arguments accord with most accounts in the Greek press that the United States did not trust the security regimes of the Athens 2004 Olympic Committee or the Greek government, and that "the US National Security Agency, the Central Intelligence Agency, or some other US spy agency have all the necessary tools and expertise for mounting such an attack. The location of the monitored phones correlates nicely with apartments and other property under the control of the US Embassy in Athens." Moreover, as Kiesling and Cherry and others argue, the inclusion of a few members of domestic radical groups and few Athens-based Arab businessmen in the phone tappings was not enough to prevent a terrorist attack on the Athens Olympics but was likely included as a smokescreen to impede investigations (Cherry and Goldstein, 2007; http://spectrum.ieee.org).

The Greek scandal and the "big sisters" global interceptions business

As the Greek scandal shows, surveillance systems used for lawful interceptions can be also be deployed for unlawful ones. Indeed, the system advertised by the Ericsson Interception Management System to allow lawful intercepts or wire-taps was the one used to illegally spy on top Greek government officials. Although it is not yet clear what role Vodafone and Ericsson played in the illegal tappings, both are routinely involved in *legal* interceptions all over the world, as are all other telecom giants. As part of the effort to "make the world safer for global capital" (Lenskyj, 2004), there now exists a collection of network-monitoring and data-mining suites made by European and American companies like IBM, Nokia Siemens, Ericsson, Verint, and others. All these surveillance systems comply with the "lawful interception" standards of both the European Telecommunications Standards Institute (ETSI) and the US Communication Assistance for Law Enforcement Act (CALEA), a wire-tapping law passed in 1994. According to *Quintessenz* (http://quintessenz.org), while the official name of such monitoring is still "lawful interception," nowadays these suites enable high-speed government surveillance. They are deployed in 60 countries and target markets in the Middle and Far East; they are ab/used to track down democratic opposition, dissidents, ethnic and religious minorities. The latest addition to these databases is the Nokia Siemens Intelligence Platform, a monster data-warehousing suite integrating all sorts of data sets: mobile-phone data and internet logs, credit-card and bank-account transactions, car registry and DNA databases, road-traffic data, phone-call transcripts, chat protocols, health and insurance data. This "trend-setting intelligence solution" is delivered either as a "Mini-Sized entry system" or "with Data Center dimensions processing mass data (www.quinessenz.at).

As the main target markets for such technologies are in the Middle East and Asia, it is likely that these systems are also deployed in Iran, Egypt, Oman, China, and India (see www.quintessenz.at).

It is not uncommon for these systems to be used for monitoring related to the Olympic Games and other mega-events (Sugden, 2008). The IBM S3 surveillance system and Ericsson's Interception Management System (IMS) have been used for fixed and mobile networks to spy on reporters, athletes, and delegates (Moechel, 2008). The surveillance system used by the Chinese secret service for the security of the Beijing 2008 Olympics was produced and deployed by American companies (Honeywell, General Electric, and IBM) and European ones like Ericsson.

The global promotion of sophisticated but flexible surveillance systems is motivated not only by economic and corporate interests, but also by Western security interests, since all these "big sisters" which comprise the "emerging surveillance-industrial complex," have deep ties to the American and European Union security establishments (see ACLU 2004 at www.aclu.org/surveillance; Barlett and Steele, 2007; Hayes, 2006:3, and in this volume).

The vulnerability of mobile telecommunications

Experts have warned that events like the Greek phone tappings are becoming more common, partly because of the technological integration of the new generation of mobile phones (smart or web phones), which are essentially small mobile computer systems with increased connectivity and data-storage capacity. This alone increases the security risk by enhancing the ability to contaminate private and corporate networks with limited defensive capabilities. Smart phones are vulnerable to the same risks as personal computers (viruses, spam, worms, phishing, smishing, and so on). Their small size and low costs make it difficult to integrate defensive systems, causing new security problems, including new developments in phone hacking. Since many people now see mobile phones as indispensable (Koskela, 2004), and they are already five times more prevalent than PCs, the security problems become even greater. All of this is compounded by the phone users, who are the weakest link in the telecommunication security chain and are often unaware of security threats (Pangalos, 2008; Alexandropoulou, 2008).

The Vodafone bugging scandal in Greece pointed out the serious problem of security responsibility and transferral among the various network partners (service provider, hardware provider, service operator, etc.). Much of Ericsson's software development has been outsourced over the last 15 years to Intracom Telecom, a Greek firm based in Athens. According to Cherry and Goldstein (2007), "Intracom has aroused suspicion because it provided key software to Ericsson and because their Greek partner company is a major telecommunications equipment supplier to Greece's dominant carrier, OTE Group" (http://spectrum.ieee.org). Prevelakis and Spinellis (2007:7) also point out that the necessary know-how for this wiretapping "was available locally and was spread over a large number of present and past Intracom developers …," raising the question of whether this could have been "an inside job."

The uncertain security responsibilities of the telecom network partners is once again receiving serious attention in Greece, since Deutsche Telekom (DT), on March 17, 2008, bought 20 per cent of the state-controlled Greek Telecom Organization, OTE. DT is a giant with close ties to German intelligence and Siemens, which was recently accused in a series of corruption scandals in different countries, including accusations about kickbacks to the ruling Greek parties to ensure Olympic contracts in the Athens 2004 Games.

Public and political consequences

The security of mobile communications and citizen-privacy protection has become a critical issue (Alexandropoulou, 2008). If a prime minister, his top ministers and officials, and telecom corporations like Vodafone and Ericsson could not protect the privacy of their cellular-phone communications, it is not surprising that ordinary people feel almost defenseless against comparable breaches. Yet, the public was not completely apathetic, and after the scandal was revealed there was strong reaction against Vodafone, and the Greek and American governments.

Vodafone has lost credibility and subscribers in Greece. In the 12 months after the scandal was revealed, Vodafone saw a sharp decline in customers compared to its competitors CosmOTE and TIM. During February of 2006 alone, Vodafone saw 22,500 of its customers transfer to its competitors (*Eleftherotypia*, March 12, 2007:59).

On February 9, 2006, soon after the phone-tapping revelations, hundreds marched against the US Embassy in Athens and the US Consulate in Thessaloniki, accusing US secret agents of being behind the taps. This reflected the findings of a well-publicized poll which confirmed that a considerable proportion of the Greek public believed that the US Embassy was involved.

In an opinion poll conducted by VPRC and published in *Sunday's Eleftherotypia* (February 5, 2006), Greek citizens expressed "insecurity as regards their rights." More than three in four Greeks, 78 per cent of respondents, believed that the phone-tapping scandal was a major political issue; 40 percent said it was the work of Greek and foreign secret services, while three in four of those thought the US Embassy was behind the tappings. Perhaps more unsettling is the fact that 80 percent of respondents believe that such taps are still occurring, something that is particularly troubling given that not even 30 per cent of respondents agree that Greece's secret services function properly and 55 per cent feel certain that the country's national security is not being safeguarded.

The credibility of the two main parties in the Greek parliamentary system has also suffered. Neither the government nor the opposition, PASOK, could convince the public that they were on top of this situation. The fact that the government did not respond in a way that reflected the magnitude of the problem is clearly reflected in the conclusions of the survey noted above, which suggested that 73 per cent of Greeks believe that the government held back information about the tapping, and 39 per cent believe that the Karamanlis government did not handle the matter properly. The other worrying aspect of this scandal is how it intensified a belief that everyone, everything and everywhere is subject to surveillance (Glassner, 1999), a view strengthened by the Greek television coverage of the scandal (Tinic, 2005).

Concluding remarks: a defenseless Greek state covers up an "Olympics-gate"

These concluding remarks clarify some unspoken truths and address unanswered questions about the Greek phone tapping scandal.

Unspoken truths

The Greek phone tapping is unprecedented in touching not only on the privacy of communications and human rights, but also on sensitive areas of national security and sovereignty. It represents a serious humiliation for the Greek government and the state apparatus. In citing national-security risks, the government, the judiciary, the parliamentary investigating committee, and even the CEO of Vodafone, have allowed evidence to be suppressed, the guilty parties to escape, and the scandal to be covered up.

This undoubtedly amounts to an "Olympics-gate" because these illegal phone tappings are closely related to the security and surveillance of the Games. As we have documented elsewhere (Samatas, 2007), to ensure the security of the Games, Greece surrendered sovereignty to a multinational security consortium. Greece not only bankrupted itself to host a successful Olympiad, including spending $1.5 billion on security (Samatas, 2007), but the Greek government and top security officials were unwittingly subject to prolonged illegal cell-phone monitoring. All of this was most likely espionage motivated by US Olympic security concerns, and informed by the American mistrust of the Greek Olympic security measures. Of course, since key evidence has been lost or was never collected, there is no tangible proof of who the infiltrators were or of their motives.

This study embraces a common-sense conclusion: given the damage done to both Vodafone Greece and the Greek government, if the perpetrator had been an individual, private hacker, or even a corporate rival, officials would have immediately exposed the breach, secured punishment, and pursued compensation. The fact that the official victims of this case acted to cover up the particulars indicates that they had adequate evidence to imply that a foreign power was involved. This necessitated the cover-up by both Vodafone and the Greek government to protect Vodafone's corporate and Greece's national interests. Vodafone had to ensure that it would continue to be viable in Greece, while the Greek government, according to Kiesling (2006), "had no desire to help Greece's rivals by harming the US–Greek relationship. Greek officials are adult enough not to take eavesdropping personally. They rely, however, on the eavesdroppers being artful enough not to get caught" (www. thenation.com).

The Greek "tapping scandal" is primarily a political scandal. This conclusion is warranted for several reasons beyond the demonstrated inefficiency of the state security apparatus in discovering and arresting the culprits. Officials also suppressed the particulars and never provided sufficient public explanations for their actions: a black eye for Greek parliamentary democracy and a slap in the face for Greek citizens.

The episode revealed the Greek state to be weak and defenseless, and left Greece's military and security leadership looking lost. Beyond the embarrassment of this episode, it likely also involved major security threats, the most striking of which is that the prime minister and senior public figures were exposed to very dangerous levels of risk in terms of their personal safety. This follows from the fact that most cell phones now contain a Global Positioning System chip, making it probable that those tracing the calls could also determine the location of their targets (including the prime minister) 24 hours a day.

These events exposed the huge democratic deficit in the contemporary Greek political system, where government retains the power to control the parliament and the judiciary in order to cover up scandals (Papadimitriou, 2008). The government of Kostas Karamanlis used its power over the appointed leadership of the judiciary to close the case and relied upon its parliamentary majority to stop the investigations of the parliamentary committee. It left the ADAE, the proper communications watchdog, effectively in the dark. This, in turn, demonstrated that the real power of Greece's several privacy-protection bodies is very limited.

Despite its promises, the Greek government did not take this opportunity to reshuffle the troubled state apparatus and failed to restructure the intelligence services. The Greek government has instead shown inexplicable tolerance towards those public officials who failed to detect this security breach. Not a single individual resigned and no one was fired or jailed. The government defended this lack of response, saying it had done everything in its power to uncover the case. "The government handled an issue of the highest national security in an impeccable way," said Public Order Minister George Voulgarakis (*Athens News*, March 31, 2006:A3). The picture that emerges, however, is of a government covering up the facts and losing the opportunity to modernize the state apparatus, especially the Greek intelligence services. This failure is ultimately more scandalous than the tappings themselves; we can expect that it will lead to future national-security breaches, as ADAE has warned. In brief, the glaring inability of the Greek state to protect its political and military leadership, much less its citizens, from phone tappings makes a mockery of the Greek state.

This episode also demonstrates the state and parliamentary democracy to be defenseless in the face of cyber crimes like cell-phone tapping and the policies of global corporate giants. The democratic control of these huge firms is a critical issue (Gandy, 1993; McGrew, 2000: 149–55; Ogura, 2006), especially for small and weak states like Greece. Telecom and other corporations are entrusted with serious security functions but remain largely unaccountable for their actions. The existing legislative framework is inadequate, the powers of the state watchdogs are weak, and the penalties for companies who violate guarantees are small when compared to their profits.

Furthermore, the fact that the telecom giants routinely promote sophisticated surveillance technology, including high-tech interception systems, to authoritarian and democratic regimes for lawful interceptions, poses threats to individual and civil liberties. As the Greek case shows, when national security is left to the mercy of powerful mobile-phone firms and the actions of senior multinational officials, lawful surveillance systems cannot be adequately controlled and can produce a negative backlash for democratic governments.

On the other hand, the Greek case has proved a huge embarrassment for these companies. Although it has denied any wrongdoing, the credibility of both Vodafone and Ericsson has undeniably been damaged. Despite an extensive advertising campaign, Vodafone has lost customers and remains third in the Greek cell-phone market. In a very public way, this case revealed that neither corporation can protect their Greek customers' communication security and privacy. This raises troubling questions for the whole telecom industry.

In Greece, phone tapping was traditionally monopolized by the authoritarian state. There is a rich history of "Machiavellian tappings" in the post-dictatorial period (after 1974), conducted by the ruling parties and directed against their political opponents (Samatas, 2004). The recent events are different because the Greek conservative government was itself a victim of interceptions conducted by unidentified eavesdroppers. If such tappings targeted only the usual suspects (leftists, the opposition, dissidents, minority leaders, Muslims, and so on) they certainly would not have produced much official publicity or fuss, and would most likely have been justified as part of the war against terrorism. Indeed, according to the joint plan drawn up by the Council of the European Union and the US Federal Bureau of Investigation (FBI) a global system is being launched to conduct surveillance of telecommunications—phone calls, emails, and faxes—against organized crime and terrorism (see Bunyan, 2005). In the context of this global anti-terrorist campaign everybody is a suspect (Lyon, 2008) and data-retention policies now make it mandatory for all phone-traffic data in the

United States and European Union to be stored for up to two years (see Mitrou in this volume).

Finally, these events have left the Greek people feeling weak and unprotected. Public confidence in the ability of state and corporate institutions to safeguard telecommunications privacy has been severely shaken (Kyriakidou, 2006). Given that corporate actors and security officials can apparently intercept all wireless conversations with relative ease, the responsibility for privacy protection is being offloaded onto individual citizens, who are offered the implausible advice that they should avoid saying secret or embarrassing things over the telephone (see Whitson and Haggerty, 2008).

Unanswered troubling questions

Years after the event, too many troubling questions still remain unanswered about the culprits, the alleged suicide of Kostas Tsalikidis, the use and whereabouts of the recorded interception data, and so on. Some other pertinent questions also need to be considered.

For instance, regarding the alleged US involvement in this case, one reasonable question is why the Americans would conduct a phone-tapping operation against a NATO ally that has a conservative and pro-American government? One answer to that question is that there is nothing unusual about the surveillance of allies. Such surveillance has occurred in the recent past. So, for example, the European Parliament has passed a resolution against the global ECHELON system which is used to intercept private and commercial communications (2001/2098(INI)–September 2001, www.cyber-rights.org/interception/echelon; Campbell 2003). Likewise, prior to 9/11, the FBI discovered a massive spy ring operating inside the United States being run by three Israeli companies: Amdocs, which provided billing and directory assistance for most American phone companies; Comverse Infosys, which installed and maintained telephone tapping equipment for US law enforcement; and Odigo, which provided services for various electronic "Instant Message" systems. All three companies are owned by Israel and have strong ties to the Israeli Defence Force (see http://www.whatreallyhappened.com). What these and other examples suggest is that spying amongst and between allies is a fairly routine occurrence.

One reason for thinking that the Greek case involved spying between allies is that the US secret services may have been suspicious of the Greek authorities in the light of the Steven Lalas case. (Mr. Lalas was a Greek-American employee who worked and spied in several US Embassies in favor of Greek national interests. He was arrested in 1993 and sentenced to 16 years in prison). Yet a more likely explanation is simply that the US secret services were involved because they had serious concerns about Olympic security and did not trust the Greek government.

We are also left to wonder if the phone tappings were limited to *only* Vodafone's mobile-phone users in Greece. What about the other mobile provider companies? If operatives wanted to listen in on the telephone conversations of senior officials they would likely want to penetrate a number of different service providers. We know nothing about the extent to which other phone networks were (or are) compromised by intelligence agencies or other extremely well resourced and dedicated intruders.

The new technological possibilities of surveillance (Marx, 2002; Simon, 2005; Haggerty and Ericson, 2000) raise serious questions about the freedoms of ordinary people (Sidel, 2004; Lyon, 2008). For example, what happens to someone who uses a monitored network to call a relative or friend who may be a terrorist suspect? Or what happens to someone who dials a wrong number and reaches a terrorist suspect? The case of Pakistani immigrants in Greece who had made phone calls to their London relatives and friends in the time preceding the July 2005 London Underground attacks is disconcerting in this regard. After the attacks the British Secret Intelligence Service, MI6, sent a long list to the Greek government containing the names of individuals suspected of being involved in the Underground attacks. This resulted in 5,432 immigrants being "questioned" during that July and August. Furthermore, 2,172 immigrants were "probed," 1,221 were arrested for "other reasons," and six of the latter were deported. Ultimately, Greek plain-clothes security agents, at the behest of MI6, kidnapped 28 Pakistani men from Athens, Oinofyta, and Ioannina. These individuals were held in secret locations, denied legal advice, questioned, and physically abused. This was confirmed in January 2006 by then Greek Public Order Minister Voulgarakis (see *Statewatch.org* article no. #26920, January 2006).

What guarantees are there that this blow to Greek national security and sovereignty will not be repeated? This scandal highlights how difficult it is for a small and comparatively weak state to preserve national sovereignty and dignity. It exposed the weakness of the government and state institutions and their limited abilities to protect themselves against serious cyber crimes. Unfortunately, the telecommunications-protection changes announced by the Greek government do not guarantee that such a national humiliation will not be repeated. Hence, a pressing basic question remains unanswered: How can a small democratic state effectively defend itself and protect its citizens in this telecommunications age?

Notes

1 See internet reports: "Italians Weary of Scandals Generated by Phone Tapping," June 25, 2006, www.nytimes.com; "Pair jailed over royal phone taps," January 26, 2007, http://news.bbc.co.uk; "MDF Hungarian phone tapping scandal," September 17, 2008, www.budapestsun.com; "Brazil Gov't In Phone Bug Scandal," September, 2008, http://news.sky.com; "Portuguese elections hit by phone-tapping scandal," January 16, 2006, http://findarticles.com.
2 Later statements have clarified that this spy software was part of Vodafone's system to allow legal phone taps, which was then hijacked or illegally reprogrammed.

References

Alexandropoulou, E. 2008. *Security Services of Mobile Communications—Citizen Protection.* ADAE Conference on Privacy, Protection of Communications and Self-Protection of Users and Customers. April 11, 2008. Available at www.adae.gr.

American Civil Liberties Union (ACLU). 2004. *The Surveillance Industrial Complex.* August 2004. Available at www.aclu.org.

Barlett, D.L. and J.B. Steele. 2007. "Secrets: Washington's $8 billion shadow." *Vanity Fair* March 2007.

Beck, U. 2002. "The terrorist threat: World risk society revisited." *Theory, Culture and Society* 19:39–55.

Bunyan, T. 2005. *While Europe Sleeps.* Available at: http://www.spectrezine.org.

Campbell, D. 2003. *Inside Echelon.* March 24, 2003. Available at http://www.heise.de.

Cherry, S. and H. Goldstein. 2007. "An Inside Job." *Spectrum* IEEE (electronic) Magazine July. http://spectrum.ieee.org.

Edwards, J. 2004. *Telecosmos: The Next Great Telecom Revolution.* Hoboken, NJ: Wiley-Interscience.

Garfinkel, S. 2000. *Database Nation: The Death of Privacy in the 21st Century.* New York: O'Reilly.

Gandy, Oscar Jr. 1993. *The Panoptic Sort: A Political Economy of Personal Information.* Boulder, CO: Westview.

Glassner, B. 1999. *The Culture of Fear.* New York: Basic Books.

Haggerty, K. and R. Ericson. 2000. "The surveillant assemblage." *The British Journal of Sociology* 51(4):605–22.

Hayes, B. 2010. "'Full Spectrum Dominance' as European Union Security Policy: On the Trail of the 'NeoConOpticon.'" In *Surveillance and Democracy,* ed. Kevin D. Haggerty and Minas Samatas. London: Routledge.

——2006. *Arming Big Brother: The EU's Security Research Programme.* Amsterdam: TNI, Transnational Institute.

Kiesling, J.B. 2006. "An Olympian scandal." *The Nation* March 20, 2006.

Koskela, H. 2004. "Webcams, TV shows and mobile phones: Empowering exhibitionism." *Surveillance & Society* 2(2/3):199–215. http://www.surveillance-and-society.org.

Kyriakidou, D. 2006. "'Greek Watergate' scandal sends political shockwaves." Reuters. March 2, 2006.

Lenskyj, H. J. 2004. "Making the world safe for global capital: The Sydney 2000 Olympics and beyond." In *Post-Olympism? Questioning Sport in the 21st Century,* edited by J. Bale and M.K. Christensen, pp. 135–63., New York: Berg.

Lyon, D. 2008. "We live in a society of suspects." *Eleftherotypia,* July 12, 2008: 40–41.

McGrew, A, ed. 2000. *The Transformation of Democracy?* London: Polity.

Marx, G. 2002. "What's new about the 'New Surveillance'? Classifying for change and continuity." *Surveillance & Society* 1(1): 9–29. Available at http://www.surveillance-and-society.org.

Mitrou, L. 2010. "The impact of communications data retention on fundamental rights and democracy: The case of the EU data retention directive." In *Surveillance and Democracy,* ed. Kevin D. Haggerty and Minas Samatas. London: Routledge.

Moechel, E. 2008. "The surveillance Olympics, Beijing 2008—Powered by European technology." Brussels: Olympic Rights for Human Games Conference, May 15, 2008. Available at http://pgp.mit.edu.

Ogura, T. 2006. "Electronic government and surveillance-oriented society." In *Theorizing Surveillance: The Panopticon and Beyond*, ed. D. Lyon, pp. 27–295, Devon: Willan Publishing.

Pangalos, G. 2008. *New Challenges for the Systems and Communication: The European Union Prospect*. ADAE Conference on Privacy Protection of Communications and Self—Protection of Users and Subscribers. April 11, 2008. Available at http://www.adae.gr.

Papadimitriou, G. 2008. *Democracy in Adversity*. (in Greek) Athens: Polis.

Prevelakis, V. and D. Spinellis. 2007. "The Athens affair." *Spectrum*, Institute of Electrical and Electronics Engineers (IEEE) 44 (7, July):26–33.

Samatas, M. 2004. *Surveillance in Greece: From Anticommunist to the Consumer Surveillance*. New York: Pella.

———. 2007. "Security and surveillance in the Athens 2004 Olympics: Some lessons from a troubled story." *International Criminal Justice Review* 17(3): 220–38.

———. 2008. "From thought-control to traffic-control: CCTV politics of expansion and resistance in post-Olympics Greece." In *Surveillance and Governance: Crime Control and Beyond*, ed. M. Deflem, pp. 345–69, Bingley, UK: Emerald/JAI Press.

Schulhofer, S.J. 2002. *The Enemy Within: Intelligence Gathering, Law Enforcement, and Civil Liberties in the Wake of September 11*. Twentieth Century Fund.

Sidel, M. 2004. *More Secure Less Free? Antiterrorist Policy and Liberties after September 11*. Ann Arbor. MI: The University of Michigan Press.

Simon, B. 2005. "The return of panopticism: Supervision, subjection and the new surveillance." *Surveillance & Society* 3(1):1–20. Available at http://www.surveillance-and-society.org.

Smith, H. 2006a. "Athens Olympics phone tapping revealed." *The Guardian* February 3, 2006. Available at http://www.guardian.co.uk.

———2006b. "Death of Vodafone engineer linked to Greek Watergate." *The Guardian* June 23, 2006. Available at http://www.guardian.co.uk.

Sugden, J. 2008. "Watching the games." *Foreign Policy In Focus*, Washington, DC. August 22, 2008. Available at http://fpif.org.

Tinic, S. 2005. "(En)Visioning the televisual audience: Revisiting questions of power in the age of interactive television." In *The New Politics of Surveillance and Visibility*, ed. Kevin D. Haggerty and Richard V. Ericson. pp. 308–26. Toronto: University of Toronto Press.

Whitson, J. and K. Haggerty. 2008. "Identity theft and the care of the virtual self." *Economy and Society* 37(4): 571–93.

Chapter 12

Surveillance and democracy in the digital enclosure

Jennifer R. Whitson

Governments of the Industrial World, you weary giants of flesh and steel, I come from Cyberspace, the new home of Mind. On behalf of the future, I ask you of the past to leave us alone. You are not welcome among us. You have no sovereignty where we gather.

We have no elected government, nor are we likely to have one, so I address you with no greater authority than that with which liberty itself always speaks. I declare the global social space we are building to be naturally independent of the tyrannies you seek to impose on us. You have no moral right to rule us nor do you possess any methods of enforcement we have true reason to fear.

(Excerpt from John Perry Barlow's Declaration
of the Independence of Cyberspace (1996))

The absence of elected governments in cyberspace, on the one hand, has increased freedom of expression and creativity, and allowed the formation of online communities that are governed from the bottom up. On the other hand, the lack of a democratic process also allows corporations to step in as de facto governments, and privatize increasing areas of online space (e.g. Google, MSN, Yahoo, AOL, Facebook). Once hailed as a place where users could escape hierarchical control and the tyrannies of government, the internet is now subject to an enclosure movement, wherein public "land" is being privatized, and citizens' creative labor is appropriated to profit the corporations that administer these places. The extent of surveillance in these spaces may surpass any in the terrestrial world, yet the façade of democracy—communities laboring together as equals to create idealized spaces—is used to attract more citizens. It is a cruel joke that the unregulated spaces idealized by techno-libertarians of the nineties have now become sites of surveillance and control. The gap left by elected governments, especially nation-state governments, allows corporations to conquer online spaces. Unlike elected governments, these corporations are not accountable to their "citizens," cannot be disposed of, and their practices and internal workings are opaque.

The history of Second Life (SL), an online virtual world with over 14 million "residents" in 2008 provides a paradigmatic example of the enclosure movement.

It is used throughout this paper to highlight the interplay between privatization, the promise of online democratic spaces, and surveillance. While these kinds of enclosure movements are taking place in many online spaces, I draw examples from a virtual world to further demonstrate how avatars, the characters that users choose to represent them in these worlds, facilitate surveillance and challenge traditional notions of online anonymity. While in time SL will likely be replaced by more technologically advanced virtual worlds, it has much to teach us about the corporate incursion into online spaces, the expansion of asymmetrical surveillance practices and power relations, and the resultant transformation of spaces originally created in light of the most democratic ideals. Second Life is just one instance where the hype of community participation and co-production of economic wealth in online spaces is underpinned by increasing corporatization, surveillance, and control.

What went before: the myth of the commons

Barlow's famous Declaration of the Independence of Cyberspace evokes the picture of an online intellectual commons free from government control. This picture is reinforced by technical descriptions of how the internet works. Originally created by DARPA (the United States Defense Advanced Research and Projects Agency), the internet was designed to ensure quick, unhindered communication in the event of nuclear attack. It is a distributed network that has no central site of control, and can be rudimentarily envisioned as a massive web, with each computer linked to and able to communicate with any other computer. Consequently, if one node of the network is inoperable, the message automatically diverts to an alternative route and communication continues. Extrapolating from this model and its attendant "protocol" (Galloway, 2004), the internet is seen by many, including media scholar Mark Poster, as a place explicitly designed "with no attention at all to questions of who is authorized to speak, when, to whom, and what may be said on these occasions" (Poster, 2004:321).

The architecture of the internet allows for easy information access, facilitates communication, and promotes the formation of communities over long distances (Rheingold, 2000). This architecture, it is claimed, levels terrestrial communication hierarchies because the identity of the sender has no effect on the priority and speed of the message, thus ensuring equality regardless of the social power or economic status of the sender. Accordingly, the internet is seen by many as a revolutionary medium that gives equal voice to all citizens, especially when compared to pre-existing media forms (e.g. television, newspaper, and radio networks), that are commonly characterized as top-down, one-way communication channels controlled by media elites. The technical capabilities of the internet are held as proof that the internet is an inherent threat to centralized, hierarchical power relations (Galloway, 2004; Andrejevic, 2007).

By definition, convivial technologies are transparent, accessible, and flexible in terms of being easy to use and modify (Torin Monahan, in this volume). While they are predominately small-scale, the decentralized network of the internet encourages participation, diverse modes of expression, and power equalization—all of which characterize convivial technologies. For example, the opportunity to make oneself heard through webpages, blogs, and video postings is believed to foster democratic engagement and empower internet users to actively participate in online environments.

Second Life exemplifies the convivial in its proclamation that it is "imagined, created, and owned by its residents" (Linden Lab, 2006). Second Life is largely the vision of Philip Rosedale, founder of Linden Lab. It was originally designed as an online 3D environment devoted to task-based games and socialization, but during an early meeting with investors, Rosedale noticed that the participants were particularly responsive to the collaborative, creative potential of SL. The most popular application in SL was the 3D modeling tool that allowed users to create avatars, buildings, clothing, and animations in-world. As a result, the initial gaming focus of SL was shifted to a more user-created, community-driven experience that was partly inspired by Rosedale's experiences at the radical Burning Man Festival (Au, 2008a).

Launched in June 2003, the SL platform started as a blank slate where the first visitors could build any content they chose. However, Linden Lab discovered that without incentive to create, SL content evolved slowly, a problem given that novel content was necessary to attract new "residents" (the term preferred by Linden Lab and SL users alike). On the verge of financial ruin, Linden Lab consulted with prominent technology activist and scholar Lawrence Lessig, and decreed that inhabitants could own and resell virtual land, own intellectual property and have the ability to claim copyright on their designs. The mixture of a community-driven experience, creative freedom, and the ability to profit from selling one's designs in-world has proved to be extremely successful. SL has grown phenomenally—from just over 1,000 residents in November 2003, to 180,000 in April 2006, to over 14 million residents. SL is particularly convivial as sections of its underlying code are open-source, meaning that residents can access the inner workings of the SL platform, determine how it works, and make modifications and improvements. Yet, when the daily operations of SL are closely examined, many elements of SL are at odds with this apparently convivial nature. This finding extends to the internet more generally.

The digital enclosure movement and the rise of the surveillant society

The myth of the intellectual commons, where ideas are freely circulated and everyone is equal, fails to hold up to scrutiny when we move from abstract diagrams to concrete examples. While at one point the internet *may* have fit the description of a convivial technology, the increasing privatization of online spaces by large corporations results in asymmetries in the power relations between corporations and individual users, asymmetries that belie the democratic ideals that the internet is assumed to foster. On top of the decentralized network model of the internet lies another model wherein the creation of privatized spaces—digital enclosures—allows corporations to control who is authorized to speak, when, and to whom. Moreover, these spaces are characterized by asymmetries in visibility, whereby corporations have significant surveillance powers while their own actions are increasingly opaque.

Communications scholar Mark Andrejevic describes a digital enclosure as "an interactive realm wherein every action and transaction generates information about itself" (Andrejevic, 2007:2). For Andrejevic, the internet as a whole provides a paradigmatic example of a digital enclosure—one in which every virtual "move" has the potential to leave a digital trace or record of itself. These digital traces are assembled into informational profiles of users, which can be used to improve the user experience, subtly shape users' desires and behaviors, or be profitably sold to other corporations (Gandy 1993). The digital enclosure concentrates an unprecedented amount of control over digital information in the hands of a few via asymmetrical surveillance practices.

The term "digital enclosure" consciously evokes the land enclosure movement of the eighteenth and nineteenth centuries, when public farmland in England and Wales was appropriated for private benefit. This appropriation of public land allowed private landowners to set the conditions of its use. It resulted in the formation of distinct classes because it separated those who owned and administered the land from those who had to sell their labor. In the contemporary case, corporations such as Google, Yahoo, and Linden Lab are the owners, and users pay to access these sites, not only with fees but also by submitting to forms of monitoring, thereby trading their valuable personal information and privacy for access. Following this, digital enclosures exemplify a shift from conceptualizing privacy as a right to conceptualizing privacy as a commodity to be exchanged for other goods and services (Leman-Langlois, 2008; Steeves, 2006).

While the term "digital enclosure" is fairly recent, the concept is similar to what media scholar Joseph Turow calls a "walled garden." Both terms are used interchangeably in this chapter. A walled garden is:

> an online environment where consumers go for information, communications, and commercial services and that discourages them from leaving for the larger digital world. The concept initially referred in the late 1990s to a safe place for children on the Web; parents would set their computers so that the kids could visit only those areas. Quickly, however, the concept morphed to mean an area where content providers could induce targeted consumers to enter—sometimes even have them pay for entry—and then

track their activities while surrounding them with ads appropriate to their demographic characteristics and actions.

(Turow, 2005: 117)

Users are enticed to enter and stay in walled gardens through a wide array of premium services that are not readily available on the rest of the internet. America Online (AOL) is a well-known example of a walled garden, complete with desirable content such as music, videos, and online magazines available only to paying subscribers. In return for access to their personal information, AOL blocks spam and unwanted pop-ups, and customizes ads according to the user, the materials they choose, and the time of day (Turow, 2005). Subscribers' behaviors are also recorded and analyzed in order to tailor content to their inferred tastes.

Second Life is also a prime example of a digital enclosure. At the time of writing countless services are accessible in one site, from financial planning (Wells Fargo Bank has an entire SL island), to university classes (Harvard, Princeton, and MIT all have SL campuses), to music concerts (hosted by Sony BMG) to purchasing a new laptop (Dell Computers has a SL store), to cyber-sex and escort services. In exchange for convenient access to all these services under one virtual roof, residents and their behaviors are subject to surveillance. Complete records of everything SL residents say and do, their virtual body movements and facial expressions, the people they interact with, the times at which they do so, their consumer preferences, and so on, can be easily collected and analyzed.

Linden Lab has relatively strict privacy policies (except in the event that they merge with another company or go bankrupt—then *all* personal user information can be put up for sale), yet data collection in SL is not restricted to Linden Lab and privacy policies are often ignored. Corporations that have invested millions of dollars to establish their presence in SL use the world to collect a significant amount of marketing information (Au, 2008a). The ability to harvest the demographic and personal information of users (including their shopping preferences, in-world travel and usage patterns, and even personal conversations) is enhanced by the "open code" of SL, which gives users access to the blueprints for the virtual world as well as the ability to modify certain areas. For example, corporations can create "Zombie bots," automated software agents that look like avatars, but are controlled solely by algorithms. These spy-bots roam SL collecting data on SL residents (Au, 2008b). Providing users, including other corporations, with access to the underlying architecture is intended to promote creativity, but it also has numerous unforeseen effects, including enabling enhanced dataveillance of other parties. It is difficult for residents to argue that these initiatives breach their privacy, as the information is gathered in an ostensibly open forum where there is little expectation of privacy. Further examples of such surveillance include the CIA and other government agencies trolling SL to investigate terrorist activity (O'Harrow Jr, 2008).

While data collection via the internet is nothing new, we are seeing an extension of the depth and breadth of the information being collected. There is a significant difference between collecting data in the physical world, collecting data online in general, and collecting data specifically in digital enclosures such as SL (Zarsky, 2006, 2004). In the physical world, corporations regularly amass a variety of data about consumers, but this data is generally restricted to a final purchase (e.g. American Express creates profiles based on consumer purchases). Online corporations can track users' actions and browsing patterns using cookies, even monitoring idle surfers who do not make any purchases. This data is then aggregated and compiled into profiles using sophisticated databasing technologies (Poster, 1996). Yet these profiles are not flawless. While navigating the internet, users divide their attention (and thus the data trail they leave behind them) among several e-commerce vendors, content providers, and other online applications. The profiles that corporations create are limited in scope and prone to errors, as the users they track are constantly logging in and out, creating piecemeal patterns as they move from one website to another. Aggregating data collected at different times, places, and sources into a single profile results in numerous overlaps and errors in the data.

Surveillance in digital enclosures such as Second Life is broader in scope: it pertains to an extended online experience and monitors a more persistent and detailed online identity. In SL, purchases, education, workplace training, socialization, and dating all occur under the same roof. Because SL residents spend a great deal of time in this monitored environment, much more than they would spend on any one website, the data trail they leave behind— including logs of everyone they ever talked to, every place they visited, and every purchase— is immensely valuable to corporations, especially those who own these virtual worlds.

Total surveillance society

In 1974, James Rule proposed a number of criteria to distinguish a society's surveillance capacity (Rule, 1974). In light of technological developments in networking and communication technologies that have emerged since 1974, David Lyon has updated Rule's original categories to include four dimensions of surveillance capacity: (1) size of data files; (2) comprehensiveness of reach in terms of institutional access to data; (3) speed of data flow; and (4) subject transparency in terms of subject visibility to monitoring (Lyon, 1994). Second Life especially, but digital enclosures in general, fit the criteria for a total-surveillance society almost perfectly. The fact that these enclosures exist in the realm of data makes the complete collection, databasing, and analysis of residents' data a realizable enterprise, right down to logging every facial expression. While avatars are not used in all digital enclosures, technology analyst firm Gartner, Inc. 2007 predicts that by 2011 80 per cent of active internet users will have avatars. This level of surveillance, especially that enabled by avatars that allow for facial expressions and body language, is impossible in terrestrial space, where many behaviors go unsurveilled and unremarked upon.

Users' anonymity is being slowly pushed aside in favor of transparency. Online anonymity was once taken for granted and valued in terms of encouraging identity exploration and the transcendence of race, gender, and class barriers. Increasingly, however, users' behaviors and lives online are connected to their offline identities, and users are cautioned to censor their behaviors and the information they reveal online. Recent controversial examples include the US military delving into personal emails and online activity logs to "out" gays, and employers performing Google searches to provide background on potential employees (Nederlander, 2008; Associated Press, 2007). A closer look at identification practices and anonymity in SL further highlights the decreasing anonymity in cyberspace.

In the short history of SL, avatars were originally anonymous. Real-world identifiers were not required, and users' off-line identities were protected. All that was needed to create an avatar account was an email address. In fact, the right to anonymity has always been protected by Linden Lab, as evidenced by their community standards. One of the six cardinal sins is disclosure, "sharing personal information about a fellow Resident—including gender, religion, age, marital status, race, sexual preference, and real-world location" (Linden Lab, 2007). Yet, this protection of anonymity is quickly reversing in the face of pressures created by both the growth and corporatization of this space.

More and more, being visible equates to having one's avatar linked to real-life identifiers. In order to do business in SL one must increasingly expose one's real-world identity as a token of trust (Lyon, 2001). Although not initially popular, residents' "First Life" pages are increasingly valued as information sources and indicators of trustworthiness. These profile pages include information on residents' "First Life" (their "real world" identities) such as their names, locations, and occupations. Such information ostensibly determines who is genuinely committed to being part of SL, to the extent that they are willing to stake their offline reputation on their participation. The growing popularity of "First Life" pages coincides with the increasing corporatization of SL (with numerous Fortune 500 Companies such as Cisco, IBM, Dell, Sears, and Reebok attempting to establish a presence in SL). SL contractors who earn a living designing content for these companies must expose their real identities, as businesses and organizations demand that avatars validate their "true" identities. For example, the avatar Aimee Weber initially preserved the anonymity of her user while brokering SL design contracts with Warner Brothers and American Apparel. This anonymity was short-lived. Ultimately avatar Aimee Weber "came out" as Alyssa LaRoche in real life in order to secure an SL development contract with the United Nations. This coming out process is familiar to many SL residents who hope to make a living from their creations (Au, 2008a).

The anonymity that SL residents were originally entitled to may be a thing of the past for all residents, not just those interested in securing employment. According to Robin Harper, Linden Lab VP of Community and Support:

> We are in the process of implementing an improved electronic age verification system that will verify Residents' ages by using different forms of identification, such as national identification numbers, passports, and social security numbers.
>
> (Harper, 2007)

The implementation of this identification measure coincides with negative media attention surrounding residents who used SL avatars to simulate sex acts such as pedophilia (Harper, 2007). Anonymity makes it difficult for Linden Lab to apply sanctions to those who violate the written rules and community norms of SL, and accordingly it is not surprising they are attempting to link avatars to real-world identifiers as the virtual world grows in size and gains more media and corporate attention (Whitson and Doyle, 2008). While anonymity is seemingly fine for games and role play, it is anathema to the more commercial practices that necessarily involve identity verification, paper trails, and accountability. Accordingly there is a shift from visible, yet anonymous, avatars to avatars that are linked to their users' offline identifiers and reputations.

Labor and creative capitalism in the digital enclosure

User-created content, alongside the user information noted above, is a valuable commodity to corporations. While user-content creation fosters creativity and productivity, it is the corporations that benefit from and control this labor in digital enclosures. Users' unpaid labor is a cheap and efficient way for corporations to respond to the demand for increased and improved content, serves to keep existing users from becoming bored, and draws in potential new users. Users' increased creative control results in a stronger identification and emotional investment in the space as well as a reluctance to abandon these spaces (Humphreys, 2007). Corporations portray user labor as a solution to alienation related to mass production and consumption, and persuade users to manufacture content for digital enclosures by promising them that their experience will be more satisfying with increased input, personalization, and effort (Andrejevic, 2007: 145). Users, in true neoliberal form, take on the duties of production in order to create a product that addresses their specific desires and needs.

Anthropologist Tom Boellstorff associates user-created content with creationist capitalism, a mode of capitalism in which labor is understood in terms of creativity, and production is accordingly understood as creation (Boellstorff, 2008). By framing labor in terms of creativity, work is framed as play

(Yee, 2006). This trend can be seen in many online sites, including social-networking sites such as Facebook and MySpace, as well as YouTube and other digital enclosures that rely entirely on users for content. The valorization of creation is key to Linden Lab's business model as it provides a way around the large development resources required to add new content to SL. For example, in 2006, the total amount of content created by residents was equivalent to the output of 5,100 full-time programmers. This labor is wholly unpaid. Instead users pay Linden Lab monthly fees and property "taxes" for the privilege of creating content (Craig, 2006). This leads to the uneven property relations that characterize digital enclosures:

> In a traditional Marxist analysis this would be seen as a form of super-exploitation where workers are unable to reproduce their needs for existence. Within a logic of creationist capitalism, such labor could be seen to have both exchange value and use value as a form of self-fulfillment ... Creationist capitalism allow[s] labor to acquire value as a form of leisure.
>
> (Boellstorff, 2008:213)

The cultural logic of creationist capitalism renders intelligible a "state of affairs where consumers labor for free (or for a nominal prize) to produce advertising materials for a product they have already purchased" (Boellstorff, 2008:210). While there is a cultural significance to content creation and it is a valued skill in SL communities, most creators make little to no money—just enough to pay their SL land taxes, or the equivalent of five or ten dollars a month.

While some user-created content can accumulate substantial real-world economic value, more things than just economic interest and property rights bind users to digital enclosures. The social networks they establish also ensure that they remain. While there exists a neoliberal discourse of the empowered consumer who can leave the digital enclosure if they are not happy with how it is governed or how they as an individual are treated, this ignores the user's role as co-producer of content, their interest in the digital goods and reputations they have accumulated, the community networks they have established, and the online identities that they have created. This further exemplifies the uneven relations that are created by digital enclosures.

Linden Lab, seemingly on the side of users in terms of instilling intellectual property rights and claiming that SL is "imagined, created, and owned by its residents," is one of the worst offenders. Linden Lab promotes the image of a self-governing community where residents can profit from their creativity, yet most of the profit goes directly to Linden Lab. By signing SL's Terms of Service (ToS) before they enter, residents agree that Linden Lab can pull the plug on the world, their avatars, and their considerable investments in the world without any legal liability or means of recourse. In fact, Linden Lab quietly dropped the "owned" from its tagline in 2007, thereby de-emphasizing the rights of ownership, if any, that residents may have in SL. The complex property relationships between corporations and users point to the need to rethink previous theorizations of the relationship between property, ownership, and power online. Although it is beyond the scope of this paper to develop this extensively, we require a new political economy of online spaces that takes into context the new network of property relations enabled by user-created content. Parallel to the real world, and despite the important role played by users as content developers, the powerful still impose their will on property relations.

Creative capitalism extends the surveillance capacities of digital enclosures by encouraging residents to develop and post their own content. This content deepens and broadens corporate dataveillance even further by incorporating residents' writing, chat logs, and digital designs into the surveillant gaze. A hidden aspect of user-created content is how it facilitates a participatory form of surveillance (Taylor, 2006b; Albrechtslund and Dubbeld, 2005; Leman-Langlois, 2008). A sizeable proportion of users engage in behaviors in order to let third parties watch their activities, for exhibitionist pleasure, personal pride, and communication. Although data from the digital enclosure may not always point directly to a specific physical individual, it does track a generally persistent identity—such as one's avatar—over extended periods of time. This level of surveillance has significant implications for the freedoms traditionally associated with the internet and with convivial technologies.

Total(itarian) surveillance society

Digital enclosures are not just total surveillance societies but *totalitarian* surveillance societies as well, where corporations exert total control over each enclosed online space. This section further highlights the uneven power hierarchy that exists between users and corporations. While John Perry Barlow applauded the fact that the internet has no elected government, this absence of government creates opportunities for exploitation. Democracy, in part, relies on a symmetry of relations. In exchange for citizens' votes, elected governments are mandated with carrying out the will of the public and remain accountable to the public. There is a symmetry of visibility wherein rulers provide the public with access to their deliberations and the policy they form. Corporate rule is, by contrast, asymmetrical: the decisions and actions of corporate entities remain opaque even as users are rendered increasingly transparent to marketers and advertisers. Rather than accountability and transparency, corporate digital enclosures offer the promise of convenience and customization as an alibi for a shift in power relations: "for the ability to discriminate invisibly and to gather information that facilitates market management and public manipulation" (Andrejevic, 2007:258).

Much of the asymmetry between corporations and users is a result of an imbalance in visibility. While the corporate ruler "sees all and knows all," including the minutia of residents' day-to-day lives online, their own practices and policies are opaque.

This has important implications for online privacy given that legal privacy rights are primarily focused on the state. Corporations such as Linden Lab are just one example of a non-state agency conducting surveillance limited, for the most part, only by the "fair information practices" they have chosen to instill, which in themselves have only a limited record of success (Haggerty and Ericson, 2006). David Brin argues that a synoptic form of surveillance may reverse some of the power imbalances between the watched and the watchers, in this case corporations and users (Brin, 1998), but, as of yet, there are few ways for users to turn the surveillant gaze upon the corporate deities that operate digital enclosures. It is difficult to be optimistic about the idea of a transparent society (a society that allows everyone equal access to information) given that large corporations continue to operate behind closed doors and few privacy laws actually have an impact upon their practices.

While corporations are happy to collect users' information under the guise of improving service, users encounter difficulties when challenging the way digital enclosures are governed. Linden Lab replaced the open forums of SL with blogs that allow only corporate employees to post (Boellstorff, 2008), and there are few opportunities for residents to discuss their concerns with Linden Lab staff given the decreasing staff presence in SL (Au, 2008a). The significant history of protests and demonstrations in virtual worlds points to an alternative method of representation. Masses of protesting avatars have occasionally presented a united front that catches the attention of the corporations, as well as the media. Collective action is relatively common, and there are many accounts of users rallying to pressure companies to address problematic issues. For example, an early protest in SL recreated the Boston Tea Party to challenge Linden Lab's taxation policy. Shortly afterwards the policy was rescinded (Au, 2008a). When Linden Lab did not respond quickly enough to a "copybot" program that duplicated residents' designs and violated intellectual property rights, shop-owners closed their shops in protest (Gonsalves, 2006). IBM's move to Second Life was quickly followed by an in-world protest in September 2007 by workers at IBM Italy that led to international press coverage and the resignation of IBM Italy's CEO. Following that success, union members again rallied for collective action, this time in response to IBM outsourcing labor contracts. The repercussions of this protest were not restricted to the virtual world—the strike was noted by AOL's stock-market resource webpage, which consequently sent waves of shareholders and potential investors searching the internet for more information (Au, 2008c).

Although at first glance such examples provide encouraging signs of democratic potential, not all public demonstrations are successful. In fact, they are more often met with severe repercussions, as officials frame protests as a disruption of the digital enclosure, a violation of the terms of service, and an offence that ultimately leads to protesters' accounts being closed and their avatars destroyed (Taylor, 2006a). T.L. Taylor, for example, details the corporate response to a protest in an online game, World of Warcraft:

> It was not met with a positive reception by Blizzard, the developers and maintainers of the game. Not unlike the kinds of warnings you expect to hear offline from police at unsanctioned demonstrations, participants at the protest were told by a Blizzard representative via the in-game communication system:
>
> *Attention: Gathering on a realm with intent to hinder gameplay is considered griefing and will not be tolerated. If you are here for the Warrior protest, please log off and return to playing on your usual realm. We appreciate your opinion, but protesting in game is not a valid way to give us feedback. Please post your feedback on the forums instead. If you do not comply, we will begin taking action against accounts. Please leave this area if you are here to disrupt gameplay as we are suspending all accounts.*
>
> (Taylor, 2006a)

Companies argue that such gatherings stress the technical limitations of the digital enclosure, result in slowed server response and the potential for server crashes, and consequently endanger other users' enjoyment of the space. Because of this, the companies argue, collective action must be halted in order to avoid inconveniencing users who are not participating in the protest. In addition, collective action is seen to violate the end-user licensing agreements (EULAs, otherwise known as the Terms of Service) that users must accept prior to entering the virtual world. Accordingly, there are few options for users to provide input into how they are governed in digital enclosures.

Game designer Richard Bartle has written extensively on the uneven power hierarchy that exists between corporations and users. This hierarchy is rooted in the relative ease with which coded rules can be used and altered by corporations to govern populations. The scope of these corporate powers is reflected in the following quotation:

> Virtual worlds are played by rules. The rules are written (embodied in the code) and unwritten (embodied in the expectations of the players). People can deny the existence of unwritten rules, but they can't deny the existence of coded rules ... You may be able to pick and choose which cultural norms to obey, but you don't get to pick and choose which rules of the virtual world's physical universe to obey—and the administrator's authority in a virtual world is embodied in those rules. You don't swear, because if you do you're disintegrated. You don't do anything that the administrator doesn't want you to do, because if you do you're disintegrated.
>
> (Bartle, 2006a:36–37)

Most legal scholars equate corporate administrators to the governments of online spaces (Lastowka and Hunter, 2003; Castronova, 2006; Balkin, 2006). It matters little whether these governments are elected or not. What matters is their unrestricted power to govern online populations.

Corporations are granted ownership of online identities, labor, and user information through the terms of service and EULAs that users must accept before entering. These companies are not accountable or transparent, and their rules are often opaque even to terrestrial courts and legislation. Accordingly, they make de facto law (Humphreys, 2007). Their powers are so absolute that it is argued that they are not governments at all, who could be disposed of by the populace, but rather dictators (Boellstorff, 2008:222; Doctorow, 2007) and gods (Bartle, 2006b). The monopoly on force and coercion, traditionally held by the state alone, has been handed over to private parties. Corporations can "banish" users without recourse, drastically alter the physics and mechanics of the digital enclosure, or destroy it at will. Given that these digital enclosures account for an increasing proportion of online spaces, and that our lives are increasingly lived online, this is a worrying trend.

Conclusion

While John Perry Barlow applauds the fact that the internet has no elected government, this means that the tenets of democracy that constrain and direct most governments in the terrestrial world do not apply. The symmetry of relations, accountability, and transparency associated with terrestrial governments, and with democracy in general, are absent. There is no public scrutiny of corporate-cum-government decision-making, policy, and actions. Corporations have low levels of accountability to online communities and ban users at will, denying them access to their communities, their user-created content, and their online identities without any requirement that their decision-making process be transparent or open to contestation by users who feel that they have been wrongly punished. The current proprietary environment that gives corporations the power to banish users without any transparent governance process and the power to alter code and erase entire online domains at the flip of a switch ultimately ends up with users being governed through the threat of losing their online identities, communities, and virtual property. While consumer activism is sometimes effective, there is little recourse if protests fail. In the terrestrial world, exploited and unhappy citizens have recourse to the rule of law, they can sue and they can elect new leaders. Users of digital enclosures lack these rights.

The forms of participation and empowerment open to users are harnessed to corporate drives for efficiency and profitability. Rather than working to correct power asymmetries in society, as predicted by the decentralized model of the internet, the internet contributes to ever-increasing levels of surveillance, concentrates power in the hands of a few, and erodes transparency and openness. While the internet is seen as democracy-promoting in terms of how it affords potentials for political organization from below, it is increasingly important to examine how new media is appropriated for corporate ends, and how this alters the democratic potential of the internet. Moreover, it is increasingly important to examine how citizenship is constantly being redefined in online spaces. Consumer relationships are replacing other practices of community and government, and act as a stand-in for true citizenship. Digital enclosures are one way in which the labor and information of online "citizens" are being exploited under the guise of community and creativity.

References

Albrechtslund, Anders and Lynsey Dubbeld. 2005. "The plays and arts of surveillance: Studying surveillance as entertainment." *Surveillance & Society* 3(2/3): 216–21.

Andrejevic, Mark. 2007. *iSpy: Surveillance and Power in the Interactive Era.* Lawrence: University Press of Kansas.

Associated Press. 2007. "U.S. military continues to discharge gay Arab linguists, and congress members seek hearing." *International Herald Tribune*, May 23, 2007.

Au, Wagner James. 2008a. *The Making of Second Life: Notes from the New World.* 1st ed. New York: Collins.

——. 2008b. *Metaverse Bots: How To Spot Them, What To Do With Them?* New World Notes, February 13, 2008 [cited April 1, 2008]. Available at http://nwn.blogs.com.

——. 2008c. *Virtual World Labor Protest Shows Up On IBM's Real World Stock Chart.* New World Notes, March 31, 2008 [cited March 31, 2008]. Available at http://nwn.blogs.com.

Balkin, J. M. 2006. "Law and liberty in virtual worlds." In *The State of Play: Law, Games, and Virtual Worlds*, ed. J. M. Balkin and B. S. Noveck. 86–117. New York: New York University Press.

Barlow, John Perry. 1996. *A Declaration of the Independence of Cyberspace.* Electronic Frontier Foundation, [cited August 22, 2008]. Available at http://homes.eff.org.

Bartle, Richard A. 2006a. "Virtual worldliness." In *The State of Play: Law, Games, and Virtual Worlds*, edited by J. M. Balkin and B. S. Noveck. 3–54. New York: New York University Press.

——. 2006b. "Why governments aren't gods and gods aren't governments." *First Monday* (special issue number 7).

Boellstorff, Tom. 2008. *Coming of Age in Second Life: An Anthropologist Explores the Virtually Human.* Princeton: Princeton University Press.

Brin, David. 1998. *The Transparent Society: Will Technology Force us to Choose between Privacy and Freedom?* Reading, Mass.: Addison-Wesley.

Castronova, Edward. 2006. "The right to play." In *The State of Play: Law, Games, and Virtual Worlds*, edited by J. M. Balkin and B. S. Noveck. 68–85. New York: New York University Press.

Craig, Kathleen. 2006. *Second Life's Must-Have Stuff.* Wired [cited October 19, 2006]. Available at http://www.wired.com.

Doctorow, Cory. 2007. "Why online games are dictatorships." *Information Week*, April 16, 2007.

Haggerty, Kevin D. and Richard Ericson, eds. 2006. *The New Politics of Surveillance and Visibility*. Toronto: University of Toronto Press.

Galloway, Alexander R. 2004. *Protocol: How Control Exists After Decentralization*. Cambridge, Mass.: MIT Press.

Gandy, Oscar. 1993. *The Panoptic Sort: A Political Economy of Personal Information*. Boulder: Westview.

Gartner, Inc, 2007. Gartner says 80 percent of active internet users will have a "Second life" in the virtual world by the end of 2011. [Cited April 24, 2007] Available at http//www.gartner.com/it/page.jsp?id=503861.

Gonsalves, Antone. 2006. "Second Life shop owners threaten suit against Virtual World's creator." *Information Week*, November 15, 2006.

Harper, Robin. 2007. *Accusations Regarding Child Pornography in Second Life*. Linden Lab., May 9, 2007 [cited November 1, 2007]. Available at http://blogs/secondlife.com

Humphreys, Sal. 2007. "You're in our world now." TM: Ownership and access in the proprietary community of a MMOG. In *Information Communication Technologies and Emerging Business Strategies*, edited by S. Van Der Graaf and Y. Washida. 76–96. London: Idea Group Publishing.

Lastowka, F. Gregory and Dan Hunter. 2003. "The laws of the virtual worlds." In *Public Law and Legal Theory Research Paper Series*: University of Pennsylvania Law School.

Leman-Langlois, Stéphane. 2008. "Privacy as currency: Crime, information and control in cyberspace." In *Technocrime*, edited by S. Leman-Langlois, 112–38. Cullompton: Willan.

Linden Lab. 2006. *Second Life Homepage* [cited December 29, 2006]. Available at http://www.secondlife.com.

——. 2007. *Community Standards* [cited April 21, 2007]. Available at http://secondlife.com.

Lyon, David. 1994. *The Electronic Eye: The Rise of Surveillance Society*. Minneapolis: University of Minnesota Press.

——. 2001. "Under my skin: From identification papers to body surveillance." In *Documenting Individual Identity: The Development of State Practices in the Modern World*, ed. J. Caplan and J. C. Torpey, 291–310. Princeton, N.J.: Princeton University Press.

Monahan, Torin. 2010. "Surveillance as governance: Social inequality and the pursuit of democratic surveillance." In *Surveillance and Democracy*, ed. Kevin D. Haggerty and Minas Samatas. London: Routledge.

Nederlander, Ned. 2008. *One in Five Employers Scan Applicants' Web Lives*. Slashdot.com, September 11, 2008 [cited Sept 13, 2008]. Available at http://tech. slashdot. org.

O'Harrow Jr., Robert. 2008. "Spies' battleground turns virtual: Intelligence officials see 3-D online worlds as havens for criminals." *Washington Post*, February 6, 2008. D01.

Poster, Mark. 1996. "Databases as discourse; or, electronic interpellations." In *Computers, Surveillance, and Privacy*, ed. D. Lyon and E. Zureik, 175–92. Minneapolis: University of Minnesota Press.

——. 2004. "The information empire." In *Comparative Literature Studies* 41: 317–34.

Rheingold, Howard. 2000. *The Virtual Community: Homesteading on the Electronic Frontier*. Rev. ed. Cambridge, Mass.: MIT Press.

Rule, James B. 1974. *Private Lives and Public Surveillance: Social Control in the Computer Age.* New York: Schocken Books.

Steeves, Valerie. 2006. "It's not child's play: The online invasion of children's privacy." *University of Ottawa Law and Technology Journal* 3(1): 169–88.

Taylor, T. L. 2006a. "Beyond management: Considering participatory design and governance in player culture." *First Monday* (special issue no).

——. 2006b. "Does WoW change everything? How a PvP server, multinational player base, and surveillance mod scene caused me pause." *Games and Culture* 1(4): 318–37.

Turow, Joseph. 2005. "Audience construction and culture production: Marketing surveillance in the digital age." *The Annals of the American Academy of Political and Social Science* 597: 103–21.

Whitson, Jennifer, and Aaron Doyle. 2008. "Second Life and governing deviance in virtual worlds." In *Technocrime: Technology, Crime, and Social Control*, ed. S. Leman-Langlois, 88–111. Cullompton: Willan.

Yee, Nick. 2006. "The labor of fun: How video games blur the boundaries of work and play." *Games and Culture* 1(1): 68–71.

Zarsky, Tal Z. 2004. "Information privacy in virtual worlds: Identifying unique concerns beyond the online and offline worlds." *New York Law School Law Review* 49: 231–70.

——. 2006. "Privacy and data collection in virtual worlds." In *The State of Play: Law, Games, and Virtual Worlds*, ed. J. M. Balkin and B. S. Noveck, 217–23. New York: New York University Press.

Index